Dr. Fisher.

Compassion can come in many forms.
But when its given in the darkest of
moments, it is cherished most.
THANK you for looking after us
until the end. You have been
a blessing for us both.

Forever grateful!

and Kim.

# Rape of Innocence

## THE LONG JOURNEY HOME

### LELAND PAGE

◆ FriesenPress

Suite 300 - 990 Fort St
Victoria, BC, V8V 3K2
Canada

www.friesenpress.com

ISBN
978-1-5255-7032-2 (Hardcover)
978-1-5255-7033-9 (Paperback)
978-1-5255-7034-6 (eBook)

*1. BIOGRAPHY & AUTOBIOGRAPHY, PERSONAL MEMOIRS*

Distributed to the trade by The Ingram Book Company

# Introduction

The silver chain I wear around my neck holds a symbol of the meaning of life. My gift to you is sharing the journey of how I came to obtain it – a journey that was fraught with the damage caused when a mother breaks the sacred covenant and commits an unspeakable act on her son.

Some might wonder why I have the need to share such a dark story. But by the end, there are cracks in the darkness that allow in a light that the world seldom sees. Because of my experience, I know it is important to give testament that the broken can become unbroken. In fact, my belief in the importance of this message is so strong, that I forced myself to write this entire book within a year, and every word was written on my cell phone. I did this because it would allow me to write at anytime, no matter where I was.

I wrote this book to inspire those who are hurting to reach out for help. There is light through love. It does exist, and it's not an illusion. My story is proof that unconditional love conquers and heals all wounds. There is hope no matter how dark your path has been. It is the symbol of this fact that I carry around my neck.

# CHAPTER 1:

# The Beginning

It was the best of times; it was the worst of times. Hell, it was the 1960s, and there was a lot going on back then. Sexual attitudes and behaviour began to change in a revolution against the status quo of the previous decade. This led to the normalization of many things, from legalized abortion to the FDA approving the birth control pill. It was portrayed in all aspects of life. Public nudity and pornography became more accepted. Music and movies become more risqué. Women began to express their sexual freedom by wearing go-go boots and mini-dresses. It was the start of the "Me Generation" – a time to find oneself and explore new things. In May of 1961, it also led to an appearance by me – an innocent baby, just getting his start in life and relying on the two people who brought him into the world to guide him through it. This is where my story begins.

The pictures I saw of my mother at this time showed she was very beautiful and had an hourglass figure topped off with a large cup size. Dad exhibited all the traits of a staunch Englishman, from the colour of his red hair to his facial features that were more prominent. Before I was born, they had already started a family with my mother giving birth to three boys. I would be the fourth. My father had an old-school mentality. Times had been tough when he was a kid. His parents, who had come from across the pond, had to work extremely hard just to survive and provide for him and his six siblings. Everybody needed to chip in where they could, so at a young age he acquired a very strong work ethic. It was not only expected but also demanded that he grow up fast and leave behind childish things. Reaching the permissible age to have a job, he found one just as his siblings had. There wasn't much time to socialize with each other, as it was all about work, work, work. You showed you cared by helping to provide. This was a trait he would carry forward as a man, husband, and father.

From what I was told of my mother, on the other hand, she had her emotions on full display along with a couple of other things. She required more than just material stability. It was attention she craved – both physical and emotional. With Father always working, she would satisfy what was lacking from him by seeing other men. Her physical attributes allowed her to have the pick of many, although it never seemed to quench her thirst for more. Dad was too busy providing for us to have the same propensity.

Living in a small town, it wasn't long before rumours and innuendos began to get back to him, causing him to become even more lost in his work. He began accepting as many shifts as he could get to allow him to hide from the embarrassment of his wife's dalliances. This suited my mother just fine, and she became more open with her encounters, not really caring if he knew or not. At times, she even flaunted it in front of him, which led to heated confrontations and, in turn, escalated his anger.

He started lashing out on a regular basis, and my older brothers were often caught in the crossfire with things usually getting out of hand. The cracking sound of his leather belt could be heard throughout the house. My brothers quickly learned that "out of sight and mind" was the best solution to minimize the amount of beatings received, so they stayed away from the house as much as possible. By the time I was a little older, my parents had become more apathetic towards one another. My father continued working as much as possible, while my mother was always out and about fulfilling her needs. Having a young child to look after didn't seem to stop her.

I don't recall much about being a toddler. My recollection starts when I was about five or six. Pictures of myself were non-existent before then, however, there were plenty of my older brothers. There might be a simple explanation for this, but I was never made aware of one. Maybe I just didn't like my picture being taken, who knows? What I can recall was the first day of kindergarten. I hadn't had the opportunity to play with many other kids, so going to school was a big deal for me. I remember standing at the entrance of the classroom, shy and afraid to go in any further. The other kids were already in small groups of friends, laughing and playing, while I sat by myself feeling left out.

It wasn't long before I could tell they were all talking about me as they whispered to one another. At times, they pointed in my direction, crossing their eyes and showing their teeth as if to mock me. It was now apparent what they thought was so funny about me. Before then, I'd never really thought about my physical appearance as being any different from other kids, but it was. I was born with an extremely lazy left eye, and my teeth were rotting inside my mouth, resulting from a daily diet of pop and candy. Not only were they disgusting to look at, they also caused a lot of pain. Later, I remember taking a sharp safety pin and scraping at the rotten parts to make them bleed – perhaps creating one kind of pain to cover up another.

All through preschool I learned to keep my head down, seldom smiling or engaging with anyone. It made me very self-conscious about the way I looked, and even though there were so many other kids around me, I always felt alone. However, I did have one loyal friend at home, a female Samoyed by the name of Chinook. She never noticed my eye and rotting teeth, and she was someone I could talk to and play with whenever I wanted. There was something else special we both shared. I'm not sure if she was born with it, like me, but her left eye was different as well – not in a lazy way, but it was a cloudy white. Anyways, she was my best buddy and only friend. At least I had her.

Our house was vacant most days, so I would spend most of my time at my grandmother's. She was strong as they come and the glue that held our extended family together – a true matriarch. She fulfilled some of the emotional needs that other children had satisfied from their mothers. Whenever I slept over, she would tuck me in so tight that I couldn't move. The smell of fresh, clean linen and the little night light above my head made me feel safe from the scary world outside. I could stay there forever. Our days were filled with making huckleberry pies, doing dishes, and then preparing all the things needed for the meal that night. Sundays were extra special as that's when the rest of the family would gather for her mandatory dinner that she had spent all day preparing in the kitchen. There was never just one type of pie, always two, and never store-bought ice cream, always homemade. She never slowed down. Her "down time" was climbing the hill behind the house to gather huckleberries, skiing at the local mountain, or skating at the rink. She was as strong as an ox and becoming more of a mother figure to me every day. We were just beginning to bond, and that was making me feel that things weren't so bad for me after all. But soon that would all change.

Our matriarch was very sick. She was admitted to the local hospital for some tests. On the surface nothing looked too serious, so her results were unexpected. They confirmed a diagnosis of late stage-four stomach cancer. The time she had left was very limited, and she would never return home again. I visited as often as someone would take me, staying for hours but never grasping the fatality of the situation. I was watching her die and fully unaware of it. Then one day, I remember seeing a crowd of my family members outside the hospital crying. When they told me she was gone and never coming back, I flailed my arms, and screamed and cried. I could not believe she was gone. *She wouldn't leave me... Not my grandma.* They tried to hold on to me, but I broke free. We only lived two blocks from the hospital, so I ran as fast as I possibly could. I didn't know why, but I had to get home. The answer was waiting on our front-porch step as she always was. I wasn't running to get home, but rather to get to the only one I had left. I needed Chinook more than ever now, and she knew it. She never left my side, as we cried and sat in the rain for the longest time expressing our sadness – mine for Grandma, Chinook's for me. Not once did anyone else come to console me.

On the day of the funeral I hid deep inside one of the nooks and crannies of the house, feeling scared. One thing they neglected to mention was that it was an open-casket funeral. I shouldn't have been there. I was too young and emotionally immature to understand. When they brought me up to view her, I thought she was only sleeping, so I put both my hands inside to shake her. I yelled out, "Wake up, Grandma. Wake up! I love you." I was freaking out so much I had to be picked up and carried home. I cried for days, never losing the image of her lying in her casket. Her death would deeply damage me, and there would come a time that would make me question if this was connected to how other tragic events unfolded in my life.

Even after attending elementary school for a few years, my simple social skills and maturity level still hadn't developed. I was always on the outside looking in. I started creating make-believe illnesses such as tummy troubles and headaches so I wouldn't have to attend. This resulted in my being at home more than I was at school. It hindered Mom's time spent away from the house and that was something she wasn't going to give up, no matter what. She began leaving me alone more often, knowing there was nothing wrong with me. I just didn't want to face the kids at school, and she knew it. She did, however, try to persuade me by enlisting the help of her doctor. His solution was to prescribe countless enemas in an attempt to deter me. I guess he figured something so unpleasant would surely make me stop faking it, but it had little effect. I'd rather suffer having a tube put up my butt than suffer through what was happening at school.

When I did attend, I was the target for every bully on the playground. I wore my gym shorts underneath my pants so I wouldn't have to go into the locker room to change for gym class. Locker-room bullies were the worst! I can still feel the flicking of wet rolled-up towels stinging my skin. One day, we were about to play floor hockey inside the gymnasium when a major bully started taunting me. Hearing taunts so many times in the past, I didn't give much thought to it, but I wish I had. During the game, he charged at me full speed, checking me into an old stand-up metal radiator. I collapsed to the floor crying out, while all the other kids were standing around laughing and calling me a baby. I was in excruciating pain and being humiliated at the same time. He had broken my tailbone, but hey, accidents happen. Its repercussions required me to bring in an inflatable rubber doughnut to sit on, which unfortunately gave the other kids more ammunition with which to harass me. The taunt of the week was: "Your ass hurts doughnut." Everybody else thought it was funny, but I couldn't find the humour in it.

Then came fifteen-minute recesses in hell, bringing with it butt kicks and trying to duck rocks or ice balls. I spent most of the time running from one end of the grounds to the other, just wanting to survive so I could get back inside. Running would become a pattern in my life. I always thought if I could survive one more year until I was high school, things would be different I just needed to get through grade seven. Little did I know that by the end of grade seven I would have to endure more than any child, or anyone for that matter, should have to endure.

The year went by with me just trying to get through each day without getting beaten up or feeling sad and alone. The only notable difference was my mother had become addicted to every sort of pill imaginable. Uppers, downers, opioids – you name it, she took it, and they were all legally prescribed over the phone by her beloved doctor. Funny, he was always at her beck and call for some reason. I knew she'd always taken pills but not to the extent she was popping them now. But how could I have known? I barely ever saw her.

The school year came to an end, and I was looking forward to summer break, or in my case, a break from being bullied. In the first week, my eldest brother invited me to go camping with him. I couldn't believe it. This was the first time he had asked me to do anything with him, and I was so excited. There was just one hurdle to overcome. He rode a motorcycle, and I would need a lift to the lake 18 miles away, so I begged and pleaded for Mom to take me. She refused several times but my nagging prevailed. By the time we arrived, he had already set up the tent. A short time later, somebody approached my brother and took him aside to inform him that Mom had driven over a steep embankment a few miles from home. The panic displayed on his face scared me as he quickly packed up the tent and found an alternative ride for me. When I arrived, my mother was in a hospital room with a broken back in five places. All I could feel was overwhelming guilt; I believed it was my fault for forcing her to take me in the first place. It was just another reason to hate myself even more.

After returning home, she needed around-the-clock attention as her body cast would only allow her to get up once in a while to use the bathroom or stretch a little. Because I was on break, I was always home. Fulfilling her daily needs would now rest on my shoulders, which was fine by me, as I was prepared to do anything to make things up to her. A side benefit was that now she had no choice but to spend some time with me. It's sad it took her being bedridden to spend time with me, but I was looking forward to it just the same. I was desperately seeking attention and needed to feel loved by someone. Barely into puberty, there were so many questions I had. The first sign of puberty was the onset of pubic hair, which didn't bother me, but now without warning I was getting erections. I didn't understand why. I rarely saw my dad, so I was hoping the time spent with Mom would give me the opportunity to ask her.

The beginning of my responsibilities would mainly consist of being a channel turner, bringing her meals, and refreshing her Pepsi, as her glass always needed to be topped up to wash down the handfuls of happy pills she was taking. Her cast prevented her from wearing any type of clothing. Underwear was difficult to pull up and down when using the bathroom so a blanket or sheet had to suffice. Within a few days not even those were being used. She knew we were always alone in the house, and it didn't seem to bother her if I saw all of her exposed bits and pieces. It bothered me, however, in so many different ways. The only other time I'd seen a naked woman was in *National Geographic* and none of them looked like Mom. It made me feel guilty looking at her, but very excited and extremely curious at the same time. Soon it would be all I could think about, and I started spending most of my time in her room whether she needed anything or not. All of a sudden, puberty was hitting me like a Mack Truck.

# CHAPTER 2:

# Loss of Innocence

**Warning:** What follows refers to maternal sexual abuse and could cause triggers. Note: At times dark humour is used. This is a tool learned through therapy to separate my child-self from my adult-self.

I wasn't aware of it at the time, but my mother was grooming me for what was to come. The next step was when she requested a sponge bath. She called me into her room to tell me she needed to wash up and asked me to get some warm, sudsy water and a clean washcloth. I brought them to her and then left her alone to bathe herself. Within a few minutes she called me back as she couldn't reach down to her legs and needed me to do it for her. She was lying flat on her back with her legs closed, revealing what had already seen before. I began at her feet and ankles, slowly advancing to her knees, afraid to go any further. She told me the water was getting cold and asked me to exchange it for warmer water.

When I returned, she had arranged herself differently, with her knees bent over the edge of the bed and her legs opened more. She explained her new positioning was to save the sheets from getting wet. It made sense, so I thought nothing of it. I had enough to think about when she told me to continue washing her above the knees. Pressing against her to reach the top of her legs, it suddenly felt like I needed to use the washroom really badly, but it was too late. It felt like I had peed myself. I was so embarrassed, and to make things worse, Mom noticed it as well. She assured me it was okay and told me it would be our little secret, but suggested I go change as we wouldn't want anybody else to know what had happened.

When I got to the bedroom, I hurriedly removed the pants. What I saw on them wasn't pee, and I worried there was something wrong with me. I didn't know what to do, so I decided I needed to tell Mom. I got dressed and grabbed my underpants so she could see for herself. As I entered the room, she noticed what I was holding. Before I could say a word, she told me not to worry about the incident because it was a normal part of growing up. She asked me to hand them to her. I was hesitant until she assured me that I could show her anything and could always "trust her". She didn't seem worried about what had happened so that made be feel better. Whatever it was, she was going to make it all better like a real mom does. "

Mom smiled and told me to come and sit beside her. Next, she explained her version of the "birds and the bees". She started out by reassuring me that what had just happened was a good thing, and she was very proud of me. She began to explain when boys and girls reach a certain age their body begins to change as they become men and women. Next she explained about how boys sometimes get erections when they think of girls. She asked if it had ever happened to me before, but she already knew the answer. I was never around girls my own age, so there wasn't anyone I could think about, so I replied, "You're a girl, Mom, so I guess so." Then I asked a question of my own. "But why does it grow?

She told me when a boy and a girl get older and become boyfriend /girl-friend, they share everything in order to make each other happy. One of the ways a boy shows a girl this is when his penis grows. I asked, "Is that why it grows, because it knows I like you?" She would eventually answer "sort of", but said it's only supposed to happen with girls my own age. "Moms shouldn't be little boys' girlfriends," she said. "They should already have their own." That statement and the following were necessary to start priming my self-doubt and continue the process of grooming me.

"You don't think you're ready to have a girlfriend yet, do you?" she asked.

Dropping my head, I answered, "No Mom. I don't even know any girls."

"Don't be sad," she said. She was positive it would happen one day.

"But I don't think any girl will ever like me," I replied. This was exactly the response she was expecting.

"I'll tell you what. If you promise me that you'll never tell anyone, I'll be your pretend girlfriend until you're ready for a real one...but only if you keep it a secret."

As I was about to leave, I suddenly remembered the initial question that brought me back in the first place. She then explained that my ejaculation was "special happy pee" and that my penis was just starting to learn how to be happy and excited. She made a comparison to playing baseball and how you have to practice to be good at it. Next, she would begin distorting any perception I had of right or wrong. She said it was okay if I thought of her naked when I practiced, because we had a very "special" relationship. She reminded me that no one could ever know besides us, because they wouldn't understand that I wasn't normal.

I told her my lips would be sealed forever. With nothing more to ask, I gave her a kiss and said, "Thanks Mom. You're the best." I actually left thinking that it had been the best day ever because my mother had said we had a very special relationship.

On a daily basis over the next two months, she would become my practice girlfriend and sexual mentor. The details are too graphic to relay, but she would teach me things under the guise of helping me become a "normal boy" like all the others. What was supposed to be unconditional love from a mother for her child turned into unspeakable evil, and what my mother did became so embedded in my psyche that it would control the rest of my life. Over time, the reality of what we were doing weighed heavily on me. Deep down, I knew it was really bad, and I felt guilty I didn't realize it sooner. Every time she told me other people wouldn't understand should have made me realize it was wrong. But then she convinced me, I had asked for it. It was all my fault because there was something seriously wrong with me. I couldn't let anybody know that. How could they love me then? All I ever wanted was for someone to love me so I wouldn't feel lonely anymore. *Why couldn't someone just love me?*

Today I know that sexual assault victims typically blame themselves. A child doesn't have the reasoning skills to come to the conclusion that it isn't his or her fault. The perpetrator knows this and grooms their victims slowly to normalize their abuse and strip the child of any control of how they view right and wrong. However, in my case, the grooming was anything but slow. The abuse didn't happen over a long period of time when some things might have been buried or forgotten. She demanded I remember it all because that's how she told me to practice being normal.

Maternal sexual abuse is rarely reported. The bond between a mother and her child is expected to be one of unconditional love. To think of it in any other way would be taboo. Who would ever believe it? It is so despicable that society would rather turn a blind eye and sweep it under the rug than deal with it. This in turn, leaves the victims with nowhere to reach out for help. It's a stigma that has to stop.

Once Mom was able to get out of the house, she started ignoring me again. I guess she got tired of being around me, so that was the last time anything physical occurred between us for awhile. However, the drug she had dealt still coursed through my veins, especially at night when it was quiet. It was the only thing that ever made me feel good, so I continued the routine of gratifying myself every chance I could get. I had become a thirteen-year-old sex addict. And just as a drug addict feels the crash after a high, I became racked with shame and guilt. This is something that followed me through all future sexual and personal interactions I had as an adult. I didn't know what to believe anymore. I felt more unloved than ever. Mom was right, there was something wrong with me. Those few short months of constant abuse would become the foundation of my life. Going forward, I would associate any type of affection with sexual contact. *God help me.*

The only constant in my life now was my Chinook. I retreated to her love, knowing she wouldn't hurt me. She was always there when I needed her, especially when Grandma died, so being with my smiling Samoyed suited me just fine. Perhaps that was why I liked being around her so much, she was always smiling.

Soon snow began to blanket the roads, and the snowplows piled a big mound just beyond our front fence. This was Chinook's castle. If you couldn't find her anywhere else, she would be buried into the top of it with a blanket of snow. If people weren't accustomed to her being there, her gentle bark as they passed by would make them jump. I thought it was hilarious. I was so happy to have her in my life.

One day, just before Christmas break, I hurried home and made a beeline for her castle. I waited to hear the soft bark, indicating she knew it was playtime. This time she wasn't there. I went inside the house and yelled for her. The sound of my voice would usually make her come running, but not this time. I began to panic as I searched the house inside and out. I grabbed her leash thinking she might be roaming the streets – something she never did, but I was desperate to find her. I took off in search of her, calling out her name over and over, knocking on neighbour's doors to see if they had seen her, but no one had. Soaked to the skin and very cold, I decided to go back home to see if she had returned. I ran inside only to find my eldest brother. He asked me where I'd been and I told him.

Without any concern for my feelings, he told me that Mom and Dad had her put down earlier that morning. She was dead and never coming back. My reaction was the same as when I had heard Grandma died. I started running around the house and crying in a total panic. *They didn't even let me say goodbye, just like with Grandma.* I had no one I could run to now that she was gone. The only ones I had ever been able to count on in life were gone. I now knew without any doubt that nothing good would ever last. I knew to never get too close to anything or anyone as it would only end in total heartbreak. Now every day was sadder than the last.

Over the winter, I had been successful in burying the previous summer in the past to some degree. "Practicing" on one's own gets boring. Don't get me wrong, I still continued, but liking myself was becoming a moot point. I could never like myself. I didn't think anybody else could either. Even my own mother had stopped liking me after she got her cast off. But in time, she stopped going out very much. Most days you could find her lying in bed as her pill addiction was becoming worse than ever. I think it made her male friends stop liking her as much as she wanted them too. Now she was sleeping more, left alone in the house until school ended. Every day when I got home, I would go up the stairs to her bedroom just to let her know that I was there. However, most times she would be sleeping, and I never tried waking her. She was always in a comatose state from the drugs.

One day, however, she was sleeping but she was also something else: She was completely naked on top of the bed. It was the first time I had seen her without her cast. *I guess I hadn't buried things that deep after all.*

All of the other times she made me touch her were now the only things I could think of. I began reliving each practice session in my head. Something triggered me physically and emotionally. Like a junkie relapsing, I couldn't resist the drug she was enticing me with – the only one that ever made me feel good. She would become my practice girlfriend one more time. Subconsciously I knew she wasn't even aware I was there, but it didn't matter. Every time she violated me, she was drugged up, so why should now be any different? She had continuously brainwashed me to think of all those things and told me there was something wrong with me If I didn't. Now it was my turn to do as I wished, whether she wanted me to or not. Like mother like son.

Afterwards when I returned to my room, the fix began to wear off. Feelings of guilt, shame, and disgust in myself overtook me. I started crying, wondering why I had done it again when I knew it was so wrong. I had just been beginning to leave it in the past. But the reality is, no matter how much a victim of sexual assault tries to believe it's in the past, the past is never dead. It's just waiting for the opportunity to rear its ugly head and repeat the cycle. All it took was seeing her sprawled out on the bed naked to trigger me to repeat the routine she had instilled. Now I would have another shameful, forever secret to carry.

I started getting worried about how upset she would be with me if she did knew I had been there. I had seen her upset and angry before and that scared the shit out of me. About forty minutes passed, and there was still no sound from her. I started calling to her without any response, so I got up and returned to her bedroom. As I entered, she was in the exact same position as when I had left. Reaching the side of the bed, I saw something I hadn't noticed previously; two empty pill bottles on her nightstand were tipped over. I shook her gently, but she didn't wake up. No matter how stoned she'd been in the past, the effects never lasted this long. I shook her even harder, demanding her to open her eyes. I was beginning to realize something was seriously wrong. I started running in circles.

"Please wake up, Mommy. Please!!!" She didn't seem to be breathing. Her mouth was fully open with a little dried vomit sticking to her chin. It hadn't been there before. *What do I do? I'm home alone?* I must have blacked out because the next thing I knew her doctor was in the room injecting her with something. Had I called him? For the life of me, I can't remember. She slowly began to regain consciousness just as my dad arrived. The doctor said she'd accidentally taken too many pills and she would be fine. I began wondering if it was really just an accident. I knew my guilt and self-hate made me feel like I didn't want to go on sometimes. The things we did were so bad and not to mention, I had just been with her while she lay there dying. That was all me.

Now any gratification I got from making myself happy was associated with her trying to off herself. I didn't want to pleasure myself anymore. Someone could end up dead. From that day forward, and for an extended period of time, I refused to gratify myself. However, I developed another compulsion as a substitution. As my pubic hair began to grow, I taught myself to shave it off. It became so much of an obsession I was doing it daily whether hair had time to regrow or not. This led to scraping my genitals with a razor to cause nicks and cuts that would bleed. The sting had become addictive just like when I used to poke at my rotting teeth with a needle. But now, I used rubbing alcohol to increase the pain.

Later, through therapy, I learned a root cause for this behaviour was that physical pain can take away emotional pain. Because it works instantly, cutting is highly reinforcing and becomes addictive. The sensation feels like a release of pressure, similar to how people suffering from bulimia describe purging. Another contributing factor was that hairlessness reminded me of an innocence lost – a time before I was able to get an erection and for it to cause so many problems.

# CHAPTER 3:

# More Rough Years

A few years passed, bringing on my sixteenth birthday. It would bring a couple of things that made me excited in another way: a driver's license and a car. I thought this would be a catalyst to my making friends as not too many kids had their own vehicle at the age of sixteen. My car was a powder-blue Mustang 2. I was styling and feeling proud. Kids would now have to think I was cool. For once, I was actually looking forward to going to school, so I could show it off. I believed the car would change everything.

There wasn't much time in the morning for anyone to really see my car, but I figured there would be plenty of time after school. The last bell of the day rang, and I hurried to my locker. I couldn't wait to get outside. Excitedly, I opened the doors leading to the parking lot. It looked like my wish had come true as all the kids were standing around my car. For a brief moment, I felt happy and cool. It wasn't until I got closer that I realized they weren't admiring it, but rather laughing, as someone had let the air out of all my tires during class. I felt so humiliated.

I spent the next two hours taking each tire off and walking downtown to inflate them. As I walked, kids drove by taunting me and laughing their guts out. It goes without saying that I always walked to school from that day forward. Things hadn't changed since kindergarten and elementary school. I was still bullied and still unloved. It was the same thing – just a different day."

About a year later, I was given the opportunity to visit my grandfather's brother in Saskatchewan during summer holidays. I thought it would be a nice change to get away from where anybody knew me. The plan was to take the bus down to visit him for a week. It was only an 18-hour ride by myself, but I guess my parents thought I could handle it. What could go wrong?

There was a three-hour layover in Calgary, during which an older man approached me. He asked where I was heading and when my bus was going to depart. He seemed really nice, and offered to take me to a restaurant to buy me lunch. Still naïve, I accepted thinking maybe he could be my friend. We went to his car to travel the couple of miles up the road to where he said the restaurant was located. As soon as we left the parking lot, I knew I'd made a mistake. The long knife on his dashboard had something to do with my epiphany. I kept asking him if we were almost there as we had travelled more than a couple of miles. He wouldn't tell me; he just continued driving, and now I couldn't see any other buildings around us. Finally, he turned down a road and parked.

As soon as he did, he grabbed the knife and put it on the floor in front of him. I was terrified! He demanded that I pull down my pants, but I refused. He then used the back of his fist and struck me in the chest. I thought he was going to kill me. I started crying, which made him say, "Okay, keep your pants on," but then he pulled down his. He forcefully grabbed my hand and put it on him. I just held it there without any motion, which pissed him off. He grabbed me by the hair and forced my head to it, telling me to open my mouth. My brain switched into survival mode. I did what needed to be done to get out of the situation. Once finished, the man did his pants back up, turned on the car, and started driving back. Just knowing I was getting out of this alive was a relief to me. As he let me off about six blocks from the depot, he picked up the knife off the floor and told me I'd better keep my fucking mouth shut. *Yeah, I know, another "forever secret".* I didn't want to go on with the visit anymore, so I took the next bus back home and never spoke of it again. I figured it was my fault anyways for going with him. Now any interaction with the male species had become polluted as well. From the bullying I received as a child to my father's indifference, and now this, I would steer away from guys as much as possible. I was just never meant to have one as a friend.

# CHAPTER 4:

# The Search Begins

After getting back home I felt safe. Things hadn't changed, but at least I wasn't in fear for my life, so I carried on. Then one day, I happened upon a poster. Disco was big back then, and it said there would be disco lessons at the old Union Hall every Sunday night for free. I gathered up enough courage and went. This was a decision that would begin to change my social status. I was a natural dancer. *Who knew?* I figured the better I became, the more girls would want to dance with me. It was a way to socialize – something I'd never done before. It also made me feel like I was good at something for once. Now I had two things going for me, I knew how to dance and still had a cool car. These two superficial things would mask my emotional immaturity and all the other social skills I still lacked.

I began to perpetuate superficiality at any cost. I would do anything to feel liked and loved, even if it meant lying. I began to create a new identity for myself. It was easy to do as I didn't have one in the first place. Now I had a lot of kids the same age as me to socialize with. Granted, there were a lot more girls, but that suited me. I had high hopes I would finally find the affection I craved so much and not just the way Mom showed it. So now with a new mission in life, my only focus was girls. Unlike before, they were all paying attention to me now – or at least my dancing anyways. I was even asked to go out on dates, something I'd never done before, as I had always felt too awkward to accept any invitations. I was clueless about what to expect.

There was one girl I'll remember for the rest of my life. She was a Filipino girl, standing about five foot four. Her long, silky, black hair reached down to her knees. She was absolutely stunning. It took me by surprise when she asked me to dance. Our styles meshed, and we danced the rest of the night together. Talking to her made it apparent how beautiful she was on the inside as well. She was modest, nice, and kind. By the end of the night, we decided to become permanent dance partners. I didn't know if she could see how damaged I was, but it didn't seem to matter if she did. She genuinely took an interest in me as a person. Not only did I have a dance partner, but now I also had my real first friend. I don't think I had ever been so relaxed in my life around a person. It was a relief for me that I didn't need to put on a show. Of course, I could never reveal who I really was, but I was feeling some sort of a bond just the same. I was learning to be a friend by following her example. But just when everything was looking up for me, she was killed in a head-on collision a month later. It confirmed what I already knew: Nothing good ever lasts. I felt a profound sadness. I had gained my first friend and lost her in the same breath. Rest in peace K. I will never forget you.

Then came another first, at least with a girl around my own age. One night after dance class, we all went to Boston Pizza. A friend of someone in the dance group had joined us and introduced herself as Kim. She was a very pretty girl and a little drunk, I think, but she appeared to take a liking to me. She told me she loved watching me dance and asked if I would teach her sometime. I said I would be happy to. Over the course of the evening, she was touching and leaning into me, laughing, smiling, and actually having a good time. I was more nervous than anything else as I had never had a girl flirt with me like this before. *Maybe there wasn't something wrong with me after all.* Leaving the restaurant, she tucked her arm under mine and whispered, "Do you want to go and watch the submarine races?"

*We had submarine races? Holy shit! How did I not know about this?* I had no Idea what she was talking about. Winging it, I just went with the flow and told her that I would love to, so we drove off with her directing me to a local river lookout. She must have changed her mind about the submarines because she started kissing me. Anyways, I knew she wanted to make-out, but I had no clue how. I guess it starts off with kissing. *Maybe that was the first base Mom didn't teach me about. But what happens at second and third? Oh yeah, something I knew all too well.*

We spent a lot of our time jockeying around to get more comfortable in the front seat. After kissing for a while, she stopped what she was doing, looked at me, and asked if I wanted to poke her. *Here we go again. What the hell did that mean? Awkward.* She realized I had no clue, so she repeated its meaning in a more direct fashion. *Oh, you mean it's happy time.* I hadn't had any real sense of that in the last two years, which was plenty enough time to make me curious again. I knew eventually interactions with girls could become sexual as a normal progression of a relationship. I guess this was the beginning of it. I just wanted to be normal like all the other boys, but I had no idea how. However, she did.

She got out of the car waiting for me to follow. She reclined down on the ground and motioned for me to lie on top of her. Before I had any second thoughts, it was happening. All the pent-up sexual energy built up over the last two years had to be released, and it was. It was over so quickly she didn't seem to get happy herself, but she didn't appear to be disappointed about it. As we both started getting dressed, she said, "This was your first time, wasn't it?"

*Not really,* I thought, but what could I say? I told her it was and I hoped I did it right. She responded with something I had heard so many times in the past. "It's okay, you just need to do it more to get better at it." She said she wouldn't mind letting me practice on her if I wanted to. I would take her up on that offer every chance we could meet up. That's all it was from that point on, with nothing else shared. In my head I thought she must have liked me a little. Why else would she let me practice on her? However, it appears there were other boys that needed practice as much as I did. In fact, I walked in on her with someone else. This lesson taught me some girls only wanted to be practice girlfriends and help as many boys as they could. Unfortunately, there was no way of telling which kind of girlfriend they were until it was too late, so I would just have to hope for the best.

Being sexually active again triggered me into pleasuring myself once more and losing any sense of self-control. I started using magazines, movies, and any image I could think of, including my mother – whatever it took to get happy. Now my only focus was sexual gratification and searching out any girl to assist me. Plus, along the way, I thought it could bring with it what I was ultimately looking for – someone who could actually love me.

My relationships would only last a short while, if you could call them that. There were a lot of one-night stands and even a few of those in the same day. Some would last a week or two at the most. Intercourse was seldom. I did what I knew I was good at. I massaged them to happiness. It was all about their gratification. I never wanted to disappoint anyone ever again. As long as I could keep them sexually satisfied, there was a chance they would love me. Isn't that what it's all about? For me, it was; for them, not so much. But I associated their physical gratification with my emotional gratification. There was nothing else I could offer them. I couldn't let them know who I really was. I felt that not so deep down there was something wrong and twisted inside me. What chance would I stand then? Out of the numerous girls I had sexual interactions with up to this point, there were only two I had intercourse with. Neither turning out very well for different reasons. As time went on and the more active I became, it triggered the progression I had learned as a student, and I needed to act out the final lesson my teacher had taught me: Boys and girls need to get happy together.

I started seeing a girl who I had met through dance class. She was very prim and proper, and wouldn't you know it, her name was Kim as well. Some coincidence, eh? She was the Homecoming Queen in our area. We went out for dinners and to the beach like normal people starting off in a relationship. It would take weeks before we even started feeling each other up. That was different and kind of nice. Unfortunately, before we could get emotionally closer, she told me that her family was moving away and she wanted to make love with me before she did. We planned a romantic evening the night before she was going to leave. I was looking after a couple of dogs while their owners were away and had a key to their trailer. When the night arrived and we started, she grimaced in pain, which was very unsettling to me. She told me it was okay and wanted me to continue, but I realized she wasn't enjoying it. Making things worse, I could see droplets of blood, so I thought I had hurt her. I stopped and said I didn't think we should go any further. Both embarrassed, we got up and put our clothes back on and didn't say a word about it as I drove her home to say our last goodbyes. Later that night, she called and revealed what had happened. She had been a virgin and wanted me to be her first. How would I've have known that? *Aw, jeez...*

I had no idea how to establish any type of emotional bond with another person. It played more and more on my lack of self-esteem; I thought I could never measure up to anybody's standards. I began sabotaging any chance I had with my neediness, which gave way to desperation. This was circle that couldn't be broken, and I followed the same loop over and over. My obsession to fill the void would lead me to do or say anything – beg, borrow, steal or lie. I became more and more promiscuous. I was running out of options where I lived, as I had either dated, danced, or liked most of the girls in town and even some of their mothers too.

Perhaps I was just looking in the wrong place. Maybe I could find what I was looking for down the road 40 miles. I was about to embark on a road trip to find love, attempting to stack the odds. Doesn't buying more lottery tickets and using new numbers increase your chances of winning? On a Friday night I was off to get as many new numbers as I could and hopefully have some luck and cash in with one of them. I was beginning to feel more confident on the drive over as none of the girls would know me. That way, I could become whoever I wanted to be and they wouldn't know the difference. I arrived at the only dance club in the next town with high hopes. Back then it was easy to get into clubs underage. I asked a few girls to dance and had a few drinks, but nothing special. Most of the girls had boyfriends, but were there without them because they wanted to dance. I started feeling discouraged and wondering if the trip had been a waste of time. But just as I was about to leave a new group of girls arrived. I decided to give it a few more minutes just in case.

One stood out from all the rest by the way she carried herself. I remember thinking she was like a bottle of bubbly. Her presence immediately brought oxygen to the joint, so I decided to stay after all. *Maybe this was the one.* It was getting late, and everyone still remaining in the club had already consumed their fair share of alcohol. The few guys remaining were now just trying to hit on any girl they could, hoping they would get lucky for the night. Miss Bubbly, on the other hand, just wanted to dance with her girlfriends. I was intrigued by her exuberance; I could definitely use some of that in my life. I needed to come up with a plan for her to talk to me. Knowing the direct approach wouldn't work, I did exactly the opposite to what my first inclinations would have been: I would wait for her to approach me. So instead, I asked her friend to dance. She told me that her friend thought I was really cute and was hoping she could meet me. *How cool is that? My plan had actually worked.*

We were introduced and hit the floor. Her spirit was contagious. We danced the rest of the night away. By now, she knew I lived forty miles away. I don't know if it was an invitation to hook up or not, but she graciously offered me a place to stay. I didn't want to drive back home, but I declined her offer. I made up some cockamamie story that I had to work the next morning at my non-existent job for half a day and then I would be starting my vacation. I said I would love to come back the next day and see her. It turns out she had started her vacation that weekend from a real job as well, so she was available to meet up anytime. We gave each other a quick hug, and I was off to nowhere really, but I certainly didn't want to make the drive home. So I drove a few miles out of town to a lookout right beside the highway and turned the car off and went to sleep.

The noise from the traffic woke me up early the next morning. I still had about five hours or so to kill before we were to meet up, so I just drove around. That was five long hours waiting to find out if she was the drug I needed. How about that for commitment? It was more like desperation, but I was still committed. We met up, and to make a short story even shorter, I had taken up residence with her by the end of the evening. It was just that quick. It was always easy for me for some reason. It could have been all the bullshit I was burying them in.

All ran smoothly for three or four weeks. I left during the day to travel to my non-existent job and returned at night. We were having fun going to the local beach and then out to the bars. She told me a lot about herself, but there was nothing I could tell her about me that I dared to share. I made stuff up and told her things I thought she wanted to hear. I gave her nothing she needed to begin forming any meaningful type of bond. It was all about having fun at the time, but that too can become old very fast. I began to see the writing on the wall. I knew she was going to dump me after awhile, but I didn't want it to stop. It was feeding me some sort of happiness I was lacking, and I was prepared to do anything to stay in a state of happiness. I began seriously thinking about ways to keep things going with her. *So, let me think, how could I get a small-town girl with very little excitement in her life to want to spend more time with me. I know. I'll offer her something she wouldn't be able to pass up. What could be more thrilling than an exotic getaway to paradise?* The minute I introduced the idea to her she was in all the way. There was only one problem. Her job. You know, the one she actually had, unlike me. She had just taken her vacation and couldn't book another one for three months, but I knew we wouldn't last that long. It needed to be now or never, so I convinced her to quit. *Asshole!*

We were heading to paradise in eight days. Tickets were bought, new luggage purchased, cash withdrawn, and we were on our way. She was very grateful she didn't have to pay for a thing. Well, that was kind of true. She wasn't cash out of hand; however, her bank didn't share the same view. They didn't appreciate she didn't have the funds to cover all the cheques that had bounced; ones she had no clue were written until some time later. I knew, however. The tickets, luggage, cash, all of it, was acquired by stolen and forged personal cheques. I was willing

to commit bank fraud in my search for love, just as a drug addict would do anything to get another fix. However, I was an emotional junky, without regard to
the consequences. I was only fixated on being liked – no matter what the cost.

It was the first time either of us had flown anywhere, so that alone excited us.
Our trip included a three-day layover at a Miami hotel, smack in the middle of
downtown. Upon checking in, the receptionist informed us there was an open-
air, rooftop club if we felt like dancing. We checked out the other amenities,
returned to our room, sucked back a few drinks, and then decided to make our
way up to the rooftop to dance and continue the party. We were having the time
of our lives. Sometimes when we danced, the other partygoers would stop and
clear the floor to watch us and then buy drinks out of their appreciation for the
show. We'd been there for a few hours, and during a break, an elderly gentleman approached us and introduced himself as the hotel manager. He said he'd
been watching us all evening and he was impressed. He offered us work as dance
coordinators for the hotel.

*Wow!* I told him we were flattered, but we were only there on vacation and
heading to Freeport in a couple of days. He seemed disappointed, but then he
told us that he had to make a phone call and he would be back shortly. When
he returned, he said he had just gotten off the phone with his brother, who was
the entertainment coordinator at the hotel and casino in Freeport. He said if we
worked for him for a few weeks, his brother would offer us the same position
when we arrived in the Bahamas. How could we pass that up? Besides, it would
also relieve a lot of money pressure. My girl was over the moon about it and
told me she was game if I was. It was a done deal. *Holy shit. I was going to make
money just by getting people to party.* With expedited work visas, we were ready to
rock and roll, or should I say shake and twist? Every waking moment became a
never-ending party with most meals and the room being comped by the hotel. I
even had money in my pocket – not much, but enough to keep the party going.

After fulfilling our obligation in Miami, we arrived in Freeport, which is a
very small island off the coast of Nassau. Its main attraction was the hotel and
casino, which brought in big gamers and high rollers. A-list guests would fly in
on private jets from around the world to gamble there and then fly back out the
same day. We would be hobnobbing it with the rich and famous. We found a
small, self-contained suite that we could rent by the month just across from the
casino. Our employment duties were basically the same as they were in Miami.

Every night, the hotel's outside lounge would have different theme nights, which always revolved around dancing. Calypso night, disco night – whatever dance you could think of, they had a night for it. Our job was to get everyone up moving. Only the locals knew that we were part of the staff. The more guests danced, the more they drank and spent lots of money. Business 101.

We hardly ever slept. We would finish at the hotel around three in the morning and then head off to the beach with some of the other staff couples to continue the party. Sitting around in the private floating bar in nothing but our birthday suits, we partook of the many party favours being offered. Booze, weed, coke – we were doing it all now, every waking moment. Day after day, night after night, we were literally living the high life and doing it with paradise as a backdrop. Now I was not only addicted to giving gratification, but also to drugs. Not the best of combinations. In my head at the time, I thought things couldn't have been better. Not only that, I had sustained some sort of a relationship for more than a few weeks. Maybe my girl really did like me after all. I know all we did was party, but we seemed to be enjoying each other's company. I thought if we could keep things going, it might give us the time needed to really have a shot at making it work

But no matter what I tried to tell myself, it wasn't real life. Not for her anyways. She was getting burnt out and needed something more substantial than just being the life of the party. She wanted to go back home to Canada; me not so much. I had no desire to return, not back to British Columbia anyway. That wasn't in the plan. *Oh, wait I forgot, I didn't have one.* What to do? Always trying to delay the inevitable, I told her there was nothing back home for us. I convinced her the humdrum lifestyle of a small town would be boring now, especially after experiencing the high life. Calgary, Alberta was the last layover of our trip home and still far enough away from British Columbia to make me feel more comfortable about returning, so that's where we would be heading. We said goodbye to paradise and left for Calgary. I had a little bit of money, at least enough to get us by for a couple of weeks.

Upon arriving in Calgary, we found a fully furnished apartment to rent. Ironically, my girl found a job at the same railway company I had made her quit back home. I, on the other hand, became a high-end ladies' footwear consultant. In other words, I was a glorified loafer pusher to the ladies, and I was good at it.

Making the lady customers feel special wasn't a problem for me. Telling them what they wanted to hear wasn't a problem either. It was who I was now – doing or saying whatever it would take to make people like me.

All was well for a while until it was casually mentioned she had talked to somebody back home. It was the first time she had connected with anyone since we had left on our little excursion. If there were cell phones back then, she would have left my ass before we even reached the Bahamas. *This is where the shit is going to hit the fan,* I thought. She must know now. It's done. Over. Self-destruct complete. But she didn't go into any details about the conversation; she just made a comment in passing. Maybe things were safe for now. But it did freak me out, so I felt like I needed to do something just in case she did know. I needed to do something to smooth things over, because if she didn't know now, it would only be a matter of time before she did.

*How could I bury myself even deeper? Got it!* Just as the gift trip to the Bahamas had given me more time, I thought maybe another gift would as well. Never thinking of the consequences of my actions, the next day at work, I took it upon myself to secretly borrow a very expensive pair of stilettos. *But what's a little theft when it comes to matters of the heart?* Anyways, this was nothing compared to what I had already done. That evening, with the shoes tucked under my arm, I returned to the apartment to surprise her with them. She was gone along with all of her belongings. She had found out the truth, but hadn't given me any clue. On the coffee table was the necklace I had bought her along with what I assumed was a "Dear John" letter, or in my case, "You Lying Son of a Bitch" Letter.

# CHAPTER 5:
# The Hooker Mommy

I knew it would only be a matter of time until I had to pay the piper, but my intention was to put it off for as long as possible. I still had a job and was still in Alberta, which would keep me safe from any provincial warrants that might have been issued. Now more than ever I needed a drink, so I walked down to a local bar to fill myself with tequila. On the way back, I saw a woman walking towards me, wearing a white mini-skirt and tight satin top. I could tell she was a lot older than I was, but I still found her very appealing for some reason. Just before our paths were about to intersect, she took a side step so she was behind me. She reached down, grabbed my ass, and asked if I wanted to party. I knew she was a hooker. I had never been with one before, but they always fascinated me as we had something in common: We both offered sexual favours to anyone who was willing to pay. The only difference was their payment was monetary, whereas mine was the replenishment of my emotional bank account that was always in overdraft.

I needed any type of affection in that moment, whatever the cost. By this time, I was already surveying her physical attributes – bare long legs and big breasts. For a brief second, I had a flashback of my mother. The amount of tequila in me made it only a fleeting thought. Now the only problem I had was I didn't have any money or anything of value to barter with. Or did I? Thinking of the $300 pair of stilettos sitting on my counter, I asked if she would be interested in a little trade. I told her my proposition, and it intrigued her, but she would have to see them first. I invited her up to the apartment so she could authenticate them. Once she did, a deal was struck. Their value insured ninety minutes of her undivided attention and unrestricted access. Her list of dos and don'ts didn't contain very many don'ts. She was there to give me anything I wanted.

Entering the bedroom, she removed her top, allowing her breasts to fall lower and rest in their natural position. The tequila must have been wearing off as a vision of my mother's boobs flashed before my eyes again. It was making me feel sick to my stomach, but I tried to convince myself it was all in my head, and I wasn't that little boy anymore. *Oh, but yes I was.* She sat on the edge of the bed and pulled up her mini skirt. The way it fell looked very familiar to me. Then I knew why. Her mini-skirt resembled the cast my mother had worn. I almost put an end to the whole situation. *I wish I had!*

All of a sudden, I was feeling a deep anger rising up from the depths of me. In a way, I had always lived with it, but it was always directed inwardly and never towards anyone else, including my mother. I'd experienced so many other emotions with her except that one. I excused myself from the room for a moment and chugged back four or five ounces of tequila and snorted a half a gram of blow. I needed all the help I could get to make it through this, as I couldn't control the thoughts that were overtaking me. I was hoping the booze and blow would bring me back to reality.

I began unconsciously acting out all my "practice sessions" I had with my mother. I couldn't control what I was saying or doing. I blacked out. A "Momma" comment I accidentally blurted out only escalated things. She thought I was role playing, telling me now she understood what her role was. That was the last thing I wanted, but it was out of my control as so many times in the past. This time, however, it would come out as rage. I was wigging out, becoming extremely aggressive and very physical. I was so fucked up. In my head, I just wanted her to feel my pain for all the things she did to me, but the hooker didn't know that, she was just playing a role.

Finally, with sweat running down my forehead and my body uncontrollably shaking from total exhaustion, I collapsed on top of her without completion. I instantly started hating myself for what I had just done. I sat on the bed beside her with my body slumped with shame, begging her to forgive me and telling her how very sorry I was over and over again. She had no idea why I was sorry, only concerned she didn't fulfill her end of our bargain. She asked me if I wanted her to finish me off. I told her that was the last thing I wanted now. It was fine by her. She got up, dressed, and left with her boxed payment under one of her arms. I sat there bawling my eyes out, confused and hurt. I thought had I left those things in the past.

I should have known that the past would always guide me through life. All it would take was one bad experience or memory unlocked to make me that little boy again, just like when I was triggered into "boy-friending" my almost dead mother. Now, however, I had shown a very ugly and terrifying side of me that I hadn't known existed. Right then and there, I promised myself I would never feel that angry again. Once was enough!

I almost slept through my alarm the next morning. At any cost I didn't want to screw up my job as it was the only thing of which I had control. I made a quick cup of coffee to go, snorted a small line, and caught the train to work. It gave me plenty of time to beat myself up about what had happened. I tried to convince myself to put it behind me as I knew I had bigger worries waiting back home for me. At least I could put that off for a while, since I still had the means to support myself in Calgary.

When I arrived for my shift, my boss was talking to a couple of uniformed city cops. When they saw me, they motioned for me to join them. It turns out that a hooker had tried returning a pair of stilettos earlier that morning. They asked me if I knew anything about it. I told them I had no clue what they were talking about and hoped my acting would convince them. One of the cops responded he knew I was lying, but I held my ground. Realizing I wouldn't confess, they said I was free to go since they couldn't prove anything in court. He told my boss she had to give me my last paycheque. However, she had more to give me than that. Just one last little turn of the knife. I guess she had quite the little girly chat with the hooker. On my way out the door, she yelled out so everybody could hear, "That's right, little boy, run home to your mommy. Maybe you won't have to pay for her." It was a low blow, but I guess I deserved it. It still hurt me deeply. She had no idea. If she had only known. Feeling dejected on my way home, I thought how ironic it was that my hooker mother had screwed me right back the next day. Somewhat like my real mom, however in her case, the effects would last a lifetime. "

Not having any source of income and no other place to go, I was forced to return home and face the consequences of my actions. A couple of days later, I bought a bus ticket with the rest of the money I had and began the twelve-hour trip back. I wasn't looking forward to what was waiting for me, but I figured I might as well get it over with. As my journey began, I sat beside a girl and told her my name was Jessie. She asked my destination, and I told her I had a performance at the coast, which of course raised her curiosity. "What kind of performance?" she asked.

I didn't lie, I told her I was a dancer. It wasn't my fault she thought I meant I was a stripper. She said she was on her way to take care of her brother's house while he was in Mexico. Her thinking I was a stripper made it easy for me to hook up with her when we reached her brother's town.

See how my life was consumed by my sexual addiction. I was always trying to fill the void by being with any girl I met. We all know what the cause was. This was just the beginning of the effect.

CHAPTER 6:

# Actions Without Consequences

I didn't know what to expect when I got home, except that it wouldn't be good. My dad arrived to pick me up. On the way back to the house not a word was said. I didn't know how to take it. On one hand, I thought we didn't talk very much anyway. On the other, he could be so pissed at me and he was speechless. *It was the latter.*

Once inside, my parents told me they knew all about my little adventure. The police had already made numerous visits to the house looking for me. Dad told me to put my coat back on as we were heading down to the police station so I could turn myself in, which also meant I would have to spend the night in jail. I was still a child emotionally so it terrified me. The next day I was released with a court date. I was guilty so I thought that was that. I would be going to big boys' jail soon. I finally had to suffer the consequences of my actions. Hopefully it would teach me a valuable lesson to help me grow.

Now it was time to face my parents again. I walked back home fully expecting it would be a very loud reception but to my surprise it wasn't. They were both very matter-of-fact about what needed to be done. They also told me they had already hired a lawyer, and not just any lawyer, but the highest-priced one in town. I wondered why they were doing this. Surely a Crown-appointed one would suffice. But I did what they wanted me to do and told the lawyer everything. I met with him only once and not again until the court date. My parents, however, were having regular meetings with him. I had no idea what they discussed, but I knew it was a given fact that I was pleading guilty. The only question now was the amount of time I would be spending in jail.

During the hearing, the prosecutor recommended I should be sentenced to a year. My lawyer objected and argued that it was a harsh sentence for a first-time offender. The prosecutor stayed firm to his recommendation. Before the judge could pass sentence, my lawyer asked for a short adjournment. During the recess I saw him talking to the prosecutor and then calling my parents to join them. After about fifteen minutes, the court was called back in session. I had no idea what was going to happen. The prosecutor stood up and told the judge that he and my lawyer had reached a consensus on my sentence, "If it pleased the court." The agreement was my parents would pay all money owing for the fraudulent cheques, and the Crown would not requesting jail time, but rather six months of probation.

It did please the court. I was released to go home after a $6,000 cheque from my parents' savings account was written. This was one of the very few times my parents had my back. In a strange way I felt they owed it to me. I think they did as well to satisfy their own guilt. Mom's guilt was for what she did to me. Dad's was for never being around to help guide me through life. Sadly, out of all the times in the past they could have helped, this shouldn't have been one of them. They should have known better and let me suffer the consequences of my actions, no matter what they were. Now with major repercussions avoided and not really having to take responsibility, another valuable lesson had been wasted. Like everything else in my life, I never got what I needed – not as a child, not as a teenager. I knew I desperately needed help, but I had nowhere to get it. I was still alone and craving the one thing that would solve it all – love.

I was nineteen now, and the lack of any form of maturity made it difficult for me to hold onto a job. Most of my money came from my mom. She controlled my parents' bank account, and I learned I had a certain kind of power over her. It entitled me to get whatever I wanted in exchange for holding on to our forever secret. She owed me big time, and I was cashing in on it every chance I could get. Still without a job, I had plenty of time to visit the bar. In fact, one had become my home away from home. At least I wasn't actively chasing skirts anymore. Now I was chasing shots. The patrons were all there to play pool and get drunk. My days were filled with drinking and only an occasional happy time. Booze was my rambunctious mistress now. One addiction had taken the place of another. Along with it came two impaired charges. I was drinking way too much, but everybody was happy when they drank. It made me think less about myself, and I never wanted to think about that. It was so damn depressing.

So there I was without a driver's license and getting bored, I borrowed some money and hopped a bus to make my way to Vancouver. I had no idea why; it was just on a whim. I had no plans for when I got there or about where I was going to stay. I was just running like I always did.

I arrived just before noon and began walking to the centre of town. A few long blocks later, I found myself standing in front of a strip club. Of course, I was going in. As I entered, the first show of the day had already commenced. The dancer on stage didn't seem to care about the size of her audience. She was just dancing in her own little world. She was so seductively innocent. Maybe that's why her stage name was "Baby Buns". She was a petite thing with long blonde hair and big blue eyes, which reminded me of Charlene Tilton from the television show called *Dallas*. She radiated an aura of unabashed sex appeal. As I continued watching, I began noticing something else about her. It's hard to explain, but I sensed a sadness in her like she also had been deeply hurt by someone. I could see it in her eyes. It made me feel for her, knowing all too well what sadness felt like. There was some sort of connection, but I never thought I would have the chance to find out what it was, as she was so out of my league.

After her performance I fully expected her to walk off the stage and go to her dressing room. To my surprise, she casually walked over to my table. She sat down across from me with her robe fully open as if giving me a private show. She introduced herself as Bonnie Marie and asked what I thought of her show. I told her she was a very good dancer. She was taken aback about my response. I think she expected to hear a comment about her body. She probably got a lot of that and hearing something else made those sad eyes have a little sparkle in them. I knew right then we were cut from the same cloth, searching for any resemblance of approval. She didn't have to say it, but I knew she was as damaged as I was. I think she could see it in me as well, and we were bonding because of it. It wasn't a healthy connection, but one just the same. *Damaged people seek out those who are also damaged. Like begets like.*

We sat there feeding each other's neediness, both of us trying to satisfy our emotional hunger. We should have been the last people on earth to try and teach each other about love, but we both needed another fix and would take it wherever we could get it. As we sat and talked, things got interesting. We queried each other with questions that two strangers would commonly ask. Age: She was 18. Siblings: She had 3. Birthplace: Well, that was curious. It just so happened she was also born in a small town in the Kootenay's. My town. *Coincidence or fate?* She would opt for the latter, wanting to perpetuate the unhealthy bond growing between us. But it didn't stop there. She fed into it, beginning to recollect that we had met before. She was positive we had played together building sandcastles at a local lake when we were very small children. It's possible. I was seldom at the lake, but then again, before the age of 7 or 8 there wasn't a lot I remembered. Her persistence of the notion was aggressive. She wanted me to believe it to pull me into her world more. It worked because I would say anything to pull her into mine and do anything to create a connection to solidify the idea that it was fate bringing us together. We were trying to convince each other that this was the beginning of something special for the both of us. I have to admit, it did seem more than coincidence. *Maybe we could learn what love was together.*

We were both all in; our journey in life together would start that day. Her made-up stories complimented mine. Truths or untruths – it didn't matter from that point on. It was all about satisfying our gluttonous emotional appetite. I told her what she needed to hear to make her feel good, and she did the same with me. She told me she only started stripping at the age of seventeen to support herself after she ran away from home. At first it was something she didn't want to do, but she became good at it and now liked performing. Oh my, oh my. I was a performer as well and my act was about to start. I took my cue and said I wanted to take her away from this life, to be her knight in shining armour. I said I was waiting on money and once I received it, I would take care of her. *After all, this was fate wasn't it?* That night, she invited me back to her place. And boy, oh boy, I had no idea what I was in for. Her sexual prowess far surpassed anything I had ever encountered. Her attention was focused on every aspect of my gratification, sometimes overwhelming me. I was entranced by everything she did. For the first time it was all about me. She was fulfilling desires I didn't even know I had. She was the female me with a libido far surpassing even mine. "

It was a connection no one else could understand unless they have been abused. We were both givers and pleasers. Superficial and perverse as it was, it filled a void we both had. We both just wanted to make each other happy, as much as we could. *After all, this was the only way we had been taught how to display any type of affection.*

We did the only thing two emotionally immature, extremely damaged, sexually addicted people could do after two days of knowing each other. We decided to get married as soon as possible. This wasn't going to be good, especially with my financial stability not exactly what I had professed it to be, but why should that little fib stop me now? So, without any means of support and no long-range plan, it was full steam ahead. We were crazy, mixed-up kids. Now all we had to do was to wait for that non-existent money that I was expecting. I didn't want her to continue dancing, even though it would have given us the funds we needed, but my jealous insecurities wouldn't allow it. I was the only one that could see her naked now. Who knows, she might meet her actual knight in shining armour, and I would be left alone again.

Besides she was also making me enjoy everything about sex for the first time without the guilt. She was my new teacher now. You could understand how delighted I was when she asked me if I wanted to go and meet her mother and stay there until my funds came through. She danced her last show that day with her final paycheque funding our bus trip to meet her mom. Arriving and meeting with some of her family gave me a little more insight into what she had run away from. She had been exposed to the same type of love from a father as I had with a mother. But who was I to judge? All I knew was that for the first time in my life what I gave was being returned tenfold. Granted it was all sexual, but it was all we both knew. It was love to us. "

Wedding plans made and executed, we were man and wife. However, we had a little setback a few days later. It appeared someone had told the police where I was living, and I had forgotten about some unpaid fines. So with no money to pay them, I was escorted to jail to pay with time served. I was worried my jig was up concerning any finances coming through, and I didn't know how my new wife would take it. Any worries I had were soon a thing of the past as she was all over me when I returned, telling me she had missed me. Well, maybe not me per se, but how we showed our love. That time it felt sort of special for some reason. *I wouldn't know how special it was until sometime later.*

Weeks had passed without an ounce of any type of emotional bonding; everything was physical. We were making each other happy seven or eight times a day in ways I was just learning from her, but even that was becoming routine now. I was aware that just like me, she was incapable of expressing real love. I knew the signs all too well. We were both living a lie. I was just more aware of mine. It wasn't going to last anyway and being the asshole that I am, I started looking around again, craving something new. However, I was married now, and believe it or not, the last thing I wanted to do was to hurt her. She had been hurt enough as it was, so I held it in my pants, but I was gone already.

There was no way ether of us could have known a phone call from one of her friends would give me the new I was looking for and be the final nail in the coffin for us. My wife had many acquaintances while she was on the dance circuit, mostly other dancers. A few she bonded with, but most were also running from their past. One day, she received a call from one who was in the area and wanted to meet up and reconnect. Arrangements were made to meet later that night in town. My wife began to fill me in on a little about her, and it turns out they had been more than just colleagues; they were also happy buddies. Well that was definitely something new. I couldn't blame her, I guess. She probably thought it would increase the odds of finding what she was looking for. I know that looking anywhere you can get what you need at the time made sense to me.

I was really looking forward to the night with visions of possibilities dancing in my head. We met up in the bar of the hotel where she was staying. There were a couple of other things my wife hadn't mentioned about her. First, she was black, which from my past experience in paradise excited me very much. Second, she was quite renowned on the circuit. Even those not frequenting strip clubs had heard of her unusual talents using certain props during her performance. Let's just say she had very strong Kegel muscles. Just thinking about it brought my thoughts to another dimension. We sat at the bar drinking, talking, and drinking some more. The booze resurfaced the affection they had for each other. They started dancing and groping each other with open-mouth kisses shared. They were dancers tantalizing the crowd. That's what they do. However, in this case it was all on the up and up. My wishful thinking was coming true without any instigation on my part. I was going to be a participant in my first real threesome. Boy…I really started liking my wife again. We all stumbled up to her room, and they began to make out.

They didn't invite me to join in, so I pulled up a chair to be schooled once again in what it really took to please a woman. This lesson was new to me, and it was all oral in nature. But it didn't stop at just one new thing learned. Now, not only was I having sex with my wife, but she was encouraging me to have sex with someone else while she participated. It was a night to remember. *Maybe too much so.* She left the next day, and the experience became a new drug for me. I thought maybe all we needed was a lot more of that to keep our relationship going, but not to the extent I would begin to pursue it. After her friend was long gone, I needed to have that rush again, so I started flirting with other girls in front of my wife. I was constantly focused on getting another girl to join us. I told myself it was all my wife's fault, and I blamed her for my newfound deviance.

She would give in a few more times passively, but she was not nearly as involved as she was with the encounter with her friend. It was stealing away from the attention she desperately needed from me. Seeing me with someone else all the time was depleting any of the self-esteem she had left. I was damaging her even more. This time she was the one who knew it was over and began telling me so. In a way, it made me feel sad knowing that if we both hadn't been so damaged things might have been different for us – or we might not have connected in the first place. It was a heartbreaking story of two lost souls linked for a moment in time. My entire life had been based on the lessons my mother had taught me sexually. It was those of my wife that were consuming me now, and I always needed to increase the dosage. I was destined to repeat the cycle. This was just an end to one cycle and the beginning of another.

My plan was to take the bus home the next day, but unbeknownst to me there was a secret my wife was keeping. One she had only learned herself that morning. Remember that time I thought was special? A purchase of a pregnancy test revealed one of my fishes had been captured. She was pregnant. *Oh, my God.* I knew with every fibre of my being I wasn't ready to be a father. Not even close. I couldn't love the expected child. How could I? I didn't even love myself. However, considering the new circumstances, we made the decision to give it another shot. Maybe a baby on the way would solve everything. *Yeah, that'll make all the difference in the world.*

Things were a little better for a while, but as she grew in size, so did my philandering. She however, started developing another bond that was pure and true – one with the child who grew inside her. It was an unconditional love that only a mother could know. *Most mothers, anyways.* It was something both of us had been searching for all our lives, and there was nothing that could get in her way of that, including me. Almost six months into the marriage and as expecting parents, divorce papers were filed. *It was another failure, but you know, I was used to it. It was just a part of who I was.* Now there was going to be a piece of me in the world, and because I was so fucked up, I would miss out on that too. The only thing giving me any comfort was that I knew my child would feel the unconditional love of a mother. At least my child would have that.

CHAPTER 7:

# From Bad to Worse

With the only option I had, I tucked my tail between my legs and returned home, retreating to the only friends that had ever given me any comfort. Booze and drugs were always there in the moment to take the pain away. Unfortunately, it also clouded my judgement to make wise decisions. Once home, the first thing I did was to take a trip with a guy I had known when I was younger. He was the same one I had walked in on with my "submarine girl". And get this: We decided to visit her in a town called Kamloops, so we let bygones be bygones, I guess. He was a little fucked up himself. Go Figure.

The plan was to fund our stay by distributing some blow in my possession. (Bought with money from Mommy). Once we arrived, he went to visit our ex "happy girl" while I hit the bar to make some cash. In no time at all, I found someone to take a substantial amount of the white powder off my hands, and she was as cute as a button. I guess she thought the same about me as we made a date for the next night. Well, not a date exactly, as we never made it out for dinner. We weren't hungry for food, anyways. Sex and Coke satisfied our appetite, and again, just like that, we moved in together. She made a lot of money working at the local mill and didn't seem to mind supporting me with it, so who was I to look a gift horse in the mouth? She worked while I just waited until she returned home, then we partied and had sex. There was no question how this would end up.

During the next few weeks, I established contact with my soon-to-be ex-wife now living back in Vancouver. I boasted how I was turning my life around. She said she missed me and wanted me to come down and see her when I could. I told her I would try, but I was super busy. *Yeah, right.* Anyways, the relationship I was in suited me fine for the time being. I knew it wouldn't lead anywhere, but the attention she gave me was welcomed. As always, it was all about sex and drugs every waking moment. Even having a girlfriend didn't stop me from fantasizing about doing any other girl I met. Not once did I think I could be friends with one without doing the nasty with them. It was a necessary evil to make them like me. I had to find a way to feel good and get me through the day. But now, it was a lot more perverse and nothing surprised me.

As expected, my present union unravelled, but in a very unusual way. My girl attended a company Christmas party without me. She was late returning home, so I was already suspicious. As she entered the house, I could see guilt written all over her face. She didn't know it, but I could also see a great big white stain on her black dress. I knew she had just gotten happy. She was surprised when I confronted it with her. She broke down and started crying, telling me what had happened. She got drunk at the party and her ex-boyfriend had offered her a ride home. Then she offered him a ride in the front seat of his car. She didn't mean for it to happen. Anyways, she apologized left, right, and centre. She asked me to forgive her indiscretion and said that it hadn't meant anything. She pledged she would do anything to make it up to me.

Outwardly, I displayed all the right emotions one would be expected to have when confronted with a cheating girlfriend – anger, sadness, and disappointment. Inwardly, I didn't give a rat's ass. I knew she was a party girl when we first met, that's why I was with her. I was just along for the ride. It did hurt my ego somewhat and I did want some type of payback, so I over-dramatized how much I was hurt and played on her guilt just to punish her a little. She repeated her willingness to do anything to make it up to me. Well, if she felt that strongly about it, I would find a way that she could feel better about herself. It was tit-for-tat time. I told her I needed someone to talk to so I could clear my head about it. The only other person I knew was her very sexy, younger sister. Maybe she could arrange a get-together so we could privately talk about the indiscretion the next night when my gal was working. Without hesitation, she told me she would call her and explain the situation and convince her to come over the next night.

My sexual corruption had always been fuelled by increasing its dosage, making me act out any demented thoughts that overtook my psyche. I would do and think of anything that would make me happy in the moment, no matter its disgusting nature. I liked dirty. It was the only thing that would titillate me; anything routine would never satisfy my satyriasis.[1] What follows next depicts the disease's progression.

---

1    This is a compulsive sex disorder in men.

She called her sister the next morning and set up our heart to heart. Before my girlfriend left for work, she brought home a bottle of tequila, saying it was her sister's favourite drink. *Was she trying to help me get her sister drunk and loose?* The sister arrived shortly before my gal left for work, and they talked privately for a bit. Then on the way out the door, my gal told us to have fun and not do anything she wouldn't. *I think she just gave me the green light to go there.* We sat in the living room, having shot after shot and line after line. She told me she knew her sister had cheated on me and said she was surprised knowing how much I sexually gratified her sister – unlike her own boyfriend who didn't satisfy her. The more she drank, the more she lashed out about her own boyfriend. The more we snorted, the looser she became. She wanted to play strip poker, which was fine by me. But before I even dealt the first hand, she said, "Fuck it. I'm going to lose anyway, so I might as well take my clothes off now."

Without any doubt, I then knew she and my girlfriend had planned this all along. My girl wanted to make up for cheating on me and her sister wanted to vent her displeasure with her own boyfriend. There was no pretence between us anymore. By that time, we were more than a little drunk, so it was one sloppy revenge act on both our parts. However, I consciously left the door wide open, so my girl could see her naked and wonder what else had transpired. *When it came to right or wrong concerning sex, I had no moral compass.* I would soon find out how damaged my gal was as well.

I was already sleeping when my girlfriend got home, but I felt her lay beside me. Later, I woke up to pee and passed by the spare bedroom, where I saw her sister still naked and lying on her stomach. I went in and finished what I had started. I returned to our bedroom only to find my gal fully awake and making herself happy. She stopped and casually got up and went down the hallway. She returned holding hands with her sibling. They sat on the end of the bed making out with each other for the longest while and then crawled in to join me. I knew exactly what my role was. My soon-to-be ex-wife was the first to deal me this drug.

It got very intense and more than a little creepy. *But I'm one to talk.* Granted it was a huge turn on, but by the end of it all, I knew I couldn't be a part of this any longer. They had to be extremely damaged themselves. *I had too much of my own shit to deal with.* The ride was almost over, but I still needed a favour from her before I would call it quits. The next day I asked if I could borrow her car so I could go back home for a day or two. In reality, I was heading somewhere else.

For some reason I still felt a connection to my soon-to-be ex-wife and missed her. I had to be sure us parting ways wasn't a mistake. She was carrying my child, so I hoped a visit would give me the answer. *If you couldn't say anything else about me, I was sure a wishful thinker.* So off I went in my soon-to-be ex-girlfriend's car, to visit my soon-to-be ex-wife.

The last time I had seen her was when her baby bump had just started to develop, but you couldn't miss it now. She was getting huge, but she was still very beautiful, if not more so. Our interaction with each other felt as comfortable as ever, and we had the same attraction as we always had. It went without saying we would share a bed that night, then the floor, and everywhere else we could. We rediscovered why we liked each other so much in the first place. In that aspect, we took up exactly where we had left off with nothing changing. *Pleasers pleasing pleasers.* However, any wishful thinking for something more never materialized, as it never could with how damaged we both were. The decision to call it quits was the right one. We didn't belong together.

The next day I said my final goodbyes and headed back to say another one, but I never really made it that far. I was close, but no cigar. It was snowing like crazy, and the three-hour drive was now in its fifth hour with vehicles in ditches all the way back. I decided to stop and rent a cheap motel room. That night, as I was keeping the ritual of shaving, I noticed some little creatures crawling on a few hairs on my testicles and between my legs. I thought they might come from the dive I was staying in, so I stood in the tub and shaved off all the hair they were clinging to. That seemed to do the trick as I couldn't find any more on me. However, when double-checking, I noticed a small sore on my penis. I chalked it up to all the friction it had endured over the last few days. It was painful to the touch, but not any more than I was used to when I cut myself. I figured it would heal, but I decided not to stay the rest of the night as I didn't want to share the room with any more of my tiny visitors.

It was still snowing like crazy, but I pushed on. I was getting close to my destination when the brakes stopped working. I slid across the highway and ended up in the ditch. I waited for a tow truck and let him know where to deliver the car. I was done with everything now. Depressed over my wife, my girlfriend, and just life itself, I put out my thumb and started hitchhiking towards home. I didn't care that I was leaving my girlfriend to wonder where the hell I went. I was sure she could find someone to fill the void – maybe her sister.

I got picked up by a guy who was heading home to Calgary. I told him my name was Jessie, not feeling he needed to know my real name. We got talking about his work as a salesman of culinary supplies, with his territory covering all over British Columbia and Alberta. He said he made a really good living at it, and a company vehicle was one of the perks. Driving and drinking a few beers, we appeared to get along. He told me he was looking for a partner to cover his expanding territory and asked if I would be interested. Sure...what the hell? I didn't have anything holding me back, so I was off to Calgary with him now. We'd travelled quite a distance, so he suggested renting a room to spend the night before travelling the rest of the way. This would allow us to head over to the bar and get to know each other more. His stature was intimidating. He had bulging muscles everywhere and stood taller than my six foot-one-inch frame. As we drank, the more the subject kept returning to his wife and how sexy she was. From what he told me, she was a little bit of an exhibitionist, and it turned her on to do a striptease while others watched. It didn't faze me. I thought it was the booze talking and just a guy's over exaggeration to impress another guy. Besides, I was still married to a professional striptease artist. *I had seen that before.*

We drank a lot more and then returned to the room with some beers to continue. Before we even cracked the first one, he retrieved a photo album from his suitcase. He wasn't done talking about his wife, and he wanted me to see some pictures of her. His enthusiasm became a little unsettling as he was grinning from ear to ear. I opened the album and then closed it immediately and asked if he was sure he wanted me to look further. He told me, "Fucking right I do." The pictures were nudes of his wife posing in different sexy positions. I could tell why he was so glowing in his comments about her. She was smoking hot. He asked me to hand it back to him so he could show me his favourite. Finding it, he showed me one her of her bending over a chair. "Doesn't it make you horny?" he asked.

I started having flashbacks about a stranger's car. "Oh shit, here we go again." Before I had a chance to say anything, he approached and dropped his pants. "Whoa...Step back, buddy!" He didn't, and he wouldn't. He grabbed the top of my head and pulled it down to him. *This had happened to me once before.* I told him "no" and that he was scaring me.

He yelled out, "Just fucking do it." Petrified, I used my hand to give him the completion he was demanding. *No matter how you look at it, I had just been sexually assaulted by a man for the second time.* After he finished, his demeanour changed, and he became apologetic for his aggressiveness, saying being away from his wife so much made him horny. He told me it would never happen again and offered me a bribe to smooth things over. He said that once we got to his place, he'd have his wife strip for me. I was getting pissed off, but holding it inside. I needed to have some type of payback. Not only for this, but also for what had happened with the other guy. I was too scared then, but now I was just angry. He hurt me, and now I was obsessed with hurting him back. This became my sole purpose in continuing on with him: I needed to exact my revenge somehow.

We arrived at his home early the next morning, and he introduced me to his wife. As promised, he told me we would have a private party at home that night. Their tenant downstairs was going to be working late, so it would be an opportune time for a little strip show. He informed me drinks weren't the only party favours we would be partaking of. He had been saving some tabs of acid, and we were going to drop a couple of hits of those. Well, that will be something new for me; one of the only drugs I hadn't tried yet. The night began with a full tab of acid for each of us, washed down with a stiff drink. Up to that point his wife had been pretty reserved. Once the drugs kicked in, things changed and she started dancing around the room. I was experiencing acid for the first time and everything began to seem as if it was in slow motion. I was in a trance as she moved across the floor. She didn't have to have her clothes off. Just watching her felt like a sexual experience. Abruptly, she stopped dancing and bolted for the bathroom, needing to throw up. I looked to her husband and asked if she was going to be okay. He said it was just the acid, and she would be back to satisfy me. As nice as that sounds, I didn't want her to notice the little "friction sore" on my penis, so I decided to keep it in my pants until I had the opportunity she could feel it without seeing it.

I went in to check on her, and after I returned to the living room, we heard the back door open. The roommate had arrived home. She entered the living room looking perplexed as the wife returned completely naked. "What the hell is going on?" she asked.

Hubby told her to settle down and chill, saying we had taken some acid and his wife decided to give us a show. No big deal. He then convinced her to take a hit herself and have a few drinks with us. By this time, the object of my overwhelming horniness went in her bedroom to pass out. She was done for the night. *Shit. I was all revved up with no place to go. Or was there?* The roommate was starting to feel the acid and let her inhibitions down. I needed to release my pent-up frustration, so I casually leaned over to the roommate and asked her if she wanted to have sex. She said sure, but she wanted to take a shower first. She went downstairs and left me and hubby to drink some more and take another full hit. We sat for a while, and then I told him "good night" and went downstairs to the roommate.

She was already naked on the bed with the lights off. Good... That way she wouldn't notice my little friction sore. I needed relief as soon as possible, so it was over in no time. She wasn't impressed, but I didn't give a shit. She rolled over and went to sleep, but I was getting more stoned. I started hallucinating about getting payback, so I crept up the stairs to see if they were awake. Nope, but they weren't sleeping together either. The wife was sprawled out on the bed still naked, and he was sitting on the floor with his back against the doorjamb of the bedroom snoring away. Absolutely perfect. It couldn't have been any better circumstances to resolve both my issues now – my insatiable desire to have the wife and at the same time exact revenge on her husband.

It was like I was having an out-of-body experience, and I wasn't prepared for how much she was needing the same relief as I was. Afterwards, I stepped over her husband, looked down at him with a devilish smile, and muttered "asshole" under my breath. My revenge had been exacted. But when I was lying downstairs again, I thought, *The hell it was – not for what he made me do.* Also, I didn't even know if he was aware of what I had done to her, so I did her twice more throughout the night. Each time I turned to see if the hubby had noticed my accomplishment, but he hadn't. My moral depravity no longer had any boundaries.

I went back downstairs, and soon the adrenaline and the acid wore off and the fear of what I had just done began to set in. I had a full and complete crash. I stayed there until I heard someone leave the house. I hoped it was him going to sell his pots and pans. I began to feel bad that his wife had to be a part of this and the trouble I may have caused her. I needed to apologize, so I went upstairs to tell her I was sorry and I was leaving. Her reaction surprised me. She wasn't sorry it happened. Her husband was a dick, and she felt he deserved everything he got. She loved the attention I had given her. Smiling she said, "He'll be gone all day, so do you want to do it again?" This time we had no other ulterior motive except our own enjoyment. Once we were done, it was time to bid adieu. There was only one problem about me leaving: I had no money. However, I remembered seeing a plastic container with money in it on the lower level. The roommate had already left, so I went back downstairs to have a better look. There was a lot there. She wouldn't miss a hundred. I knew what I gave her wasn't worth two cents, but I needed enough for the bus ride home.

CHAPTER 8:

# Round, Round I Go

In less than a week, I'd been with a total of five different women. Oh yeah, I forgot. On top of that, I had been sexually assaulted by a man for a second time. Yet, it was just another normal week for me. I was becoming more despicable every day. Perversion, sexual deviations, or total debauchery were the only things that ever made me feel good. Mom had been a damn good teacher.

But the week wasn't over yet. On the bus ride home, I sat beside a young pregnant woman, who was very pretty and all aglow. She was married, but her hubby wasn't with her as he was working in the oil fields. The fact that she was married didn't stop me from flirting with her. Why would it? As for her being pregnant, I had slept with my wife a week earlier and that told me how horny pregnant women could get. This wouldn't be hard. So before we reached her destination about ninety miles from where I was heading, I talked her into inviting me up to her trailer. *It always amazed me how little commitment girls had towards their significant other. Unfortunately, it just confirmed my belief that girls couldn't be trusted when it comes to matters of the heart.* The next morning, I left on the bus and rested on the seventh day.

I was playing a risky game, but I would risk everything I had to find what I needed, and when you spend every waking moment believing sexual contact is the basis of expressing any type of affection, your morality becomes a casualty. None of my interactions were made in good faith. How could they be? I had nothing to offer in return. What's worse is that I never used condoms, and upon returning home, it became apparent my penis wasn't in the clear. The sore wasn't healing, and now I had burning, yellow puss coming out of it. A trip to the doctor confirmed I had a dose of gonorrhea. I guess I wasn't the only one who had it now. Share and share alike. Anyone normal would have felt bad for possibly spreading it around, but I was anything but normal. I did feel a little bad about the pregnant women, but they both let me go there. I did reach out to my wife to let her know, but she had already taken care of it. She said she may have shared something with me as well – crabs. You'd think it would teach me a lesson about using protection, but it didn't. After I was given a clean bill of health, I continued with what I always did. *I was running away from things rather than running to something.*

As always, I jumped at any opportunity to keep in motion. So when an acquaintance of mine asked if I wanted to hitchhike and visit his girlfriend in Kelowna with him, I jumped at the offer. *What the hell? I had nothing to lose. Maybe I could find someone to love there. Anyone would do.* So with backpacks around our shoulders and a Mickey bottle or two, we stuck out our thumbs. Our destination was 200 miles away, and our first ride brought us to the halfway mark. The second gentleman who picked us up informed us he would be able to take us the rest of the way. Unfortunately, he was travelling with a mickey of booze of his own. Now all of us had a little buzz on. Then our chauffeur decided we needed a pit stop. We pulled in at the last bar before our destination, which was just sixty miles away. *Surely a few beers wouldn't hurt.*

I don't even remember getting back into the car. My next memory was waking up in pitch-blackness. I was strapped in my seatbelt and hanging upside down. I was in the passenger seat, my buddy was in the driver's seat, and the guy who owned the car was lying in the back. It seems we had driven over a 150-foot embankment leaving the car on its roof. None of us seemed any worse for the wear. The man in the back was still asleep and snoring loudly. My buddy began to freak out. We climbed the embankment and flagged down a car, hitching a ride the rest of the way. We just left the man there. We knew he was okay, but it was still a cowardly thing to do. We all could have died that night. I have no idea what saved us.

Upon arriving at my buddy's girlfriend's house, she informed us we couldn't stay there as her parents wouldn't allow it. It was the end of summer, but still unseasonably warm, so we went in search of a place to stay. We came across a baseball field. The dugouts were enclosed and unlocked, so we decided this would be our motel room. During the night I was awoken by a gurgling sound. I turned my head to see my acquaintance shaking uncontrollably with froth coming from his mouth. The shaking subsided, and he started to regain consciousness. I'd seen this several times before with my aunt as she used to have seizures. I knew we had to get him to the hospital, so we used the last of our money for a taxi. He was admitted and I waited for news for hours. Finally, the nurse came out and informed me that he had indeed had a seizure. He was epileptic, and he didn't know until then. I was told he would need more tests and would have to stay in the hospital for the next few days.

I was now left to my own devices. I had no cash, and I was very hungry. Again, without thinking of the consequences, I made a stupid decision to shoplift a cooked chicken from Safeway. I may have had certain other skills, but shoplifting wasn't one of them. I was caught before I even left the store. Police were called and I was arrested. The stupid words I had thought to myself before embarking on this adventure were ringing in my head. *Nothing to lose, I had said.* In the last twenty-four hours, I had come very close to losing my life and now I was possibly losing my freedom.

The judge decided to make an example of me, and the fact that I already had a fraud conviction didn't help. I was sentenced to three months to be served at a correctional facility a short distance away. Finally, I would be held accountable for my actions. However, I thought it was funny that I had once stolen $6000 and received probation. Now I was getting jail time for a measly eight bucks."

I had heard bad stories about jail. However, I adapted well. It was kind of nice having a structured setting. There were three meals a day, and I didn't need to worry about a place to sleep. It was still better than having to face my demons back home. My parents didn't even give a shit that I was in jail. I think they always thought it would only be a matter of time. Anyways, it wasn't that bad. I wasn't even behind bars. It was an old converted motel for minor offenders, like a little vacation of sorts without girls. *And did I mention it was in Kamloops? The home of my previous girlfriend and her sister. I couldn't go there again, could I? Not after I had rolled her car and left without saying goodbye.*

But just having male inmates to talk with was getting old fast. Let's see, it took about four days. With audacity I reached out to her in a phone call just to tell her I was sorry. *Some balls, eh?* She was neither excited nor overly pissed off from hearing from me. I let her know where I was and asked if I could put her on my visitors list. She asked when visitors were allowed and said she might come on the weekend. Sure enough, my name was called that Saturday to meet her in the office. I signed her in and we walked out to the courtyard to sit at a picnic table. We talked for a while about little things. She mentioned she had smuggled in some Percocets, but she wouldn't give them to me until just before she was going to leave. She started talking about our adventure the last night we had been together and how hot it was. So hot, that when I left the next day, they repeated it with her sister's boyfriend. Then she told me she had lied about her ex-boyfriend and the party that night. It was true that he had sex with her, but so did four of his friends. *But what could I say? I deserved what I got.*

Just before leaving, she told me to sit in front of her so the guards couldn't see her retrieving the pills she had brought. When I was in position, she placed a condom containing the pills into my hand. Her last words to me were, "By the way, you might want to get yourself checked out by a doctor. Me and Sis may have shared something with you." And with that, she was gone. You got to give her credit... She played it well. It was just another reminder of what a loser I was.

A second sad reminder of my loser status would come two days before my release in the form of another phone call. I received the news I had become a father to a six-pound, eleven-ounce, healthy baby girl. I knew she would be better off without me in her life. I was way too damaged to offer her anything a father should, but that truth hurt me to the core of my soul. In fact, there were times I truly believed not only my daughter would be better off without me, so would everyone else. No one would miss me. These thoughts possessed me more than a few times, but I didn't have the balls to end it all. I desperately needed to find some peace in my life.

Papers were served for child support. At the time I had nothing or any other place to go, so I returned to where I always had. I couldn't really call it home, but rather a stopover and a place to sleep until my next adventure.

I found work for about six months in sales, but the memories of the past still haunted me. Living with my parents only made it worse. I always wondered why they couldn't love me the way they should. I still believed I was to blame for it, just like everything else in my life that went wrong. I wasn't a boy anymore, but the guilt and shame about my mother and myself followed me into manhood. Whenever I looked at her, all I could see was my inner child buried in her. Even though I had a myriad of sexual experiences to think of, sometimes it was the thought of her that still helped me get happy when I was alone. If that wasn't enough, the thought of already having a soon-to-be ex-wife and a daughter whom I had never met, put me over the deep end. I began drinking heavily, which affected my job, and I was let go. My demons had a stranglehold on me. No matter what I did, I couldn't break free of them, so I did what was familiar to me. I continued running in the race of the never-ending quest to find a love that would finally fix me. It was more important to me now. I felt that once I knew what true love was, it would offer me the chance to be in my daughter's life and truly love her like I wanted to be as a child. Until then, all I could do was fill the void with anything I could get – sex, drugs, and alcohol.

CHAPTER 9:

# The Beginning of the Beginning

I knew I had to get another job, but this time, my quest started off a little differently by first researching available work. I found an advertisement that a club was looking for a dance teacher back in Kelowna. I was confident that with my previous experience, I would at least have a good shot at getting hired, so quick as a wink, I was on the road again and arriving at the club for an interview. Upon hearing my work experience, I was hired on the spot. It would be the same routine as in the Bahamas, but this job also involved teaching those who paid to learn. Maybe this would turn my life around. It had to be more than coincidence I had found my dream job for a third time. Dancing was the only thing I was capable of doing well, besides sex.

It was a fresh start, and I grasped at any resemblance of hope that somehow things would be different. I had been there for a few weeks, and everything was going great. The management of the club was happy, which in turn made me happy. They scheduled dance classes separately for VIPs, and this was an opportunity for me to make some extra cash and to send a little child support. That meant a great deal to me and made me feel like I was actually getting my shit together and becoming a little more responsible. Of course, another benefit would be all the girls. I began putting the law of averages to the test. In other words, the more girls I saw, the better my odds were I would find that special one. It was a good theory anyway. I seldom returned to my motel room alone. I was rolling the dice over and over again and taking anything I could get, even if it was just for a few hours at a time. It was better than nothing at all. I wasn't fooling myself. I was still desperately sad and alone, but I pushed on. What else could I do? Maybe a miracle would happen and love might stumble into me.

In all the encounters up to this point, I had objectified all women equally. No matter their size, shape, race, colour, or age, I only had one purpose for them.

Ugly girls, pretty ones, fat or skinny, they need to be happy too, so I'd be with any girl that would let me. It was my *modus operandi* and I hadn't even turned twenty-two yet. My motel room became a den of ill repute. I applied all the skills I'd learned throughout my life's experience. As I said, there wasn't much I hadn't done sexually. This gave me a certain power over those who weren't as versed as I was.

However, things started to get out of hand when I was booked to teach a class to a bachelorette party. They all wanted the lesson to continue afterwards back in my room. Someone brought MDMA (Ecstasy). This was a new drug to try. Before long, clothes were being discarded. I never had so many hands and naked bodies rubbing against me in all my life. It certainly didn't hurt my ego. I was pumped that I was the centre of attention. I was higher than a kite, floating around like a hyper bee between five flowers planted on the bed; the bachelorette being the final flower. On the way out, each gave a contribution to the cause. I came away with a couple hundred bucks. To think by any other accord, these were good girls, ones without any damage...

I was quickly booked for more private lessons, becoming nothing more than a gigolo or a male whore. I used the money to send to my ex for child support. I couldn't feel good about that: It was fuck money.

I had reached rock bottom and had two new drugs to contend with: MDMA and the attention I was receiving, which gave me a distorted sense of self-worth. The situation left me distraught and believing true commitment doesn't exist. It was an illusion. I was giving up hope I would ever find the love I needed to save me. I was resolved to the fact that I was never meant to be loved. It was time to face the reality of my life and embrace it. I was a morally corrupt, damaged, and sick human being. *How could anything ever change that?*

Most nights at the club I had a plethora of girls hanging around me. This in turn made guys try to befriend me, thinking if they did, it would give them a shot of hooking up with one of the girls. There was one guy who showed up every night and bought drinks just so he could hang out. I figured he was just a typical guy doing what he could to get laid. *No big deal.* One night, the club was virtually empty because there was a festival in town, so it was just me and my new buddy drinking. After last call we went back to my room to drink a bottle of Jack

Daniels he had brought. Then out of the blue, five or six of his friends showed up to party with us.

I should have realized it was a set-up. How would his friends know where we were? But I was never really good at piecing things together. The party continued and I got up to go to the bathroom. By the time I had returned, one of the guys had poured me another shot. After that I can't remember a thing. I had been "roofied". The next morning, I found myself spread out on the bed, lying on my stomach totally naked. The bed was soaked all around me and smelled like urine. I was feeling groggy from the effects of the drug, and when I sat up and put my full weight on my ass, I flinched in pain. I instantly knew I had been assaulted. Stumbling to the bathroom mirror, it turns out my ass wasn't the only thing violated. My reflection showed dried-up semen on my face, in my hair, and covering my chest and groin. As I looked down further, my testicles were black and blue. I suppose the smell of urine was because they had pissed on me. *Oh well. I'd been pissed on my entire life anyway.* I didn't see how anything could be gained by calling the cops to report the assault. It was just a bunch of guys exacting their revenge – probably for me sleeping with some of their girlfriends. I remember a couple of times in the past I had been obsessed with getting revenge myself, so how could I blame them? I deserved it. *I was just too dead inside to give a shit.*

With that, the private lessons in my room screeched to a halt. Well somewhat, I was just more careful who I invited from then on. Then one night I was scheduled to teach some VIP's from Toronto. There was a bunch of girls travelling together, and they all worked for the Ontario Provincial Police (OPP). None of them were actually cops. Most of them worked as switchboard operators fielding 911 calls. I thought it would be a nice change and give me a break from my nightly routines. Besides, I was a little more paranoid about any encounters I had.

Of course, there was an open bar, and just like any group of friends out together, they wanted to have fun. It was my job to provide it, and they had me for a full two hours. So, I broke them up into groups of two and asked one to volunteer to be my teaching partner. The girl who volunteered introduced herself as Kim. *Why is every girl named Kim? My true virginity was lost to one, I returned the favour on another, and now this one. Maybe this is what is meant by third time lucky.*

The lesson turned out fun for everyone. Afterwards, Kim and her friend invited me to go for another drink in the bar. I can't believe I'm saying this, but I could tell it wasn't about her wanting to hook up. It was refreshing, so I gladly accepted their invite. During a conversation, she told me she was off to Vancouver in the morning to break up with her boyfriend in person. *Wow! She admitted she had a boyfriend. Chalk up a bonus point.* She said the distance between them was a major factor for her calling it quits. As the night progressed, we began flirting with each other just a little, without blatant sexual overtones. She wasn't like all the other girls who had visited my room. We were actually enjoying each other's company. So much so that she asked if I wanted to travel to Vancouver with her the next day and stay overnight. I thought, *What the hell?* I could take a couple days off work. I knew certain parts of me could use a break, so I gladly accepted her invitation. We didn't have any type of sexual interaction that night. It wasn't something she was comfortable with until she broke up with her boyfriend. *Well how about that? Maybe there are some truly good girls out there after all.*

Upon arriving, we went up to the hotel room and she phoned her soon-to-be ex-boyfriend to meet up. I stayed behind and waited for her return an hour later. She told me it had gone well, and they were both good with it. I guess there was only one thing we could do now. There was nothing spectacular about our hook-up, but it was nice. This was an unfamiliar feeling to me when it came to sex, and I kind of liked it. We got back to Kelowna, and I went to her hotel room so she could pack her things up and we could say goodbye. We assured each other we had a great time and then exchanged phone numbers with the promise to talk soon. And that's all it was. It was a welcome break for me, as she was a very sweet girl. *It rekindled a hope in me not to give up.* It was just too bad we lived so far away from each other. For the next few weeks, I continued with both my jobs – the one vertically on the dance floor and the horizontal one back in my room. I even had a visit from the cops investigating if I was running an escort agency or a massage parlour. Nope, I was just a slut. I never asked for money, they just left it.

Then, as promised, Kim gave me a call, asking if I wanted to come and stay at her place in Toronto for a couple of weeks. It really took me by surprise. I knew she wasn't like all the other girls, so the prospect of getting to know her better made me want to go. The next day, I talked to my boss and asked for a leave of absence. He wasn't pleased and told me if I left that would be it. As always, my decisions were made by the seat of my pants, but I couldn't resist finding out if she was the one. I booked a flight and let her know when I was going to arrive. She didn't know I was planning to stay much longer than a few weeks. I wanted my stay to be permanent.

Upon arriving, I took a taxi to her apartment and settled in. Kim worked during the day, so I stayed in the apartment until she returned at night. Over a period of a few weeks, she began to see I had no direction in life and I was emotionally unstable. Even though she honestly liked me, she was looking for something more substantial in her life. Unbeknownst to me, she had even called my mother because she was worried about my behaviour. She basically told my mother what she already knew: I was broken. *Thanks Mom, you're the best.* It was over before it got started. I was to leave in two days, but she said I could stay there until I did. I really didn't want to go back home, so the following night, I took the train downtown to go bar hopping. Maybe I would get lucky and find a way to prolong my stay, if you know what I mean. Maybe Toronto girls were different. Kim appeared to be.

I walked into a bar with numerous pool tables, and only one was being played on by what I thought was a couple. I watched them play and realized they hardly knew each other, so I challenged her to a game. We played pool and drank for hours. She needed to be at work in the morning, so she wanted me to rent a hotel room as her place was too far away. The only money I had left was for my bus ticket the next day, and I certainly couldn't use that. I guess I should have thought of that before renting the room. Anyways, before she left for work the next morning, she told me she wanted me to call her at work so we could meet up for lunch. After checking out, she gave me a gram of hash to occupy myself, and she caught the bus to go to work. I once again had no place to go and no money. I just walked around until the time we were going to meet up, which gave me plenty of time to digest everything. Now going home didn't look all that bad, but I still needed bus fare. *Think Lee. Think.* When we met for lunch, I told her I had lost my wallet and asked her to lend me a hundred dollars, so I could pay for new identification. Once I got it, I could withdraw some money from the bank and pay her back. She went to the bank, handed me a hundred-dollar bill, and we made plans to meet up later. She went back to work, and I went directly to the Greyhound station.

This was the lowest of the low. More than ever, I just wanted to die. The continuation of the cycle was crushing me. I had searched so long and hard for what was missing in my life and to regain the innocence that was maliciously taken from me as a child. I just wanted to start over without all the pain and sadness I carried with me. I knew in that aspect there was no going home. How could there be? I could never find anyone to guide me back.

*But little did I know because of time, circumstances, and what must have been some type of divine intervention, things were about to dramatically change for me. I would begin a journey that would take me to the place I had been searching for my entire life. It was a long tortuous path at times, but in the end, I would finally reach my destination. I was about to embark on the road to my salvation and discover an unconditional love like no other. My long journey home would begin with another greyhound trip.*

CHAPTER 10:

# Who Is This Girl?

The depot wasn't very crowded – just a smattering of people here and there. The bench straight across from me had the most people at it. Four or five guys were standing around in a semicircle as if they were talking to someone sitting down. I couldn't see who it was, but it didn't really matter to me, until I heard laughter emanating from that direction. The guys were chatting up a girl. I began to watch more closely to see if I could make out what she looked like. It wasn't until one of them moved a little that I caught a glimpse of a girl and her smile – one like I've never seen before. It captured joy within it and immediately had a calming effect on me. It radiated gentleness and made me feel I was fortunate just to see it. I was gobsmacked how it stirred so many different emotions in me.

The PA announced my bus was about to depart, and it became obvious the group of guys were departing on the same one. They headed towards it, leaving the rest of what carried that smile behind just sitting there. As I got across from her, I noticed she was getting up to leave as well. She was struggling with the amount of luggage she had, so I offered to give her a hand. As she was making sure she hadn't forgotten anything, it gave me a chance to have a closer look of her. I was instantly smitten. She had no need for make-up as it would only mask her natural beauty. It was if I could feel her inner spirit penetrate my being.

Once she was ready to go, I carried her luggage without a word as we were in a hurry to get to the bus. I don't think I could have said anything anyway. She left me speechless and more than just a little off balance. I placed her luggage outside to be loaded. She smiled to thank me. No words were needed: All the thanks I needed was seeing that smile up close. I let her go ahead of me so she could find a seat on the bus. She picked a row where two were vacant, but by the time I arrived down the aisle, one of the guys had moved up and sat beside her. I found myself a seat further back. Any pipe dream I had about getting to know her better was now confined to getting to know the back of her head. About two hours in, we made our first stop along the route, and the group of guys left with their buddy who had been sitting with her.

When I reached her, she looked up and asked if I wanted to move up and sit beside her. She didn't have to ask me twice. I didn't have any luggage, so I removed my coat and placed it on the seat to make sure nobody would take it while we were inside. Well, we didn't go inside actually; we both needed to have a smoke, so we went to share one together. After lighting up, she told me the guys had given her some hash. I told her I had some of my own and offered to smoke it with her, so we moved a little further away from the depot for a few quick puffs and properly introduced ourselves. I told her I was Lee or Leland. She said it was such a unique name, and it suited me. Did that mean she thought I was unique? I sure hoped so. She then revealed hers. *I'll give you one guess. We have now entered the* Twilight Zone. *I began wondering if the universe had been telling me all along that I just needed to meet the right Kim. This was more than coincidental. I just knew it was.*

We returned to our seats gigglier than when we had left them. It was good hash. The bus had gotten underway, and I needed to know how long I would be able to sit beside her, praying her destination was as far away as mine. She told me she was heading to Victoria to finish her degree in Fine Arts. I said I was returning back home about 400 miles short of her destination. She said she was relieved and happy to have a seating companion like me, as there were a lot of assholes out there trying to hit on her. I didn't quite know how to take that, but then she said I seemed like a really nice guy. I told her I was flattered she thought so, but added that the long journey ahead of us might give her the time to change her mind about that. She inquired what I did back home. What could I tell her? I said I was a dancer and a masseuse and offered her a free foot massage later.

As I was looking at her more, I couldn't get it out of my head she reminded me of somebody famous. I just couldn't pinpoint it. When I told her she laughed and responded, "With the way my hair looks, it's probably Phyllis Diller." It definitely wasn't her. She turned to me, so I could have a better look at her face to help spark my memory. Staring at each other made her silently giggle, lifting her cheeks up. That did the trick; now I knew. I teased her a little before revealing the name of Audrey Hepburn. The comment took her by surprise. She responded, "You're crazy. Audrey Hepburn was beautiful."

"Well, duh... So are you." This was probably not the most romantic way to respond. I felt like an idiot, but it made her blush anyway. She was truly flattered somebody thought she was that beautiful. She had no air of pretentiousness about her, which made her even more desirable. She was everything she exhibited to be, nothing more nothing less. She was real beauty, inside and out. I knew in that moment she was special. It had to be her or no one at all. She made me feel differently than all the others. I didn't know why, but I was never so sure of anything in my life. She awoke something pure and innocent deep inside of me. Of course, there would be one crucial hurdle to overcome. Was I the one for her? I thought if we could make if through the next ninety hours of sitting beside each other on a bus, we should be able to make it through anything. But that might not matter anyway. Maybe she didn't want a relationship, or she was already in one. I didn't know yet, but I would have lots of time to find out.

She told me she had just left someone, which was the reason for the decision to come out West. In fact, the guy had asked her to marry him, and she showed me the engagement ring in her bag that he had bought her. She just knew in her heart it wasn't right for her. She said she would know when she found that special someone. She then gave me the first sign that she was interested in me. She took both her hands and placed each one on either side of my face, turning me to her. She said she could stare into my soulful, brown eyes forever. She could see my life's story in them. Well that did it. She had no idea of the magnitude of what that gesture meant. It was so simple and innocent, but it shook me to my core. I started crying in front of a complete stranger, one who wouldn't let me turn away to conceal my tears. She began crying herself, not knowing if mine were happy or sad ones. She asked me what was wrong, hoping she hadn't hurt me. Her sincerity made me comfortable opening up to her somewhat about my lazy eye and the anguish from the bullying about it that I still carried with me. For the first time in my life, I told somebody one of the things hurting me deep inside. This complete stranger displayed more compassion for me than anyone ever had. *Who was this girl?*

We wiped each other's tears away with our fingers. Then with a devious laugh, she added that if she had been around back in the day, she would have taken names and kicked their asses. *Yep, I was never going to let this one go.* It was time for me to start giving it everything I had, so I reached down and lifted her foot, reminding her of my promise of a foot massage. She kicked off her shoe and told me to go for it. She said I had very strong hands and her foot was in heaven. I said if that were the case, heaven would have to give it back so it could stay with the rest of the angel sitting beside me. That made her blush again. I finished the rub and placed her foot back down on the floor. She leaned her head towards mine and gave me a quick kiss on the cheek to say thank you. We decided to curl up together and take a nap, covering ourselves with a blanket she had brought with her.

As we cuddled, she allowed me to give her a soft and gentle orgasm. Soft and gentle was definitely not routine for me in regards to anything sexual. She looked up at me, closed her eyes, and rested her head on my shoulder and soon fell asleep. I put my arm around her and held her close to me, wanting her to feel safe, the same way she was making me feel. As she slept so many things were populating my little brain. *After all this time of pain and inner turmoil, could this be the defining moment when love enters my life?* I just couldn't get it out of my head. I needed to know, so as she slowly opened her eyes from her nap, I removed my arm from around her so I could turn to face her. I told her I had a question I needed to ask and blurted out, "Will you marry me, Kim?" Not thinking I was serious, she just smiled and kind of fluffed it off, giving me a kiss and returning her head to my shoulder. *Aw, crap! Now I wondered if my question would scare her off.*

In time, our undercover blanket sessions were upgraded to the bus lavatory. No clothes were removed; it was just passionate touching and kissing. It gave us more room, and we didn't think anybody would take notice or really care – but they did, including the bus driver. Upon exiting one time, his voice came over the PA system announcing if he caught us doing that again, we would be thrown off the bus. We walked back to our seats to a series of cat-calls, which embarrassed Kim beyond words. I assured her it would be okay, and I'd make everything all right. I told her when it was time to follow my lead. The next pit stop would allow me to clear it up with the driver. I held us back until everybody exited the bus, so we would be the last ones off. Once I reached the driver, I offered out my hand to shake his. I told him how sorry we were, but Kim had been in a really bad accident and had burned both of her legs. She periodically needed my help to put ointment on them. Now he was apologizing to us and saying how sorry he was for embarrassing us. Then he asked our destination. He assured us from now on, all the other drivers would be informed of our situation so we could have access to the bathroom from here on out. Not only did I make things right with Kim, but now we had a free pass to continue. Once out of sight of the driver, Kim and I bowled over laughing. She couldn't believe how clever that was. She was tickled pink about it. We then got something to eat, had a few puffs of both kinds, and returned to our seats to continue our journey.

I decided I would give her another foot massage, but I just couldn't let the question I asked her earlier go unanswered. I looked up and told her I was serious about wanting her to marry me. She put her foot back on the floor and brought her face within a few inches of mine. She was so close I felt my bad eye continuously trying to adjust itself to keep it straight to focus on her. She looked right past it, so she could look deeper. She placed one of her hands flat on my chest over my heart and then turned away so she could retrieve the engagement ring her ex-boyfriend had given her. She handed it to me saying, "Well, don't you think I should have a ring on my finger then?" I couldn't believe this was happening, but before she had a chance to change her mind, I placed it on her. I joked how happy I was in picking the right ring size. It fit her perfectly. Her acceptance surprised me so much I had to know why. She told me that it was simple enough. She just needed to look into my eyes once more for her heart to know if I was the one for her. She always trusted her heart. I couldn't believe it then, just as I still can't believe it now.

I asked if she still wanted to continue her schooling in Victoria. She said she was with me now, and her plans to attend had been just an excuse to leave her hometown of Guelph anyways and to visit her dad who was in Calgary, as he had recently divorced her mother. She didn't see him much anymore, and it made her sad as she had been Daddy's little girl growing up. She missed him taking her up in his home-built Cessna. He was a Learjet pilot, who flew corporate bigwigs all over the world. I could tell she really missed him. I said I hoped to meet him one day. What a stupid thing to say. She reminded me I would be meeting him shortly when we reached Calgary. After all, I would be his future son-in-law, now wouldn't I? I said I was apprehensive and maybe she should visit him alone. She said it would be fine, adding she was a little pissed off at him anyway for leaving her mother. I had never met a girlfriend's parents before, so I had about another twelve hours to dwell on it. But for some unexplainable reason, I believed her reassurance that it would be okay – like I could believe and trust anything she told me. *That wasn't something I was used to. I never trusted anyone.*

When we arrived, we checked into a dive downtown as she didn't really want to stay with her father. Whatever she wanted was fine with me as it was all on her dime anyway. She knew I didn't have any money. Once we got to the room, she said she needed a long, hot shower as she was feeling a little scuzzy. She went in and turned on the taps and steamed things up. Upon finishing, she poked her head outside the door and asked if there was another mirror in the room, as the bathroom one was covered with condensation. I told her there was a full length one on the wall. She exited fully naked and carrying her hairbrush and a bottle of body lotion. Like I said earlier, I hadn't seen her with her clothes off, so this was the first time. Standing in front of the mirror, she said she shouldn't be long. She just needed to comb her hair out and apply some lotion. I told her to take as long as she needed, as I was quite happy looking at the view.

I sat back on the bed with neither of us saying a word. I watching her reflection in the mirror watching mine. I began feeling dizzy. The sight of her was like seeing the heavens opening up and revealing all of it secrets. *It is her spirit I am talking about.* The way she looked, the way she moved, was of a natural grace bestowed on her by God himself. Her eyes were like supernovas, emitting a brightness that could be seen a thousand light years away. Her lips like two delicate petals of a rosebud inviting you in to partake of its nectar. She wasn't perfection, but what perfection aspired to be. I was so very blessed to see her magnificence.

Just as she was almost done, I leapt from the bed and lifted her in my arms, carrying her like a newlywed bride over the threshold. She wrapped her arms around my neck as I went to the bed and gently placed her on it. I took a seat on the edge and took both my hands and lightly pushed her damp hair back behind her ears. We gazed at one another for what felt like a millennium. *It was a simple intimacy I had never experienced before.* With tears in my eyes, I told her how very beautiful she was. She grabbed my arms, pulling me down to her for a long passionate kiss. What followed could not be described by a thousand poets, so I will not try. But I will say it was the most tender and passionate thing I have ever experienced in my life. We were as one. I think I had just made love for the first time.

We fell asleep wrapped in each other's arms, and I never wanted to let go of her. It gave me a semblance of peace at long last and a safe place to be. I could only pray to the heavens above that she felt the same way. When we woke up, I just had to know, so I asked her how she was feeling about everything, hoping she hadn't changed her mind about me. She repeated what she had said earlier, adding she knew I was the one from the first time she laid eyes on me. She also said I was the first guy to make her orgasm. She would never allow herself to have one in the past, as she had wanted her first to be with the one she would spend the rest of her life with. So I was stuck with her now. *Here comes the waterworks again.* She took my hands in hers, telling me I could cry as much as I needed to, she was here for me now. *It was as if she knew everything about me. How could she possibly know?*

We had about three or four hours to kill until her father was to come and pick us up. I was not looking forward to it. The last time they had talked was four or five days ago. He knew she had just broken up with her boyfriend, and now she was showing up at his doorstep with a fiancé. Her father might not be too impressed. I had very little clothing with me, and what I did have was dirty, tattered, or torn. Kim wanted me to make a good first impression on her dad, so she insisted on taking me shopping to find an outfit. She dressed with a certain artistic flair, so I hoped maybe she could do her magic on me. Little did I know our trip to the mall would come close to exposing my sordid past.

We were making our way from store to store when we heard a female voice calling out the name "Jessie". My heart stopped beating for a second as I turned to see who it was. *Shit, shit, shit.* I pretended to ignore the calls, but she ran up to us and asked my name. Thinking fast, I pulled out my wallet and showed her the name on my license. Nope, not Jessie. It appeared to satisfy her as she apologized for mistaking me for someone else. I wonder who? Maybe a guy who had used her, probably given her gonorrhoea, and stolen $100 from her. It could have been over between Kim and I right then and there. There had to be a reason why my past wasn't divulged. I was beginning to believe that anyways.

So off we went to continue to find an outfit for me. I don't know whether her choice was a playful joke, or if she just didn't give a shit about what her dad thought. The shoes were black-and-white chequered loafers. The pants were a see-through pale-blue pair of Hammer pants in full puffiness from the ankles up. She topped it off with a shirt to match that can only be described as a pirate shirt. You could see me coming from miles away. I asked her if she was sure this was what she wanted me to wear. Trying to contain her increasing laughter, she asked, "Don't you like it?"

She was teaching me a life lesson. Something that had been instilled in her own psyche long ago. She knew how hurt I was about the way I had looked as a kid. She wanted me to understand that looks are just superficial. Happiness comes from within. The outfit was just a reminder of that. I also think she wanted to freak her dad out a bit. I told you there was something special about her. But folks, hold on to your seats. You ain't seen nothing yet.

Her father came to bring us to his apartment for a seven-course meal and to meet the "panther" for whom he had left Kim's mom. He was shocked and concerned about our engagement to say the least, insisting we come and stay with them for a few days. Kim and I both knew he had an ulterior motive of wanting to convince her she was making a mistake, but she accepted his invitation in spite of it. She wasn't daddy's little girl anymore. That had ended the day he had left her mother, and she was not too happy with his choice of a partner either.

Having consumed a more than adequate amount of wine at dinner, Kim began to voice her displeasure, not blatantly, but by subtle comments. This in turn set her dad off, resurrecting his previous conversation with Kim and I and voicing his contempt about our decision to marry. Arguing back and forth, something he said to Kim finally got my back up as I had been doing my best to stay out of it until then. He told her how stupid she was to be giving up everything she had and to leave her family behind to marry me on a whim. At that point I interjected four words: "Oh, like you did? "You could hear a pin drop as Kim just looked at him with a questioning gesture, waiting for his response. He had nothing. Silence!

Kim motioned for me to get up and announced we were going out for a drink to let things cool off. We ended up at a sushi restaurant across from the apartment. Who knew saké had so much kick to it. We were blitzed. I had been drunk plenty of times before, but this was definitely in the top five. All she could do was laugh. It was like music to my ears. We held each other up so we could get back up to her dad's apartment. They were none too pleased about the condition we were in, as they helped us into our bedroom. As soon as we hit the bed, we were out. Our little adventure only confirmed to her dad that she was making a mistake. He and his girlfriend would now conspire to prove it to her.

Once we woke up, he informed us he was taking Kim out to brunch – just the two of them so I wouldn't be able to run interference. It made me nervous thinking he might be able to convince her that he was right. Kim knew I was feeling uneasy about it, so she assured me not to worry, but it was something she needed to do. So off they went, leaving me and the panther behind to entertain each other. This was the second step of their devious plan.

I started watching television in our room with the door shut. The sound of the running water coming from the bathroom made it obvious the girlfriend was taking a shower. I heard the water turn off and then the bathroom door open. She tapped lightly on my door and said she needed to come in to get a towel from the closet. She entered the room wet and completely naked, with not even a smidgen of bashfulness. I just continued watching the boob tube, without having a reaction to hers. She was trying very hard to direct my attention to her body. She asked if I would mind reaching a towel for her on the top shelf. After I retrieved it and handed it to her, she held it for a second, then purposefully let it slip out of her hand to the floor saying, "Oops." She turned her back to me and bent over to pick it up. By the time she stood up, I was already sitting back on the bed watching TV again. She approached me and asked if I thought she had nice breasts. I had to end this quickly before she had a chance to do anything else. I looked at her and asked how much Kim's dad had paid for them. She looked down at her store-bought boobs and then stormed out of the room, so ending her ill-fated attempt in trying to seduce me. That was a pinnacle moment for me. If I had been with anybody else but Kim, I would have been all over her without hesitation. This time it didn't even cross my mind. My moral turpitude was a no show. Something had to be changing in me for that to happen. *And to think this was only within days of knowing her...*

Now all I had to do was wait and see if her dad had convinced her. When they returned, Kim told me we would be continuing on our journey the next day. When we had a chance to be alone, she told me everything her dad had said. He told her he wanted her to stay in Calgary and was willing to buy her a small business or support her until she found out what she really wanted to do, but she turned him down flat.

I never told her about my experience with the girlfriend. I knew it would hurt her that her dad was capable of such a thing. He was willing to embarrass her so he could be proven right. Look at me go. I was concerned about someone else's feelings besides my own for once. I was still worried it was only a matter of time before she came to her senses, but I was all in now. I would take it as far as she would let me. I needed her in my life for however long I could have her.

Now that we had gotten visiting her dad out of the way, it was time that she met my parents. I gave them a call and told them when to expect us. They had only been expecting me, not knowing I had met someone. I told them I was getting married again. I can just imagine the conversation they had after hanging up. But they were well used to it by now. My history with girls didn't give them any reason to believe this time would be any different. I had received my final divorce decree from my first wife two weeks earlier, and here I was jumping right back into the fire.

# CHAPTER 11:
# Husband and Wife

Our trip through British Columbia amazed her. She had never been this far West, and the beauty of the mountains made it easy for her to fall in love with the province. She was looking forward to seeing where I had grown up. I was more nervous than anything else. The people back home knew a lot more about me than she did. She didn't even know I'd been married before and had a child. I knew I had to tell her before we arrived. If I didn't, surely my parents or my brothers would. I was as honest as I could be about it when I told her. She paid no mind to it saying that there was nothing we could do about the past, but learn from it. She did say she was a little disappointed that I didn't wait to meet her first before I got married. She should have been the one and only. *Yes, she should have!*

We were getting very close to arriving home, and this was making me very anxious and worried. The bus trip and the visit to her dad's had been a cakewalk compared to what I thought might lie ahead of us. I hadn't really discussed my family with her, and she hadn't asked about them either. All she knew was my father was a workaholic, my mother basically sat on her ass all day, and I wasn't very close with my three older brothers. She didn't seem nervous at the prospect of meeting them, but why would she be as there was nothing she had to hide. Of course, I knew she hoped they would like her, but if they didn't, that would be fine as well. She was just that type of person. I had no doubt whatsoever they couldn't help but like her. I was more worried they'd like her too much and would try to convince her she was making a mistake, just as her dad had tried.

Our intentions were to stay with them until we could find a place of our own. She told me she had enough funds to cover us for a few months or until we found work. When we arrived my father was there to offer taxi service back to their place. They still lived in the town I was born in, but were now living in an apartment after selling my childhood home. The entire way, I couldn't get a word in edgewise. I'd never seen my father take a liking to someone so quickly, and they talked back and forth the whole way. I said, there was just a certain "Je ne sais quoi" quality about her. It wasn't like she was trying to impress him; she was just being herself.

Once inside, Kim met my mother and they exchanged pleasantries but not much of anything else. Things hadn't changed over the years for her. She was just killing time by being stoned, drinking Pepsi, and watching TV. Mom wasn't cold to her, but she was too wrapped up in her own existence to care about anybody else's. My father asked us if we wanted to go down to the local and have a beer with him. I thought, *Who is this man?* He had never asked me to go anywhere with him before.

So off we went. He ordered us some beers that were crafted by a local brewer and which all the locals took great pride in, including my dad. He told Kim once she tried it, she would never drink any other brand again and watched her in anticipation of what she thought. I will forever remember that moment. She put it to her lips and swigged a little just as she was about to cough. It was the best spit-out ever, ending up all over the front of my dad. She cracked up laughing and stood up with a napkin to wipe him off. I thought he would be pissed, but he was laughing as much as she was. With napkin in hand she gently wiped the sides of his face off and told him, "I see what you mean; that's pretty good beer." Then she leaned in and gave him a kiss on the cheek. It was absolutely priceless and so heart-warming. The rest of the afternoon till early evening we shot pool and got a little drunk. It was the most time I'd ever spent with my father in a social environment. Kim brought out a joy in him that was almost like a fatherly pride. He took every available opportunity to proudly introduce her to anybody he could. This the beginning of a bond between the two of them that my dad would come to rely on down the road.

Once we arrived back home, my father held me back from going inside, saying he needed my assistance with something. We went back out and sat on the stairs leading to the building and lit up a smoke. He told me I had one chance to come clean with Kim about my past. I knew he wasn't talking about what happened with my mother but referring to everything else. He said she deserved to know everything, as she wasn't like any of the other girls I had brought home. He said he'd be damned if I hurt her by lying, especially if she was going to make a commitment of marriage. He said I had until the end of the night to do so or he would. He then patted me on the leg and said, "Good luck." I think he might have thought it might not go so well for me. If he wasn't, I sure was. I decided I better get it over with and asked her to join me in a walk.

I spilled my guts out, except of course about the horrible things involving my mom. There was a lot to tell her: Grandma, Chinook, the true extent of being bullied as a child, my mother's accident and how I blamed myself for it, my excessive drinking and drug use, my criminal convictions, and all of my insecurities. There was so much for her to digest, I told her she might want to take some time and rethink her acceptance of my proposal. She didn't even bat an eye. She grabbed both my hands and pulled me closer to put her forehead on mine. She said it must have been hard for me to tell her the truth, but even harder going through it. She knew I had a lot of pain inside me, she could see it in my eyes, but more importantly she saw something else: a very kind and sweet soul. There was no need for us to put off getting married and nothing was about to change her mind. She now knew more about me than anyone else, and she not only wasn't going to run away, it appeared to be one of the reasons why she wanted to stay. *To know someone could like me without the facade brought me a happiness I'd never experienced before. It relieved my spirit that she could see some of my pain.*

We went back inside to join my parents with smiles ear to ear, making my dad question if I had told her the truth about things. He got up and took her into the kitchen to find out. It was only a few minutes before they returned, and as I stood up, he reached out his hand to shake mine saying one simple word, "CONGRATULATIONS!"

Everything this girl said and did gave me more hope for myself. Perhaps one day I could share with her the pain she didn't know about. Maybe, but until then, we had a wedding to plan, and the quicker the better. I asked if she had any vision of what she wanted for the wedding. Smirking she told me, "Yes silly boy, to marry you." *Wow, just wow.* A big fancy wedding held no weight with her. She would be just as happy to have a courthouse wedding, so that's what we decided on. The next day we went down and applied for a marriage licence. I needed to bring my final divorce decree from my first marriage to help speed up the process. They told us it would take 72 hours, and then we would be free to get married. We booked a reservation with the justice of the peace on the fourth day.

**March 9, 1984 was the day we became man and wife.** We still needed to find a place to live, and we knew we couldn't be too picky with the funds we had. We viewed several rentals that day and secured one that allowed us to move in a couple days later. It was such a dive with cracks in the wall and a heater that continuously made a buzzing sound, but she didn't care. It had an enclosed porch at the back of the house where you could watch the mighty Columbia River flowing by and see most of downtown. No matter it's pitfalls, the view made up for it. We decided to wait until the day of our marriage before we moved in. It was kind of corny, but she wanted our first place together to be as a married couple. We had no furniture or linens, absolutely nothing, so my parents helped us out with what they could for the time being, and we got whatever else we needed later at one of the local thrift stores.

On the big day, our wedding party consisted of the four of us and the justice of the peace. Afterwards, my dad treated us to dinner and drinks at a local hotel. During the meal, he handed Kim an envelope containing $250 cash as a wedding gift from them. It was still early, so Kim and I decided to take a stroll through the local shops in town before we headed up to spend our first night together in our new place. We entered this little boutique that sold wicker and rattan. She fell in love with a small wicker loveseat. We used some of the money my parents had given us and carried it out. We trudged up the hill and finally arrived. I put the love seat down to carry her over the threshold, feeling excited about our honeymoon night. As we stepped inside, we felt a wave of dry heat blast against us. The heater was going full blast and it was so hot, Kim had to retreat outside as I continued in to rectify the issue. I would just need to turn the thermostat down and let it cool off for a bit. There was just one problem: I couldn't find it anywhere.

By the time I gave up looking and joined Kim, I was soaked with sweat. She thought for a moment, then ran inside and opened the door to the back porch, which was secluded from the rest of the house. She told me to bring in the love seat, while she opened up the porch's numerous windows. The outside breeze flowed in making the temperature very comfortable. That would be where we would spend our first night as man and wife, on our little love seat enjoying the view and talking until the sun came up. It didn't bother her one iota. However, now she needed a morning coffee and braved going inside to make it. Within a couple of minutes, I heard her laughing and yelling out, "Oh, my Lord." I could see she was staring at something inside the kitchen cabinet. Once I reached her and looked inside, I felt like such a fool. There was that elusive thermostat, What a buffoon. We spent the rest of the day sleeping to make up for the lack of it the night before.

When we woke up, we needed to get some food in the house, so I told her to make a list and I would go down and pick it up. I had an ulterior motive for going by myself. I'd come up with a plan to melt her heart and make up for the previous night. The following day my mother and her were going out thrift store shopping, which would give me ample time to initiate what I was planning, but I needed to do a few things first. I paid a visit to a local print shop and asked them to print up a twelve-foot-long banner. Next, I made a call to the radio station to talk to a disc jockey that I used to know from when he supplied music at the Union Hall. Everything was going according to plan. Look at me: I actually had a plan this time. Still very tired we just slept that night away. The next morning, they left for the day of shopping together and I quickly ran downtown to pick up the banner I had ordered, even though I had no money to pay for it. The banner was already made, so what could he say? A slight chance of getting paid for his work was better than none at all, I hurried home to hang it and turned on the local radio station. When Kim returned, I met her at the door telling her to close her eyes. I guided her through the house to achieve a position where she would have the best view of the banner. When her positioning was right, I told her to open her eyes so she could read the words scrolled across. I - L O V E -Y O U. She turned and hugged me softly saying, "I love you too."

I can still hear the whisper of those words. I knew we didn't truly love each other yet, but I hoped in time we would with all our hearts, believing we had connected paths for a reason. At least that's how I felt. Hearing the "I love you" words gave me hope that one day, with time, she would. And as for me loving her, no matter how much time I had, I wouldn't know if I did or not because I had no clue of what real love encompasses. My only hope was that she would be able to teach me.

Then with perfect timing, I began to hear the DJ on the radio fulfilling a special song request. I ran and turned it up as loud as it could go. "This Dedication is from a very happy groom to his new bride, Kimberly. Congratulating you both, and may you have all the happiness in the world." The song he played was made a hit when used in the very popular dance movie, *Footloose*, which had been released a year earlier.

This song was called "Almost Paradise" by Mike Reno."[2] We were pressing against each other so hard our feet became stationary, just rocking to the melody and shedding tears to its words. She kissed me and said it was the most romantic thing anyone had ever done for her. We moved to the bedroom and for the first time in our new place, we made love. That was the only way I could describe it now. The graphic depictions of my previous sexual encounters would now be left in the past. They were too vulgar and obscene.

We spent the next couple of months visiting the local taverns. I was so proud to show Kim off, however, it also brought out my insecurities as well. Every guy and even a lot of girls would attempt to make a move on her. She always put them in their place, but I was still worried she would come to her senses about me. Deep down, I still believed that nothing good would ever last.

We ran out of all the funds that Kim had brought with her and nothing had changed in my ability to find work, so we applied for Social Services. The money basically covered our rent and bills, leaving us with about $200 to live on a month. Each time when we needed more, we would hit up Ma for it. At one point we moved to Calgary. Not for very long, as I couldn't find work there either. Not that there wasn't any available; I was just emotionally incapable of holding any type of job. We had to move back, leaving us in the same boat as when we left.

Time went by, and one morning, Kim became violently sick. It only lasted for an hour or so, but it continued day after day. We had a sneaking suspicion what was causing it. A doctor appointment and test confirmed our suspicions. She was going to be a mother, and I would be father for the second time. I can't say we were overjoyed knowing our circumstances, but what could we do about it now? We needed to change our financial situation immediately. The baby wouldn't be able to survive on noodles and potatoes, not to mention all the other expenses that come with raising a kid. There was a very small town about sixty miles away with a family-ran sawmill that employed most of the town. We decided this would be our best shot for me to find work. My dad was fully behind the move

---

2    Three songs are an intricate part of our story. Because of copyright laws, I can only give you the titles as they come up. Please give them a listen as it will become clear why they are so important to our story.

and bought us an old Rambler car as he didn't want us to be without transportation, especially with Kim's pregnancy. *Did I mention he really liked her?*

We moved and found a tiny house close to the mill. Now all I had to do was wait for them to hire me. I don't know if it was my lack of work experience, but the call still hadn't come after a couple of months. When Kim had studied Art, her speciality was realism, so she began offering her services to draw portraits of the locals and their pets. It would supplement our income enough to make sure she was at least getting the proper nutrition. She had always taken very good care of herself, no matter what. She was getting that rosy glow about her, her belly was beginning to show just a little, and considering everything else, we were doing okay. She actually was looking forward to starting a family. Her bond was growing with the life that grew within. She would be a fantastic mother regardless of how I would be as a father. It was making her happy now. But as so many other fucking times in the past, I would be reminded of the one and only truth that was certain.

It was just after midnight when she woke me up and said something wasn't right. She was feeling sporadic bursts of sharp pain in her lower abdomen. We weren't about to take any chances, so we quickly dressed and were off to the closest hospital, which was sixty miles away. The mountain-side highway was difficult to navigate in daylight, never mind in pitch darkness. I had to drive at half the speed limit with valuable time being wasted, but I didn't think it would have made a difference. Kim curled up on the bench seat beside me with her pain increasing, holding the cries it caused under her breath. I was telling her everything was going to be all right, but I felt so helpless. There was nothing I could do but drive as fast as I could.

When we got on to the main highway, she started crying uncontrollably and curling herself up even more. I frantically asked what was wrong. She couldn't answer me through her sobbing, so I pulled to the side of the highway and parked. I turned her around so I could gently move her to see her face. She was hesitant at first, but eventually started to unfurl her body to sit up. As I put my hand on her leg, I felt a warm dampness. It was blood. Her tears streamed harder as she threw her arms around my neck and cried out: I lost the baby... I'm so sorry. Please forgive me!!!"

I sat there feeling a deep sadness overtaking me. Not for me, but for her. I actually could feel somebody else's pain rather than my own. I could feel hers in my heart. For the first time in my life, I was feeling empathy. *It felt unfamiliar to my soul.* I held her hand, telling her she had nothing to be sorry about. Everything would be okay and I loved her no matter what. I knew she was blaming herself, and it was tearing me apart. We sat and held each other for the longest while and then continued on to the hospital. Once we arrived, they told us that other than the miscarriage, she hadn't suffered any other complications. However, the next morning they would have to perform a D&C. She was very tired and needed sleep, so I left her to rest. We would have plenty of time to talk after the procedure in the morning. I stayed at my parents that night, and I could tell my dad was very concerned for Kim. Ma couldn't give a crap and went as far to say it was probably for the best. *Well, I didn't get my new-found empathy from her, now did I?*

The next morning, I sat beside my angel waiting until she woke up from the anesthesia, trying to think of what to say. As she slowly regained consciousness, she reached for my hand to hold in hers. She gave a small smile and softly said, "Hey baby, are you okay?" She had just gone through one of the most heartbreaking experiences of her life and her first thought was of me. I told her I was only concerned with how she was doing. She said she was still a little tired and felt fine physically, but she needed to talk to me about something. She relayed with much pain in her voice that she didn't want to have kids anymore and hoped I understood.

This would be the only thing ever said again about the subject, but I felt with everything in my being she was crushed by the experience. Her eyes still had so much light in them, but now some of its flicker had stopped. I wish I knew how to help her get it back, but no one knows the pain of a mother's loss. She would carry it forever in her heart. To help, I started doing something I had always refused to do in the past and began wearing a condom. She didn't want me to, but I couldn't chance her getting pregnant. I just didn't want her to experience that kind of pain again or lose any more of the light in her eyes. There was something deeper going on inside of me, and I didn't even know It. That is very sad in itself.

# CHAPTER 12:

# More Family Secrets

We decided to move back home. At least if there was another emergency, we wouldn't be too far away from getting help. Kim was depressed about the baby, and we began drinking almost daily. She drank out of deep sadness, whereas I drank to drink. It's tragic, but I didn't feel any connection to our lost child. I didn't have the emotional capacity for it. I was still that damaged thirteen-year-old boy. After all this time, I couldn't even tell you if I truly loved Kim or not. I just didn't know. She didn't know it, but she was about to assume two roles in my development: one as my wife, the other as a mother figure. That was so much to expect from her and so very fucking selfish of me. "

Our lives for the next few years were about survival to meet our daily needs. The reliance on my mother's weekly generosity started to get under Kim's skin a wee bit. She knew there was something deeper for the reason behind it. At times I had to deflect some of the questions she asked. She never pushed too hard for the answer, however, it made me believe my forever secret was more vulnerable now. I was sure if she found it out, she would be so disgusted our lives together would come to an end. I couldn't let that happen. It had to remain a forever secret, no matter what.

One day she came out of the bathroom with a pair of scissors in hand. I was informed that I was her hairdresser today. We couldn't afford a real one, so I had been chosen to cut her hair. "Oh boy!" I never knew it was in me, but Edward Scissor Hands would have been proud. Kim was overjoyed with the cut and started thinking of another way we could make a little extra cash. I started a new career cutting hair on anybody wanting to save a buck or two. Unfortunately, before long, it also turned into another service I offered. Most of my clients were women, and for an extra twenty, they could receive a relaxing massage. Kim knew I was giving them, but I didn't know if she knew to what extent. It was always done at our place, with Kim there reading in the bedroom. Not all massages had happy endings for the girls; some just wanting legit relaxing ones. I preferred those, but old habits die hard. There was absolutely no sexual gratification for me as all I could desire I had with Kim. It just allowed me to do what I was good at. I was still a pleaser. In all the times I had given them, Kim never peeked in once, not out of curiosity or to display any sort of jealousy or mistrust. I have to admit I was a little worried why she never did, thinking maybe it was because she had already given up on me. I would learn many years later, that was the furthest thing from the truth.

There was about to be a celebration. After forty-three years of dedication to his job, Dad announced his retirement. We were all looking forward to his dinner at a local spaghetti house. Friends, family, co-workers would all be in attendance. Kim and I were so proud of him, and it was shaping up to be a memorable evening – unfortunately, for all the wrong reasons. Everyone was getting fairly drunk, and loose lips sink ships. I still have no idea why or who said something to Kim, but it would bring my childhood to the forefront, revealing a deep family secret concerning myself. Nope not that one. TONIGHT, I WOULD LEARN DAD WASN'T MY DAD. The implications would confirm that indeed there was something wrong with me. I was somebody's mistake in life. No wonder everyone treated me so differently when I was a kid. Maybe that's why there weren't any pictures of me.

I was in shock. Kim however was pissed. She retrieved her purse, took my hand, and as we walked by my mother when we were leaving, she offered her three words: "YOU FUCKING BITCH." Arriving home, we went and sat on our little wicker loveseat with questions beginning to surface. Why didn't they tell me? Who else knew? And of course, the one I wanted answered the most: Who in the hell was my father then? A short time later, there was a knock on the door. It was the secret keepers wanting to make sure we were okay. Kim told them we didn't want to talk to them right now and asked them to leave. The rest of the night we just sat and talked.

If it wasn't for her, I don't know what I would have done. I was still carrying the secret pain of my mother. Now, there was this one about father. Sorry, meant to say "the guy who raised me". My entire existence had been a lie. No wonder bullshitting came so natural for me. Kim knew the only thing she could do was to listen and help put things in perspective. Like yes, my dad wasn't my dad, but he had been there for both of us lately, and it must have been hard for him to keep it a secret. She didn't want me to blame him, and even though we hadn't bonded, he had done the best he could. What she said made me see things differently. However, the things I felt about my mom raised anger in me that I had promised myself I would never bring to the surface again; one that Kim had never witnessed before. She had never heard me raise my voice in all the time we had been together. Thankfully, it didn't frighten her when I finally did. She told me I should be angry and how dare my mother keep this from me. Kim said she knew there was something not right about my mother, and she couldn't imagine how hard it must have been for me growing up.

Oh my God, with every fibre of my being, I wanted to tell her how bad it really was, but I just couldn't. At least now she could see a small cause and effect of some of my pain and why I was so fucked up. Granted it was a new cause, but at least I didn't have to carry the pain alone this time.

The next day we went on a mission to get the answer to the question I had a right to know. My dad was outside when we arrived, and I think he was expecting us to be in a rage and not receive a hug from us both. We told him we were sorry his retirement party turned out the way it did. He said he couldn't blame us for our reaction and understood. He knew why we were there, but what we wanted to know couldn't come from him. He had made a promise long ago. Kim and he were a lot alike. They kept their promises." So inside we went. I won't get into every detail of the discussion, however we left an hour later with the answer, or should I say answers. At first, she said my father was the guy she worked for. Digging deeper, it became a native hockey coach, then her beloved doctor, then a one-night stand with an out-of-town visitor. The final one would be the icing on the cake. She said I was the product of a rape. She covered all the bases, basically telling us she wouldn't tell us. It could be she didn't actually know, but it was very cruel of her to let me ponder if I was a rapist's son. If the story about the rape were true, that would make me a son of two rapists. It was yet another piece of shit to add to my emotional baggage.

The rape story made more sense to me than the others. I had flashbacks of the time she lost control and yelled out as if someone else was in the room, It could be why she blacked out that one time, just like I did with the Hooker

It was in the realm of possibility if you think about it. I can only imagine what she thought every time she looked at me. She could only see him. No wonder she hates me as I do her.

The only time we would talk to my mother after that was when we needed something. Kim didn't feel bad about taking from her anymore, and it's damn hard to say Kim disliked anybody. It just wasn't in her make-up.

# CHAPTER 13:

# What Goes Up Must Come Down

Time went on with my dad actually enjoying his retirement and becoming the caretaker of a government-subsidized 60+ apartment building they lived in. He was always on the go, making sure everything ran tip top. He had been retired for less than 6 months when he called and asked us to stop by. It turns out his body wasn't as tip top as the condition in which he kept the apartment building. A biopsy was done on a growth in his neck with the diagnosis of stage-four lymphoma cancer. After working hard all of his life, he now faced the possibility of death. It was heart-breaking and the news really affected Kim. She wanted to make sure he wouldn't face it alone. He had no one else; definitely not my mother. He had become close to one of my brothers over the years, and he would be there whenever he could, but besides him, it was just us. And the sad thing about it was that I wasn't even his biological son. But I knew what it's like not to have anyone, and I didn't want that for him. He was always there for Kim and I, and she loved him. We brought him to every single chemotherapy treatment, Kim always holding his hand and reading to him as they put poison into him. Months went by with hair loss and daily bouts of vomiting, but it paid off. His last chemo check-up showed the cancer had been eradicated. We were so happy for him. Now with being able to look forward again, he made the decision to buy a small house; one with ample space for a garden that he could putter around in.

By fluke, things started to change for the better for us as well. I had written poetry since childhood, so I decided to let my imagination run wild one day and write a story. It was about a fictional historical character and his best friend, a mule named Ennie Essau. They travelled the mining camps of the area selling supplies. The main character was Mesome Wares. His name derived from the folks at the camp asking: "Are you here to sell Me-Some Wares?" I thought my story was a little lame, but an elderly couple that owned a service station just down the road from my parents had a chance to read it and said they thought it should be published.

To keep a long story short, we teamed up and created a company called Mesome Wares Inc. We were able to secure a business grant from the BC Government. I wrote content and Kim created all the artwork needed. Not only that, we manufactured a complete package to accompany the book. A soft-sculpted doll, a narrated cassette tape, and a poster that Kim designed were included. Our company even wrote cartoons for the local paper. Kim and I were having the time of our lives spending sixteen hours a day creating and manufacturing. Our main character was even named a Goodwill Ambassador for British Columbia by the Tourism Board. It was just symbolic, but it was still pretty impressive that it got that far. Things were better than they had ever been. Kim and I meshed creatively as I described the vision I had in my head and she put it on paper. We loved spending every minute together. We always had, but now we were making money. Kim even hand-painted a thirty-six-foot by twenty-four-foot historical mural to donate to my hometown. It was so big that it had to be delivered by crane to rest on the local arena. We were just so proud of each other.

With our confidence in our abilities growing, we felt we didn't need anyone else's input anymore. We were having too much fun collaborating on our own, so we decided to sell our shares to our partners and start a business of our own. Go big or stay home! We went really big and left home. We located our new business in Vancouver and moved within the week. Kim came up with our new business name: ARTSY FARTSY. We did everything from logo creation, window painting, and signs to complete print media campaigns. We became so busy we had to turn away clients. For once I actually felt I was contributing something more substantial to our marriage and giving back just a little of what she had given me. I had put her through so much already, and she remained loyal through it all. Things were really looking up for us. What's the old saying? Oh yeah. "What goes up must come down."

We received a call from my parents and Dad's cancer was back with a vengeance. The treatment they could offer him in a small town would give him little chance for survival. We were devastated by the news and felt helpless that we couldn't be there for him. It only took a few minutes for Kim to come up with a solution. She said we had to convince him to move to Vancouver with us. At least he would have a slightly better chance to prolong his life here, and he wouldn't be alone in his fight. Can you believe that? She knew it meant we would no longer be able to keep our business going – at least not if we were going to take proper care of him. She was willing to give up our first glimmer of a secure financial future. I knew she didn't make the decision lightly as it also meant my mother would have to live with us. She really loved my dad.

Now we just had to convince him. He had never lived anywhere else, so accepting our offer seemed like a long shot. But to our surprise, his decision only took twenty minutes. He accepted. To this day I have no clue why he did. I honestly believe he trusted Kim and felt her love. There could be no other reason behind it. Just like me, Kim was all he had. It certainly wasn't on my account, but I was determined to be there for him as well. So, to do my part, I needed a job to help support all of us, which now included four cats and two dogs. All of them were Kim's babies, so I guess we did start a family after all. I found one the very next day by being at the right place at the right time, as if it were meant to be. They even let me start the following week so we could move my parents down. We rented a U-Haul, packed up their belongings, and Dad dropped the house key off at the bank. He had no intention of returning. I think he knew his time was limited.

His medical team implemented a course of treatment, and we were with him all the way. He was getting weaker, so we set up a bed in the living room to be closer to the only bathroom, as both bedrooms were upstairs. I spent my days at work, while Kim looked after him. My mother always stayed in her room. It was just sad. That is all I can say about that. Then one night we heard a loud thud downstairs. We raced down to find my dad in the bathroom on his hands and knees. This proud man had been reduced to crawling just to pee. It broke our hearts. From that day forward, we never left him alone again, taking round the clock shifts. Kim was there during the day, and I curled up in a chair at night until I had to go to work the next morning. Days turned into weeks, then to months. Kim and I hardly slept, making sure he didn't want for anything. Stress and emotional exhaustion led to a bad decision on my part. We needed help staying awake and coke filled the bill. We had it "under control" and only used it when absolutely necessary, which for me, of course, was every day. I was addicted again. Kim had an allergic reaction to it, so she seldom did it. That was a blessing in disguise. To our surprise, Dad got better for a time. In fact, he insisted on preparing a turkey dinner for all of us. It took all his strength, but he did it. He wasn't able to eat any himself, but I knew it was his way of showing how much he appreciated everything we were doing for him. I also think it was a distraction to allow him some type of normality. Knowing you're dying must get overwhelming at times.

His improvement didn't last long and he lapsed into a coma a short time later. Now with a catheter in place, a home nurse would visit twice a week to help us with any medical needs he required. We never left him alone, applying ice cubes to his lips, moving him the best we could to prevent bedsores, and anything else we could do. Returning home late from work one night, I continued on downstairs. Upon reaching the bottom landing, I noticed Kim wasn't sitting in her usual chair. I turned the corner to where my dad was, and curled up beside him was Kim fast asleep with her head on his chest, holding one of his hands. I still had no idea what love was, but in that moment, I saw it with my own two eyes. IT DOES EXIST. Words can't do justice to her purity of heart and how she sacrificed of herself for myself and now my father. It made me think I didn't deserve her, knowing I could never return it in kind. I wanted to so badly, but the demons of my past were still holding me captive. The one and only secret I still held from her. I owed her everything, but I just couldn't bring myself to reveal the truth of how despicable I really was.

Not long afterwards, I could tell my dad didn't have much time left. I think Kim knew it the night she was beside him just to let him know he was loved and not alone. I phoned my brothers back home to ask them to come down so they could say goodbye. All of them except one made up excuses why they couldn't come. It was so very sad, but I guess they had their own demons concerning dad. My one brother hopped on a plane the next day, and I went and picked him up. We arrived back to the townhouse as quickly as we could. I was relieved it wasn't too late. I just knew in my heart it was very close. My brother sat with him for a time then joined us in the kitchen. I soon retreated to the living room to be with him. I held his hands and told him how strong he was to hold on to see my brother. With tears in my eyes, I let him know it was okay if he had to leave us now. He'd suffered enough. Then I lied to him by telling him I loved him. *What my mother did to me even robbed me of that moment. But I needed him to hear it just the same, whether I knew what love was or not.* He heard everything I said because I could see him trying to breathe harder. Then there was one last gasp for air. I watched as he took his last breath. HE WAS GONE!

There was nothing we could do but call the coroner. Kim and I were trying to console each other while my mother never left the kitchen, not to say goodbye or shed a tear. She must have been in shock. Yeah, I know... But at least I tried to understand her reaction.

The following months were difficult ones as Mother had to wait for all of his benefits and insurance to kick in, so she had to continue living with us. I was still using cocaine; not to stay awake any longer, but to help with the pain of losing Dad, plus the pain in the ass who was still living with us. I never handled stress too well for some reason. We desperately needed to do something to feel good about ourselves again, so we got back to creating. I came up with an idea not only to satisfy what we wanted to do, but also to honour the memory of Dad. He loved his cats, and so did Kim, so thought I should write what I knew. We decided to do a large adult cartoon book depicting our lives with our fur babies, entitled *Here Kitty, Kitty, Kitty*. All proceeds would be donated to the provincial SPCA in my dad's memory. We worked tirelessly on it day and night, and once finished, I arranged to have it printed. It took all the money we had to pay for the first run of two thousand copies, but we were hoping any sales would pay for more if needed. I then went to hit every major grocery chain and bookstore to try and convince them to carry our book. The second door I pounded on was the buying department for Sobeys. They loved it and agreed to carry it as long as we would be willing to make appearances for any book signings they might want. They ordered basically our entire first production to be distributed throughout twenty-five stores in the Lower Mainland. We went from store to store for various signings, feeling proud to be sitting there all dignified. Well, maybe not with too much dignity. Kim had the brilliant idea we would make our appearances in costume, wearing little cat noses and whiskers. It was hilarious and certainly grabbed customers' attention. Sales were steady and the SPCA was going to get a fair chunk of change in my dad's memory.

Once Mom finally left and Kim and I were alone again, we had to face the reality of our situation. #1. We were running out of money. #2. I was still using coke. All of the money from the book was being donated, and we didn't have enough to resume the business. I could feel myself slipping further into the drug use. Kim never harped on me about it. I don't know why, but like I said, it was as if she knew there was something deeper going on inside me – something I just couldn't reveal. Not yet anyways. We knew we had to leave the big city as drugs were just too accessible. We made the agonizing decision to return home. We really had no other alternative.

Back on Social Services, we were fortunate enough to rent a house right across from where my grandma used to live from a family who had known my family for years. They could have charged us double the rent than what we were paying. The only stipulation was that we were to take care of all their feeding stations for the wildlife on the property. This was something the family had done forever. I knew all about it, having spent a lot of time at my grandma's as a kid. All creatures big and small became our extended family. We fed the raccoons dog food on our porch nightly, which in turn ensured they left our kitties and small dogs alone. There were suet bags in the tree for the birds, saltlicks for the deer, and sunflower seeds for the squirrels and chipmunks. No matter how hard it was to make ends meet, it gave us a real joy interacting with nature. Things were okay, except the daily reminder of my past, now that I was living by my grandma's old house next door. My mother was living there now. The burning question of my true heritage still festered inside me. Why wouldn't my mother just tell me? It was like she was protecting someone. I felt I was always on the outside looking in, just like when I was a kid. It wasn't just about who my true father was, but now it was reasonable to think I had other half siblings out there. I could pass them on the street and not even know it. More stressing, I was starting to relive the things I had shared with her. I was getting more depressed than ever.

The only thing allowing me to face each day was the fact I still had Kim. I don't know how or why, but through everything she was still there. She could have made her life so much easier without me. I told her I loved her constantly, but it wasn't any semblance of what she gave me. Granted I was giving her every-thing I thought love was, but it was still an illusion. It's so true that it is impossible to love another without being able to love yourself. *For me the end of grade seven destroyed any hope of that.* I thought in time it would get better, especially if I did find the one I was looking for. However, time didn't change a thing. My thoughts were getting in the way of any intimacy I had with her. I couldn't risk making love with her only to have something snap in me again and reveal my past. She would surely be disgusted with me and leave. I just refused to let that happen.

No longer having coke accessible, I started medicating with forty to fifty tabs of codeine and Gravol a day. Lack of proper nutrition when I was younger caused my bones to not develop properly, and I now needed a cane to assist my walking at the age of thirty-six. It wasn't as bad as I let on. It was more psychological than physical, but it gave me an excuse not to look for work and at the same time receive pity from others. Social Services granted me long-term disability, which gave us a little extra money every month. We spent most days doing nothing except playing with our babies and picking huckleberries. Kim did find work at a local hotel restaurant as a waitress. The pay was crap, but the tips helped out a lot. Besides that, we basically kept to ourselves. We were never social pariahs, but we just didn't care for all the fake personalities; for me it was my own when I was in public. It was just too much of an effort to put on a show. I'd done that all my life, and I was tired of it. Kim would have been great in any social environment, but her commitment to me was more important to her and she knew how uncomfortable I was around others. It was just one more thing she sacrificed for me. Besides my addiction and the lack of any intimacy, we were comfortable. I tried to remain optimistic that one day I would be able to repay her for all the sacrifices she made for me. However, soon even those were nothing compared to what was heading down the pike.

CHAPTER 14:

# Cycle Reborn

"It was the epoch of belief; it was the epoch of incredulity. It was the season of darkness; it was the season of light. It was the winter of despair. It was the spring of hope."

All this would be brought on by a complete stranger: my twelve-year-old daughter who I hadn't met yet. We received information that Family Services in Kelowna needed me to reach out to them immediately, so that afternoon I made contact. They told me my daughter and her three siblings had been placed into foster care, and by law, they had to inform me. They strongly encouraged me to come and meet her. She needed me in her life. *Really? Things must be really bad then.* Of course, I wanted to, but I was scared shitless and felt no attachment to her whatsoever. As I said, after twelve years of marriage, I still couldn't honestly say I loved Kim, so how could I love my daughter? Kim saw it differently, wanting to do everything and anything to facilitate a meeting. For her it was a no brainer, and it was our responsibility to do whatever we could to be there for her.

I know the situation forced her to feel her own pain of the past and was bringing back memories of her miscarriage. I could see it in her eyes, but as was her nature, she was guided by her unconditional love for me and her morality to do the right. We contacted the worker the next day to arrange a time to visit her. To say I was nervous would be a gross understatement. I had no idea of what she looked like and or of what she knew about me. *I was just hoping it wouldn't be a disaster.*

It was a Wednesday morning, and unfortunately, we had to borrow my mom's car to make the trip, so it also meant she would be travelling with us. Four and a half hours later, we arrived at the address given to us. I had only taken a few pills that morning as Kim insisted I had to have a clear head, but I still felt like I was going to throw up. Pulling into the driveway, we saw five kids playing in the yard – four girls and one boy. Could one of these possibly be my little girl? They all stopped playing and faced the car to see who had pulled up. Kim then said, "Oh my God... Do you see her?" How could I see her? I had no idea what she looked like. It was soon obvious how Kim had picked her out from the crowd. It was freaky. It was like looking at myself in a mirror. Kim grabbed my hand knowing meeting her was already emotional for me, but to see the resemblance just added to it. Before we had a chance to exit the car, the foster mom and social worker were heading towards us. The kids resumed playing, but my daughter not so much. I couldn't imagine how she felt knowing she was about to meet her father for the first time. Her attention was now directed more our way than towards her playmates, as she waited to be introduced.

So many things rushed through my head. What would I say to her? Would she like me? My heart was beating out of my chest. We exited the car and introductions were made between the grown ups, but all the while, I was keeping my one good eye on my rambunctious little girl. All of a sudden, she ran up to me. I guess she decided she wanted to break the ice first – but not with an introduction, but rather a joke. "Knock, knock."

"Who's there?"

"Ketchup."

"Ketchup who?"

"Ketchup up to me, and I'll tell you."

Oh my God, she shared my same lame sense of humour. She then ran to sit on some outside steps, waiting for me to "ketchup to her". I sat beside her, and I couldn't get a word in edgewise. She told me more jokes, sang, and danced for me. She did anything she could think of to get my approval and attention. Not only did we look alike and share the same humour, but I knew she was also hurt like me. It brought me back to when I was her age. *I could tell she was damaged to her core. Just as I was and just as her mother was. Fucking cycle.* We hadn't been fully informed yet of the circumstances that led her to her placement in foster care, so I needed to talk to the social worker. I called Kim over who was already talking to one. The look she gave me with her eyes as she passed me told me a million things.

From this point on, I will not divulge anything my daughter had to endure. That is her story, and only she can tell it. There will be only a few things I will relate to put things in context. I want to make it perfectly clear that my daughter's mother loved each of her children the only way she knew how. Her efforts were made with the best of intentions. However, she was fighting her own demons. She was always in search of someone to show her love as I had been. Unfortunately, sometimes she was preyed on by the wrong type of man. I will not make excuses for her just as I will not for my future transgressions, but she just had no hope in hell. The only difference between the two of us was that by the grace of God I had Kim. She had nobody!

I was briefly filled in about her circumstances. She didn't go into much detail, as our time was short. However, she told me there were things needing to be discussed and asked if I would call her the next day. Over the next hour or so Kim and I were thoroughly entertained by C. (I will use C to respect my daughter's privacy.) She has read everything I've written and agrees it's a story that must be told.

The only time we were interrupted was by C's concern for the other kids. No matter what, she made sure they didn't get too close to the road or play too rough. She developed a strong commitment to looking after other children and assuming the responsibility of a mother figure to her younger siblings. This was the first time she had been separated from them that we knew of, with all of them in different foster homes, so that only added to any other sadness she already felt.

It was hard to say goodbye to her. She made us promise with a pinky swear we would come back. We both gave her the biggest hug we could, holding back our tears. As we were about to leave the driveway, she ran up to the car and knocked on the window. As I was rolling it down, she smiled and said, "Knock, knock."

"Who's there?"

"Orange."

"Orange who?"

"Orange you glad you met me." Then she ran back to play with the other kids.

Well that did it. I couldn't hold back my tears any longer. We had no idea what she was going through yet, but she was an absolute delight – on the outside, anyway. Over the course of the next week, we were given a few more details of her home situation. Some of which triggered my own distress about what I'd held secret all these years.

Children Services wanted to meet with us the next time we came up. C had been returned home briefly, so our next visit would be held at home with her mother present. We arrived early afternoon to a greeting of goats and chickens in the driveway. My ex was trying the best she could and was getting eggs from the chickens and milk from the goats. I was concerned about how my ex would view our intrusion and especially with having to meet my wife for the first time. Kim, however, held no pre-conceived judgements towards her. No matter what we'd been told, she would have to come to her own conclusion based on fact and not hearsay. As soon as we reached the top of the driveway, C was there to greet us. She was so excited we had come back and wanted to introduce us to her brothers, sister, and then the goats and the chickens. After a brief time outside, she took us both by the hand to bring us inside where her mother was.

My ex hadn't changed a bit except for looking a little haggard and worn out from the stress of her daily life. She knew we were informed of her situation, but she wanted to tell us her side of things. We were surprised to learn that one of her boys was not actually hers. He had been signed over to her by a friend who was dealing with a serious drug addiction. It was obvious how overwhelmed she felt. Her desperation even led her to ask us if we wanted to move into the household with them. *Can you imagine that?* Well, for a brief moment we did. It would mean we could be in my daughter's life full time. However, we realized it wouldn't be one of the best of solutions.

With regards to our personal interactions between us, the visit couldn't have gone any better. The only concern we had were the living conditions. The house was very unkempt and dirty. It looked like the laundry hadn't been done in months, and there was very little food in the house. Just before we left, Kim pulled me aside so we could see how much cash we had between the two of us. She wanted to give it all to C's mother to help her out a little. It was our weekly grocery money, but she knew she could hit up Mom for more. We said our good-byes and then it was off to see the social worker. I had mixed feelings about our meeting. For the entire two hours, it was as if they were trying to recruit us, with their intent being to facilitate our relocation, play on our emotions, and then basically bribe us. They didn't hide their desperation to make it happen. They offered to cover the cost for our move and to pay for our living accommodations. They had also been in touch with a family lawyer to represent us concerning getting proper access to my daughter.

They really had no idea of who we were. Never once did they ask about our background. Would they have felt the same way if they knew I had a criminal record? It didn't appear so. You would think at the very least, they would want some type of testing done to see if we were emotionally stable enough to be put into my daughter's life. *Don't you think? This would be their first fail, not only for my daughter, but for me as well.* It might have shown I was in need of help myself and by no means had the emotional capacity required to raise a child. They didn't want us to make the decision that day and gave us until the end of the week to make up our minds. *Really? Did they just actually give a time limit on their offer?* The point was moot anyways. I already knew what Kim's decision would be. Just as so many times in the past, she would put aside any self-interest as her only concern now was for that of my daughter.

They found us a self-contained motel suite about three miles from where my daughter was. It wasn't the best of living conditions with the constant parties going on, but we stayed to ourselves, so it served its purpose until our lawyer could get proper court-ordered access. In the meantime, I would steal thirty minutes a day to visit her at school. It meant a three-mile walk both ways, but I promised her I would. Each time she went out of her way to introduce me to someone new – teachers, classmates, it didn't matter. I think she was proud to let everyone know she had her real dad now. It made me feel pretty damn good too.

Now with having proper access over the next few months, we enjoyed each of our visits. Not once did C express any clue that things were getting worse at home, but you couldn't blame her for her silence. I know she was worried if she said anything it might separate her siblings from her again. They were all she had. The whirlwind of events to come would blindside us. Our best intentions would lead to things causing more damage to C and causing Kim great pain as well. Unfortunately, it would take both their pains as a sacrifice to redeem my spirit and soul. But I get a little ahead of myself again.

We were called into my lawyer's office. He had been contacted by Child Services and filled in on how grievous my daughter's home life had become. They were preparing a case to permanently remove all the kids from the home. They told him they wanted us to initiate a full custody hearing not only for my daughter, but for her siblings as well. *What the fuck?* We could barely manage daily living ourselves, never mind adding four to our family. Why were they even suggesting such a thing? My lawyer surmised that it was a ploy to make us more concerned about my daughter's situation. Surely if we couldn't take them all, we would at least apply for custody of her. It was their intention all along. *How dare they play with children's lives?*

The pressure we felt to comply was overwhelming. Of course, we wanted to be there for my daughter, but was it really the best option for her? I couldn't give her the love she needed. They would have known I was damaged if they did their due diligence. I was between a rock and a hard place. Once more, the only saving grace about the predicament was Kim. I knew it would be easy for her to cultivate a love for C, so I convinced myself that she could fill the void for both of us. Again, how fucking selfish of me.

From this point on, things would move rapidly, beginning with Social Services informing us we were moving within the week. They had acquired a two-bedroom townhouse for us as we couldn't gain custody if we were living in a motel, now could we?

Please understand that our lawyer had no collusion in what Child Services was doing. He only pursued matters by what was told to him. He was truly concerned about my daughter and even did something amazing that wouldn't come to light until she was an adult and had kids of her own.

So now we had a nice place. The cupboards were still bare, but on outward appearances, we had a suitable home for a child now. They even fudged the books to get us an old beater car to get around in. We rarely had enough money for gas, but it would serve the purpose of picking up my daughter for her scheduled visits and would look better to the court. Proceedings began and continued week after week. My ex wasn't going down without a fight. Our impression was that it was going to be a very long process, but one day my ex didn't show for court so the hearing was adjourned to later that day. We had no idea why and neither did our lawyer. It only became evident when court was back in session. Her lawyer stood up and informed the judge that my ex was now, without prejudice, conceding full custody to us. *What the hell? We couldn't believe it. Kim and I never really thought we would be victorious. We shouldn't have been.*

One stipulation of the court was that Child Services had to conduct an in-depth home visit first just to make sure our living conditions were suitable. Kim had always kept a clean house no matter where we lived, so that wouldn't be a problem. Even if we had feces spread throughout, it wouldn't have mattered. The in-depth visit consisted of two workers pulling into our driveway and having a conversation with us without ever leaving the confines of their vehicle. We even invited them to come inside, but they told us it wouldn't be necessary. I guess they had a long day as fifteen minutes later they said they would initiate moving arrangements for C. *And that's all, folks.* Kim and I were now the proud parents of a sixty-five-pound little girl, with no parenting classes or previous experience. But that's okay. Surely they would at least mandate counselling for my daughter with all she went through. Nope... not a word about it. Despite all this, things would turn out just fine. *What could go wrong? What couldn't go wrong was more like it.*

The honeymoon phase of our new family had begun. The first couple of months were about getting accustomed to each other. Kim taught C the proper hygiene that had never been taught to her – just all the little things that most would take for granted. Making sure C had proper nutrition was more difficult towards the end of the month when Social Services money ran out, but my mother always sent us a little to tie us over. We hated relying on that. Kim thought about getting work, but having C was a full-time job for her. I couldn't possibly look after her while still being addicted to codeine, not to mention I was still a child myself. Their relationship began to grow, and they developed more of a bond everyday. I had no idea what type of bond I was developing. It saddens me to say, but I don't think there was one. Not on my end anyway. It just wasn't there.

There were times I even felt jealous of their interaction. Kim and I used to spend all of our time together, but now most of it was being taken away from me. I should have been overjoyed they were getting close, but in a strange way, I thought I was losing Kim. It didn't make sense, but nothing ever really did for me when it came to love. All I knew was Kim loved me for some reason and I was a glutton for it. I was not capable of understanding there were many types of love – like romantic, parental, friendship. All these should have been cultivated in me as a child. Now the same thing that I desperately needed back then from my mother was what my daughter desperately needed from me. It was some-thing I could never give her. Now I was feeling depressed but also angry that I couldn't give her the emotional support she needed. I was letting everybody down again. My fucking past was robbing me of the most important things in life and robbing those around me of the love they deserved. I tried to do the right thing by burying my jealousy. She needed Kim as much as I did, if not more. All

I could do was to try and convince myself that all I needed was more time to feel the things I should be feeling. I thought, *Just give me more time.* However, time can do a lot of things – some good, some bad. The latter would take precedence through a series of events, beginning with Social Services deciding their generous support would become a thing of the past.

They told us our financial aid would be cut in half. Now we couldn't even afford to pay the rent, leaving us only one option. It was not a very good one, but one we were forced to take. We were moving back home to reside with all my past demons. It would also cause a great deal of distress for my daughter to be moving her away from her siblings. It is something I still regret to this day, but it would turn out to be a small issue in the grand scheme of things. The sins of a mother passed down to a son would rise from the hidden depths in a generational cycle.

As stated earlier, I will make no excuses for my actions. The pen that I write my life story with is held in my own hand. I take full ownership. Judge me as you will. My disclosure, I pray, will serve as awareness for others to reach out for help and end the cycle of abuse. I wish to give hope that there is light at the end of the tunnel, no matter how dark your path has been.

CHAPTER 15:

# The Point of No Return

Now back home, we were forced to live with demon Ma until we applied for Social Services. We thought it would be a week or two at the most before we got funds, but the Ministry would bite us in the ass again. Leaving our previous location, we were unable to give a month's notice. Usually when this happens, it would be settled in small claims court if the landlord wanted to collect the missing rent. Our landlord, however, worked at the same Social Services office that had issued our checks in Kelowna. I still don't know if it was legal or not, but they confiscated the first check back home to pay her off. This meant two weeks would turn into six weeks of living at mother's. *God help us all.*

Her two-bedroom apartment was quite small. Kim and C were in one bedroom, my mother in the other, while I slept on the couch. They adapted well as I was trying to hold back my disdain each day as I watched my mother being a doting grandma. Her phoniness sickened me. A lot of time had passed since I was a kid, but it felt like yesterday as I watched their interactions. It would have helped if she had made any attempt to make things right with me, but there was not even a small acknowledgement of the past or of the transgressions that left me without the capacity to develop a bond with my own child. I felt so lost inside myself and confused how Kim, or anyone, could possibly love me. The overwhelming stress of this, plus having to see Ma on a daily basis, made me retreat further into my adolescence. Now I couldn't even look at her without visualizing our forever secret in all its explicit detail. It was consuming me so much that even the slightest intimate contact with Kim became completely non-existent now. Any attempt would result in a quick dismissal on my part.

For the first time, Kim voiced her concerns, repeatedly asking me what was wrong. *I knew she wouldn't understand. No one could. Fuck...I didn't even understand what I did.* It was beyond comprehension that Mother and I gave continuous happy massages to each other and that I had "boy-friended" her two or three times daily over a period of two months, plus once when she was almost dead. After all this time, I still believed I had asked for it, and it was all my fault. I was so confused as to why I had enjoyed it so much at the time. That's what was fucking me up the most. I couldn't risk losing Kim by revealing how sick I was. I just couldn't, so I told her things were fine, but it was just so stressful living at Mother's. Needing to numb the torturous pain inside, I discovered where my mother stashed her pills. She had so many that I could be numbed for the rest of my life. She had no idea any were missing. *I was my mother's son in every sense of the word. All I detested in her I had become. I was void of any feeling whatsoever. The cycle she had created was now evolving.*

By the time we found a place, C was about to be enrolled in school, bringing on a whole new level of stress. Social Services gave us a little to pay for her supplies, but her clothing and lunches were on us to provide. We were barely able to afford two meals a day, never mind any added expense, however, Kim had a solution for her apparel. Now her time would be filled visiting any one of the three thrift stores we had in town. She began to realize finding adult clothing was much easier than children's, and we were becoming a little desperate about putting together a suitable wardrobe for school. We told ourselves there would be other kids that didn't have much so she wouldn't stand out that badly. School began and by all appearances, C was fitting in, so I assumed the clothes were okay.

It was a relief for me when she was at school. I just didn't want to deal with her. I knew the lack of any emotional attachment I felt towards C was wrong and that getting custody was the worst possible thing ever. Kim could handle it, but I definitely had no business in rearing a child. Now there were days I was so stoned I couldn't remember anything about them. However, this was just a precursor of a bigger storm to come. The clouds started rolling in with the realization that C was not actually doing well at school after all. Her grades were outstanding, but she was keeping a secret to herself. The other kids made fun of her every day for what she was wearing. Not because it looked bad, but they knew it came from a thrift store. In fact, she was wearing some of their old clothes that were donated by their mothers. Compounding matters, some of the parents knew of my past history in town and didn't want their kids to associate with C because of it. Many mothers were even recipients of my happy massages, but I bet they didn't tell them that. It left C isolated with no friends just as I was as a kid. Not thinking straight would lead to a decision that would rapidly give way to the point of no return. We decided to pull her out of the public system and home school her.

Looking back, the decision was made out of spite and hurt feelings on my part. It was essential for her to learn socialization skills with kids her own age, but how would I know that? As I said, it was the worst possible decision and one that would change all of our lives forever in so many different ways. All the pain inflicted upon me as a child would be returned in kind. The burden of its weight, I will carry with me forever. It would be my eventual salvation, but at what cost?!

We arranged to have C's lessons mailed to us every week. She would spend hours in her room completing the necessary assignments given to her. Kim and I were busy just trying to survive. Well, Kim was doing everything she could do to help. However, my day consisted of inactivity due to all the pills I was digesting. It was beginning to take a toll on her. My lack of help would now be the topic of many heated discussions, which made me retreat even further. We had never fought before, but I knew it was my fault for the situation we were in. We never had enough food, and the power was shut off frequently for delinquent bill payments. She would often hand wash C's clothing and hang them out to dry even in the middle of winter. I started resenting ever meeting my daughter. I know things weren't all rainbows and roses before then, but things had been a lot better between Kim and I. My daily interaction with C now consisted of one of two things at a time – anger or indifference. I only felt sorry for myself.

*Self-pity is the most destructive of non-pharmaceuticals narcotics. It is addictive and separates its victim from reality.*

—John Gardner

As they had done for my mother, the pills were used to escape reality and keep me emotionally comatose. Most days I didn't even get dressed with my robe becoming my daily apparel. Kim was so busy keeping things afloat the best she could, I didn't even see her very much throughout the day. I think it might have been more of her choosing and rightly so. I can only imagine how much stress she was under. So much so, she began lashing out at C. I was putting the world on her shoulders, and its weight was crushing her and making her do things she would never normally do in a million years. At times, she even got physical with C. Kim was never angry and now she was. She was thirty-seven and had a damaged teenager dropped on her lap. She didn't know how to be a mother, but her commitment to me forced her to be one, not only in regards to my daughter but to me as well. *C deserved so much more from both of us. Kim deserved so much more from me.*

Even though circumstances were as bad as I thought they could be, they weren't even close. Its progression initiated when Kim was out of the house one day. C knocked on the bedroom door, holding a stack of homework that needed to be checked over before they were sent off that day to be graded. Kim was in charge of that, but she was out, so I grudgingly told her I would look them over. Handing them to me, she took a seat at the end of the bed. As I was trying to see straight, she kindly began to rub my feet. As I read, we began to talk. Not about anything special, just a pleasant conversation. It was the first one we'd had in ages. It made me feel a connection with her – one that was very familiar to me. It was the one I had with my mother as a child concerning parental love. Just as Mother, I was drugged up and only wearing a robe, not caring if my daughter saw me naked as she massaged me. Thanks, Mom.

Of course, there were sexual overtones, but I associated it as a sign of affection. I knew it was wrong, but in my mind, it was the only way to express it. I was dealing the same drug I had been dealt so many years ago. Now I was teaching C that it was the only way to receive any attention from me. *I had become the perpetrator of a new cycle.*

As time went on, what began as innocent foot rubs would turn into rubbing my legs front and back, with me returning the favour. I learned through therapy, that unlike my mother, it wasn't about getting off sexually but emotionally. Not once did I think about happy endings, but it was just as damaging to her. It was an evil violation of the covenant between a parent and their child. *Evil is and will always be evil.*

It went on for quite some time. She even told me she wanted the massages to stop. They would for a while and then needing the affection, they would begin again. I couldn't use the excuse that I didn't know it was wrong because they always happened while Kim was out. She never touched my happy, but close enough at times. She couldn't say the same about the things I touched. I even introduced some picture books into the situation like Mom did, thinking maybe looking at other vaginas and breasts would make her happy as it did me as a 13-year-old. FUCKING DESPICABLE. THIS HAS TO STOP!

*By the grace of God and the inner strength of a little girl, it would all soon come to a crashing end.*

Periodically my daughter would have overnight visits at my mother's. I was not something I would have allowed if I wasn't so fucked up myself, but I knew at least she was getting fed. We didn't have a phone, so the only way we could get in touch was by a pay phone downtown. The initial plan was for her to stay Friday and Saturday night and return Sunday morning. Sunday morning came and went, and there was still no sign of them. We didn't think much of it as we thought she might have wanted to stay a few more hours. Kim suggested I go down and give them a call to see what the delay was. There was no answer. Maybe they were on their way, so up the hill back home I went. But there was still no sign of them. Hours passed with more calls made but nothing. Then bright and early Monday morning, we heard a knock on the door. *Okay, there they are.*

Upon opening the door, instead of seeing an old woman and child, stood two female police officers. Before they could speak, Kim questioned them whether C was okay, concerned that they might have been in a car accident. They assured her she was safe, but they needed me to come down to the station with them. Deep down, I knew what was happening. Kim had no idea. I kissed her goodbye and left. Once in the back of the police cruiser, the officer verified my suspicion. I was going to be questioned about **inappropriate touching with my daughter.** Their tone was very curt, as if they were interrogating me, expecting me to deny everything of which I was accused. Their demeanour quickly changed when I told them I would not deny anything. All of a sudden, I felt a wave of relief overcome me. I couldn't say whether it was because I knew my daughter had the courage to say something or because now I couldn't inflict any more damage than I already had – not just through the massages but also by not giving her everything I was supposed to give her as a father. *I had failed to give her the things that every child deserves: peace, knowledge, stability, and most of all, unconditional love.*

We spent the next hour going over everything my daughter had told them, and for the most part, there wasn't any dispute over the things that had transpired. I signed a statement acknowledging total and complete responsibility. All I asked in return was a simple request to relay two things to my daughter. First and foremost, how sorry I was that I failed her as a father. Secondly, how very proud I was that she had the courage to speak up and to never feel guilty for doing so. *I sure wish I had her strength as a kid. If I did, we wouldn't be here now.*

They told me they would let her know and then issued me a promise to appear in court a few weeks later. I left the station feeling completely drained, and my walk home was filled with many thoughts. First, I thought how ironic it was that my mother was a part of this. I wondered if she felt any remorse herself for creating who I was. Then I realized something I hadn't even thought of yet. I sat on some steps and began sobbing. Now I was facing losing everything that was good in my life. It wasn't hard to convince myself that just like my daughter, Kim would be better off without me. There was no chance in hell that she could possibly go on loving me after everything I put her through and now this. I truly believed my life was over, but I owed it to her to tell her everything so she wouldn't have any remorse about finally being rid of me. She was still young and beautiful and had plenty of time to find the happiness she deserved. So, I wiped away the tears and proceeded home.

I was visibly shaking when I entered the house. Kim was sitting with a cup of tea. She got up and went to the kitchen and poured me one as well. When she sat down, I looked into her eyes, which brought tears to mine. She reached over to comfort me, but I pulled away and told her I didn't deserve her comfort. I needed to tell her something, and she would hate me for it. She said, "I'm listening." I talked for almost an hour, revealing everything. She listened intently, showing no emotion. At the end, I briefly touched on my mother's abuse and surprisingly this was the only time she would say something. "I knew long ago she had hurt you badly." She got up, went into the spare bedroom and retrieved some empty boxes.

*Yep, just as I thought, she was getting ready to pack her things up to get as far away from me as possible.* Not able to watch, I retreated outside knowing I deserved everything that was happening and feeling no self-pity. She had given me chance after chance, and I always failed her. The only thing I could think of now was ways for me to end my life to stop the pain I was putting everyone through. *This season of darkness would be my last.* Sitting there, I decided I would delay my demise until I knew she was moving on with her life and that she was finally happy. No matter what, I truly always wanted that. I had so foolishly believed I could be the one to give it to her. I gathered myself up and went back inside to face the inevitable. I had to at least let her know how sorry I was that she had wasted a majority of her life with a wretch like me.

I opened the door to see her neatly folding clothes and gently laying them into the boxes. After watching her for a minute, I realized the belongings were not hers but that of my daughter. I walked to our bedroom only to see all of her clothes were still hanging in the closet. The confused look on my face when I returned must have told her what I had initially thought. She stopped what she was doing and told me to sit down. She gathered our cups and refreshed them. She placed them on the table and then asked me to stand up. She took both my hands in hers and raised her eyes to stare deep into mine. I saw something I only had seen a few times before: a single tear falling off her cheek. She leaned forward and kissed my lips, uttering words I thought I would never hear from her again: **"I WILL NEVER STOP LOVING YOU!"**

I fell to my knees and wrapped my arms around her as a cascade of my tears fell against her legs. After a moment, she helped me up so we could sit together. She told me she wasn't going anywhere. She didn't mince her words about how the consequences of my actions didn't only affect C, but her as well. I took away someone she loved and that alone would take a long time to forgive. She told me there were no more excuses. It was all up to me now to make things right. No matter how hard it is, no matter how long it takes, **I couldn't hide from the past anymore.** She said she knew all along I was carrying a hurt like no other. She only wished I could have shared it with her and regretted not forcing me to tell her of my pain. Maybe if she had, I could have gotten the help I needed. She felt she had let both of us down and asked my forgiveness.

"How dare you blame yourself!" I told her if it wasn't for her and all she did for me, I would have been dead long ago. The reason I couldn't tell her was because I felt so ashamed, believing it was my fault that I let it happen, and I didn't want her to be disgusted with me. We talked into the night, having no idea of what the future would bring. But she promised me that whatever happened, we would face it head on together. It would be a new beginning as long as I dealt with the demons that haunted me. Now I didn't have to face them alone anymore. She's pretty fucking incredible, isn't she?

The uncertainty of the upcoming court proceedings cast a dark shadow above us, but she assured me no matter the outcome, she would always be at my side.

As much as I hated myself, it was the first time in my life I finally felt any true hope towards the future. Kim's unconditional love was a beacon of light that would shine on the path to my redemption. I knew it was up to me to follow it and to cast away my demons and to be born again in her love. There was always something so special about her: the way her kindness was never forced, the empathy towards others she had displayed her whole life, and the strength she carried inside her soul. Until that day, I couldn't put my finger on what made her so different than most. Now I realized the one quality she had that guided all the rest: She walked in God's grace. She was filled with patience, kindness, goodness, joy, forgiveness, but most of all, love. Yes, she was blessed with physical beauty, but even that radiated from what was within. I think that was the spirit that I had felt so strongly from her when we first met. By the Almighty's grace, I could feel his through her.

*Grace is the love that gives, that loves the unlovely and the unlovable.*

She had always been my grace. I was blind, but now I could see. I just prayed I had enough time to redeem everything she had given me and what God had graced me with. Never before had I felt a sense of peace inside my soul. Now I knew my journey in life was meant for something. It had to be. I must do everything in my power to make things right, no matter the hardships of the unknown to come. We both knew it wasn't going to be easy, but it would all start with me taking full responsibility for my actions. It would all begin with my day in court.

# CHAPTER 16:

# Finding My Voice

The morning of my hearing, I hiked up the hill six miles to court. I thought it would be pretty cut and dried, as I was pleading "guilty". At least this would spare my daughter any more damage from having to testify against me. I entered the court when my name was called. The judge went over the charges and asked for my plea. In a firm voice I said, "Guilty Your Honour!" It took him aback for a moment, then he stated that this was a very serious charge and wouldn't accept my plea until I arranged representation through Legal Aid. He looked down at his calendar and said that we would adjourn this for forty-five days to allow me ample time to discuss my plea with my court-appointed lawyer.

I received a letter from the lawyer with the date and time of my appointment. As I was getting ready to leave for it, Kim started getting ready as well. It surprised me a little that she wanted to come, but as she said, we were facing this together. No more secrets. I guess the lawyer wasn't accustomed to having the spouse present because he said it was an unusual occurrence. With that Kim looked at him and returned, "I am here to do whatever I can to support my husband. I love him and he needs help." He smiled back and told her he was here to help me too.

For the next two hours, we went over all the statements made and a brief history of my childhood and everything leading up to this point. We told him we didn't want any more hardship on my daughter, and I was guilty as charged. He discussed what he thought would be the best course of action. Because of my past, there were mitigating circumstances, so he would ask the court to provide a thorough psychological evaluation before sentencing. This would not only help in reducing my sentence, but also might get me the help I needed. He couldn't promise anything, but he would do everything he could to spare me any jail time. It depended on a couple of factors: the outcome of my evaluations and which judge would be adjudicating the case. It would also mean Kim would be interviewed and evaluated as well. Before my next court date, he put forward a motion of a guilty plea, with the stipulation there would be a complete pre-sentencing report. There were no objections from the prosecutor, so the motion was granted.

We had no idea of what to expect. We not only had to comply with all the court-ordered evaluations, but just day-to-day living became harder now. We could deal with not having our daily necessities met, but now rumours began to fly. It came to a point where we wouldn't even leave the house. I think a lot of it was my own paranoia through the guilt I felt, but it was as if the whole world was judging me. We became even more isolated than we already had been. I felt so bad Kim had to be a part of this. She was innocent of any wrongdoing, but people can be cruel just to be cruel. It is the nature of the beast in a small town. Kim took it in stride, as she never gave a rat's ass what others thought. If she did, she would have been rid of me long ago. She continuously encouraged me to focus on the tasks at hand and reminded me we knew it was going to be hard, but we would get through it together. Then she realized something that encouraged us. I had stopped medicating myself. It wasn't consciously trying to quit, but there were so many distractions, I just forgot to take any pills. Wow! It made me feel a little better about myself, especially with all the appointments ahead of me. I knew I would need a clear head dealing with it all. It was a small step, but one necessary to be void of any excuse to face things head on: the good, the bad, and the really ugly.

My first appointment was with a psychologist. His purpose was to evaluate my emotional state, regarding things in my past that cultivated who I was now. Of course, it all began with my childhood and the relationships I had with my parents and siblings. So here we go. The things hidden deep inside of me, I now had to reveal to a complete stranger. He felt my apprehension when the subject of my mother was broached. He calmed me by saying he didn't want every detail of what had transpired between us, only a basic knowledge of our relationship. He told me this wasn't a therapy session, but just a small synopsis of the overall events of my upbringing. I felt relieved I didn't have to go into great detail. For the first time in my life, besides Kim, I revealed I had been sexually abused by my mother. Once that was out of the way, it was easier to open up about everything else. By the end of the appointment, I felt emotionally drained and he hadn't even gotten to my teenage years yet. There would be three more sessions with him and then on to my next evaluator – a psychiatrist. Her job was to discover if I had any redeeming qualities. *At that point, I couldn't think of any.*

The meetings between the two head doctors were similar, repeating things over and over in different ways. The only change was how they differed in the follow-up questions. The psychologist was more clinical with what I revealed. The psychiatrist was more about wanting to know how it made me feel. For me, the sessions were giving me a little more insight into my true feelings that I had buried long ago. I knew it wasn't the purpose of the appointments, but it was helping me just the same. *I was slowly starting to uncover the demons in my past, and more importantly, it was allowing me to find my voice.* As my sessions continued, Kim also had a few of her own. A totally different psychologist travelled to our home to meet with her. I had to leave the house when they met. I don't know why, but Kim and I seldom discussed our various meetings with any of the shrinks. I think we were just too emotionally drained to go over everything again. I never felt uneasy about what she might have said. I knew it would be the truth, and that's all that mattered to both of us now. *The truth shall set you free!*

Only three requirements were left to finish my evaluation. Two were in the form of psychological written tests. Each was designed to affirm or refute the one-on-one meetings that had already taken place. The third was a meeting with a probation officer so he could offer his opinion to the court. What an angry man he was. He might have been having a bad day, but I was unable finish any of the questions he was asking me. His abrasiveness frightened me into keeping silent for the most part. It was apparent he had already made up his mind about what he was going to recommend to the court. Within thirty minutes, I was out the door, and that was that. Now it was a waiting game. Everything had to be compiled and sent to the court, the prosecutor, and my representation.

I received a letter about two weeks later from my lawyer confirming the evaluations were done. Kim and I were greeted by my lawyer. I desperately tried to assess his demeanour and was comforted by his genuine smile as he led us to his office. He said he had an adjacent office for us to read the evaluations in private, but beforehand, he wanted to give us an overview of the doctor's findings. The nitty gritty of it all was that the three most important evaluations were all in agreement. They concluded serving any time in jail would only cause more damage to the fragile state I was already in. It would also tear me apart from the only support system I had ever known, namely Kim. They were confident I was not a danger to society and at a very low risk to re-offend. However, I was in need of prolonged and intensive psychological counselling with the court's supervision. In other words, I would be able to finally receive the help I desperately needed. "That was the good news," he said. The probation officer had recommended jail time. That put a downer on things, but he told us not to concern ourselves too much about his report. The court relies more heavily on true professionals when considering such matters. He was confident the probation report wouldn't carry as much weight as the psychological evaluations. He then led us to a private office where we could read a copy of everything submitted to the court for ourselves. As Kim read, she reached for my hand. There were still things she was discovering about my past for the first time.

She wasn't outright crying, but pools of water covered her eyes. Continuing to read, she squeezed my hand even more tightly as she nodded her head occasionally, as if she was agreeing with the findings. I was more concerned watching her than reading it myself. I had wanted her to know everything for such a long time. Now she had a little understanding of the things below my surface. Things she previously had no idea about my life were now written down in front of us in a neat little package. It didn't go into much detail of the events, as that would come later through therapy, but there was no more hiding the truth. It would was the first step in my journey to self-awareness and to cast away my demons.

After Kim finished reading everything, she turned to me and said, "Thank you." *What the hell was she thanking me for?* Then in a quiet tone she said, "Thank you for finally revealing all of the stories I could see in your eyes when we first met." All I could do was grab her and bawl my eyes out. She did see it all those years ago. *From that day forward, I promised myself I would never let her down again. No matter what it took, one day she would see something else in my eyes: unconditional love for her.* Now we waited for the final judgement. No matter what the lawyer said, we were still nervous about how the judge would see things. Maybe he would lean more towards the probation report. Two days before sentencing, my lawyer made us aware that the prosecutor would be leaning that way.

My fate would be known today. The court was located forty miles away, and we didn't have a vehicle, so my lawyer offered us a ride with him. He knew we were on pins and needles and offered us some comfort in the knowledge that the judge who was presiding over the case usually relied on the advice of the doctors. When he mentioned the judge's name, I looked at Kim and whispered that I knew it from somewhere, but I couldn't remember how. When my case was called, we walked into the courtroom. I took a seat beside my lawyer, and Kim sat directly behind the rail where the spectators were located. For the first ten minutes or so, the judge went over the charges and acknowledged I was pleading guilty. He informed the court he had gone over all the reports extensively and asked the prosecution to make its case for jail time. He basically reiterated the probation report, suggesting two years and also implying the psychological evaluations couldn't be believed. Then it happened. The Judge looked at the prosecutor and told him he had heard enough, as if he were scolding him. He then looked at my lawyer saying, he didn't have to rebut the prosecution as his decision was already made. He paused for a minute, looked at me and then Kim, and this is what he said.

(From Court Transcripts)
"In full disclosure, I have known this defendant and his family for many years, including when the defendant was a child." (That's how I knew his name. He used to be a lawyer in my hometown, and I went to school with his kids. He then went on to explain why he basically shut the prosecutor down.) "Everything I read that the defendant revealed about his past, except the revelation of him being a victim of sexual abuse rings true to what I knew about his family. I also witnessed firsthand some of the bullying he endured as a child. As I know that to be true, then I would have to surmise that his account of abuse is also true. The defendant does have a chequered past, including a criminal record. However, as I read the psychological reports and the progression of this young man's life, I can only feel that society has let him down. Abuse was seldom reported back then and in turn never having the means to get the help he needed."

Then he paused, looked directly at Kim, and continued. "It is also apparent to the court, that there has been one saving grace in his life: a well-educated woman that has stood by him through thick and thin. I have read her evaluation as well. Who knows where this man would be without her by his side. I want to commend her for never giving up on him. Now it's society's and the judgement of this court to return the favour. It is my ruling that the defendant receives five years of probation, in which time he is ordered to undergo psychological therapy three times a week, for the full length of his sentence."

Then the gavel came down. My lawyer turned to shake my hand and said with a smile, "Now go hug your wife. *Already there my friend.*

What were the chances the judge knew my family? I wasn't going to question it any further. All I knew was once again, Kim had saved me. I was positive now there was a higher purpose for us being together. I just knew there had to be, just as Kim had always believed. Why else would she stand by me through all this? Why else would I be given another chance to make things right?

Now I would receive the help I needed to rebuild my soul and restore my innocence. We were just at the beginning of a long, hard journey, but the first step was taken. We knew it would be difficult to continue where we were living and always under the scrutiny of the local townsfolk, but also it would increase the chance that we would run into my daughter at some point and time, now living with my mother. Considering both factors, we decided to move. This way at least my daughter wouldn't be concerned about running into us. She had suffered enough, and we didn't want our presence to be a continuous reminder. Also, we were truly alone, and our journey was going to be hard enough without the local gossip.

We needed a fighting chance to start over. So my lawyer asked the court for permission for us to relocate to a different town. The court granted the motion and off we went. Nothing else changed about our finances, as we would still have to exist through Social Services. I wasn't really in any position to find work. Who would hire a sex offender? Our main goal was to survive and attend all of my counselling sessions. We did ask for one amendment in regards to my counselling. Kim and I both agreed she needed to be present at as many sessions as she was allowed. The judge that sentenced me approved it without hesitation. *Again, there would be no more secrets between us.*

We found a place located in a small town around seventy miles away. We moved into a mobile home situated on the property of an older couple that lived in a house at the lower end of it. Within a couple of days, I met with my probation officer as the court ordered, and he seemed like a very pleasant man. It turned out he lived just down the street from where we were living and had known our landlords for years. He then told us it was a requirement for us to inform them of my charges. Oh boy! I didn't know how the older couple would take finding out about my background. Maybe once again we would have to move. However, it turned out that the older gentleman seemed to take it with a grain of salt.

I began my counselling almost immediately, attending three appointments a week as was ordered. The doctor had to travel from his home base from a town forty miles further east. We lived in a rural area of town, so we had to hitchhike the two miles in to see him. The first couple of weeks comprised of us getting to know each other a little better and establishing some trust. We went over the basics of my history and what he had planned for me over the next year or so. Kim and I began to feel at ease with him, as he appeared to be one of those health professionals that took his responsibility seriously. He seemed non-judgemental and truly concerned about helping his patient. There were times that Kim wasn't able to attend, so we could just have a one-on-one discussion. Each time she was left alone back home. At the same time, our elderly landlord would always be outside our trailer digging something up or feeding the horses. Kim said he would even knock on the door to see how she was doing once in a while. *How caring of him.* On this day, however, his true motives would come to light.

I returned home and once again he was doing something outside our place. When I went inside, Kim quickly ushered me to the backroom worried our land-lord would overhear what she was going to tell me. She was shaking. She told me that when she was outside our landlord approached her and said that she had a beautiful naked body. *How the fuck would he know?* And that is exactly what Kim said to him. His response left Kim terrified. He openly told her he would peek in the windows to watch her and pleasure himself outside the trailer, and some-times he even watched us having sex. He told her he loved her. Kim didn't know what to do after that little revelation, so she just retreated inside. What could we do now? I had to confront him, but it was like talking to a brick wall when I did. He admitted everything in a casual manner and told me that Kim should experience a real man. I left dumbfounded. How could we stay there anymore? But our hands were tied. We had no other place to go.

We decided we needed help, so the next time I saw my probation officer I relayed what had happened. I could tell he didn't believe me, but said he would talk to him. For the next few days, Kim and I never left the trailer. Then there was a knock on the door. It was our landlord's daughter with an eviction notice in hand. We had to be out in two weeks. In a way, it was a relief, but we had no idea what we were going to do. Talking to my probation officer didn't help, as he basically took our landlord's side since they were friends. Thankfully, my therapist believed us. With his help, we found another place to rent that was located further down the road where his home base was. If he was trying to show us we could trust him, he succeeded. Again with a petition to the court to relocate, we packed up as much as we could and took the journey forty miles down the road. It was meant to be. From that day forward, we would never look back.

Day to day life was still a struggle, but we had overcome those hardships so many times in the past. With full trust in my doctor, I began opening up to him, detail by detail, and recounting my entire life from childhood. As I did, I was able to release all that was repressed and slowly rebuild my emotional and psychological wellbeing and recognize the triggers that would interfere with their development. Stress was one of my main triggers. When it came to fight or flight, I always ran. Just as I had in the schoolyard of my youth. *That's how long I had been running.* Another contributing factor came to light when I was diagnosed with manic depression. I was given the tools through therapy to recognize when I was falling into it. Kim also did her part, never allowing me to get too stressed out about things.

Now we could actually talk about everything. She knew it all now, including where and how active my happy had been. There was absolutely nothing we couldn't tell each other. She also answered a question about the past I had. Remember how I questioned if she knew about the massages I gave, and if she did, why it didn't make her jealous? Now I knew the answer to both of those questions. Of course she knew, and it did hurt her a little, however, she never based her love on something as superficial as sexual gratification. *How about that? That was the exact opposite of what I had been taught.* Once she knew I wasn't receiving anything in return, she put up with it, always trusting her heart that I was the only one for her. *How could I ever repay that kind of love?*

Therapy would be the start in rebuilding my emotional bank account by working through every emotion I had. I learned to take the ones having no worth and replace them with those that did and to build new emotions that were never taught: empathy, love, trust, self-awareness, and the most importantly, self-forgiveness. It was gradual, but I started to feel differently about who I was. Kim felt it too. I still relied on her encouragement and patience, but she was the mirror of who I was becoming. If she could see the change in me, then it was happening.

The love I could never feel was now beginning to take hold and every morsel of it was directed straight at Kim. She deserved it all, plus the twenty years when I couldn't give it to her. *I had a lot to make up for.*

CHAPTER 17:

# The Best of Times

It was in the fourth year that I truly broke through. All the hate I had towards myself and my mother dissipated. I finally started to like who I was becoming, mainly because of the love that I finally felt towards Kim. If I didn't know anything else, I knew that to be true now. As for my mother, I learned to be empathetic. I now realized she must have had her own demons that were never dealt with. As I mentioned earlier, it also strengthened the belief that I was indeed the product of a sexual assault perpetrated on her. I could understand now why she couldn't love me the way I needed her to. It was sad, but in her eyes, she detached herself from me as her son; I was only his. She probably hated and blamed herself for it, just as I had. So how could I possibly forgive myself without forgiving her? Everyone deserves a second, third, and fourth chance to be loved. I couldn't honestly say I loved her, but I knew I didn't hate her anymore. I empathized and felt sorry we didn't have a better relationship.

The bond between Kim and I grew stronger every day. The one she had always had with me was now being reciprocated. The stars in the heavens were starting to align in perfect order, and soon our financial situation would change as well. When I was almost at the end of my therapy and probation, two events occurred as if they were meant to be. It was preparation for things to come so I could re-enter the world brand new. We had always relied on the local food bank to fulfill our monthly needs, and Kim saw a notice that they were in need of volunteers. I have no idea why she signed us up, but it was one of the best things she could have done at the time. Three days a week, six hours a day, we would religiously be there to pack up hampers for the locals that were in need. Not only did it bring us out of our isolation, but it also gave me the confidence to face the world. Participating in an unselfish act made me feel good about myself. It was second nature for Kim, but we were doing it together and that meant more to her than anything. Then again, as if it were meant to be, Social Services mandated us to take a job skills course. Ironically it ended on the last day of my probation order. Throughout the course, we had befriended the coordinator, and she asked if we would stay to talk to her after the last session of the course ended. She informed us she had a job lead that would be perfect for one of us. The only kicker was that it was located sixty miles up the road at a popular hot spring. She said if we were interested, she would not only set up an interview, but would be willing to drive us up for it. How could we pass it up?

Our intention upon arriving was for me to apply. The employer was a husband/ wife team who owned a service station, mechanic shop, and Greyhound depot. *Hey, how about that? Kim and I met on a Greyhound.* They were pillars of the small community, having been there for thirty years. By the time the interview ended, we were both being asked for our shirt sizes. Yep, they hired us both with full-time positions. They also secured a place for us to live at a local motel that was self-contained. *If this wasn't a sign, then please tell me what is.* Not only would it take us off Social Services, we would be working together as team. This was something of which we could have only dreamed. Now we were a team in every sense of the word – not only in life, but in love as well.

We took our new jobs seriously. I still had bouts of depression and self-doubt, but now I had the tools to deal with it. Just Kim's pride in how I was doing was the very best medicine. The promise I made to myself about never letting her down again inspired me to do even better. Before long, we even acquired an old beater truck. It was as if we had a second chance to start our marriage over again, and what better place than in a beautiful paradise? It was as if we were on a never-ending honeymoon. Every day off we would walk up to the hot springs, and at night we would visit the only local tavern. Every time we entered, we were greeted by the locals as the "lovebirds". Damn right we were, and we wore it proudly. It was during this time, I wouldn't let a day pass without holding her in my arms and dancing every night, just like we did when we first married. But now we danced to a new song. It was called "Dance Me to the End of Love" by Leonard Cohen. Every word belonged to us now. We didn't want for anything.

We received so many blessings along the line – one of which was a casual meeting at work with a gentleman who was passing through. He told me that through his weekly commute, he always stopped at the station. I kind of remembered, but we had a lot of patrons coming and going. He then went on to say he always saw how friendly I was and how I kept busy cleaning and dealing with customers. He then mentioned there was another girl who was just as committed to her work. Go figure! By his description, I knew it was Kim. I told him she was my wife, and I would relay the compliment. He then asked if we would consider relocating forty miles up the road, as he also owned a service station and mechanic shop. I told him I was flattered, but we were happy where we were. He said, "Just think about it and talk to your wife and see what she says." A week or so passed and it was just about closing time at the station, so as always Kim was there to meet me. The gentleman showed up again. What he did next took us by surprise. He offered me almost double the salary I was making at the time. Plus, he had already talked to the owner of a major shopping chain to secure an interview for Kim if we decided to move. We thanked him, but we needed time to think about it. Exchanging numbers, we told him we would let him know the next time he came through.

Wow! Kim and I were truly flattered. Over the next few days we hummed and hawed over it, questioning if we really wanted to leave when things were so good where we were and risk any security we had at that point. The one mitigating factor that finally led to our decision was something I learned in therapy: "In all things in life, you can't progress by standing still. You always need to be moving forward." We knew our love was strong enough to take the chance, so we decided to take his offer. It was the right decision. Not only was I making a substantial amount of money, but also Kim was promoted to head cashier within weeks of starting her new job. Things couldn't have looked brighter. We worked and played hard, but loved each other even harder.

Kim even got into her first bar fight. Okay not a fight, but more of a quick reckoning. Our local had a lot of tourists coming and going. Kim and I were always playing pool and, on this occasion, we were challenged by two men from Germany. One stood about six-foot-eight and weighed about 390 pounds. He was the mouthy one, always making rude comments about how beautiful Kim's ass was. It was a little annoying, but we had heard it all before and just let it slide. Talk was one thing; however invading Kim's personal physical space was quite another. He was about to learn a painful lesson.

As Kim leaned over the table to take a shot, all I remember seeing was a gigantic hand grabbing in between the bottom of Kim's bum. Before I even had a chance to defend her honour, Kim had already taken it by the balls, so to speak. I watched her calmly look behind her and tell him "FICK DICH!!" ("Fuck you" in German). Then with one quick motion, she brought back the butt end of the pool cue and returned the touch forcefully between his legs. *Perfect shot baby. Right in the centre pocket. TIMBER!!* He fell to the floor on his knees, almost blacking out. The bouncers came and dragged his ass out of the building to a round of applause from the other patrons in the bar. If you decide to goose Kim, you better be wearing a cup. As I said, she was a strong girl in more ways than you can imagine. I was so fucking proud of her. We were so proud of each other.

Time passed and our finances allowed us to bank a tidy amount, growing more substantial every year. All the love that had been vacant from me for so long was coursing through my veins and filling my heart. I only had to think of Kim to feel it flow. There was so much I had to make up for, and I took every opportunity to repay her unconditionally, day in and day out. It felt so good to be able to give this much love, but it felt even better receiving it.

Then without warning, my manic depression started to creep back in. It was more on the depressive side than the manic side. It wasn't overwhelming, but it was there. Kim could feel it as well. We had to find out what was triggering it and nip it in the bud. Night after night, we would talk about my thoughts. Soon it became obvious there was still one crucial thing absent in my healing. Even though I had forgiven my mother, she was unaware that I had. I needed to re-establish contact with her in order to let her know. We both knew I was strong enough now, no matter how it would turn out. It had to be done to give myself true peace of mind, so I bit the bullet and tried to find her number. At that point, I didn't even have any idea if she was still alive. The only number I could find was for a relative, so I called and left my work number. If she wanted to get a hold of me, she could. *At least I had done my due diligence.*

The very first call I answered the next morning was from her. We exchanged pleasantries at the beginning, and then I let her know how well Kim and I were doing. She filled me in a little about things back home and then she told me that she talked to my daughter once a week. I was shocked to be informed she was married, had kids of her own, and was now living in the land down under. What really surprised me was she always inquired if my mother had heard from us. I didn't know what to say. Our conversation ended with the exchange of personal numbers and a promise to talk again. *Okay, the first step had been taken.* The next night, we received a call from a number we didn't recognize. I guess my mother had given our number to one of my brothers. He was the other black sheep of the family. Over the years, his "therapy" was the same as mine before I received help – drink, drugs, and womanizing. He told me he was married again and wanted us to come visit. We told him we would see what the future brought, but made no promises. Over the course of the next few months, we spoke regularly with them both. We knew eventually we would have to visit for the final step of my healing to be complete. Standing still wouldn't bring any true closure concerning my past. Go big and go home. We decided we would meet my past head on. We were moving back. *Now that's a leap forward if I do say so myself.*

We gave no clue to my brother about our true intentions. We just said that we would come and visit during our summer holidays. We asked him to keep it a secret so we could surprise my mother. We were confident about our decision. I would be lying if I said I didn't feel a little apprehensive, but it took a backseat to the progress I had made over the years. Just like Kim, now I couldn't give a shit about what others thought of me. I had paid my dues and knew myself inside out. We had worked too hard to let anything get in the way of that, so we packed up everything we had in our little Tercel and off we went. The plan was that once we reached town, we would meet up with my brother and his new wife at a local tavern. From there, we could go and stay at his place.

They must have been waiting for quite some time – at least that's how it seemed by how much alcohol they had already consumed. We sat and ordered a few ourselves with my brother and I catching up. His wife conversed with Kim about how much of an asshole my brother was. Things hadn't changed much over the last ten years concerning him. That night at their place we drank some more to pass the time and found out his health was failing. Years of drinking and drug use had taken a toll on his liver. He now had Hep C. Maybe that's why he was so persistent in seeing us again, knowing he was living on borrowed time. You would think he would at least watch his alcohol consumption, but it was of no concern to him or his wife. They drank from the time they woke up until the time they passed out. It made us feel sad that he had ended up like this, not to mention he was married to an enabler. All we could do was to be as kind as we possibly could. I probably would have followed the same path if it weren't for Kim and my daughter. It made us even more grateful for where I was in life, so Kim and I promised each other we wouldn't turn our back on him. *Maybe in some way we could help and repay kind with kind for the help I received.*

The next day, my mother was about to get a surprise. I don't think she could believe her eyes that we were standing there. The first thing she said was how beautiful Kim looked. They hugged and then she approached me. "You look so different" was all she said. I told her it's because I was so happy now. She looked a lot older and a little frail, but besides that she looked the same. We spent the next hour or so chatting and making arrangements for me to cook her dinner at her place the next night. Before she left to go back home, she turned and said how proud of us she was. It was a small thing that made us smile, but she had no idea of how far we had really come. It was nice we would have the opportunity to show her that despite the past we came through better than ever. *I was ready to heal wounds inflicted and let sleeping dogs lie. I wanted to show her she was forgiven no matter if she felt any remorse herself or not. That would be on her; it wasn't on me anymore.*

My only wish was to get to know her again without having any contempt in my heart, which would start with dinner the next night. Kim and her talked, while I played master chef. Kim had also let go of any animosity she had once held against her. If I could forgive, then so could she. It would turn out to be an evening we would never forget. Mom noticed Kim wasn't wearing any wedding bands and asked her why. She told her she didn't need them to remind her or anybody else she was married. With that, my mother retreated to her bedroom and returned with a closed fist. She took Kim's hand and said Dad would have wanted her to have the bands he had given her so long ago. It made us both well up with tears, but it had more meaning for Kim to have something of my dad's. She truly did love him and missed him. Kim placed them on her wedding finger, and wouldn't you know it, they fit perfectly as if to say they belonged with her. *Those bands would come to mean the world to us.* As for the reason my mother gave them to her, I could only guess it was her way of saying she was sorry. We were very happy to convince ourselves of that.

Then just like it was in the movies, the phone rang. Mom spoke briefly, almost in a whisper and then turned to hand the phone to me. She smiled and said, "Your daughter would like to speak to you." *Oh my God. My little girl actually wanted to talk to me after all this time.* I guess she wasn't so little anymore, but in my head she still was. After everything she suffered at my hands, she was reaching out to me just as we were reaching out to Mom. I was speechless. She must have known it was hard for me to gather my thoughts, so she took the lead. Then I heard her voice for the first time in over ten years. The tone was recognizable, however, the accent wasn't. I had to really listen closely to understand everything she was saying. One thing hadn't changed, she still liked to talk. I think she was nervous as well, but it didn't matter, I was just so happy she was talking to me. Questions were asked and answered and we caught up on things. I was getting very emotional throughout, but before I completely broke down, she asked to talk to Kim. They talked to each other for a lengthy amount of time. Before the call was about to end, we told her we would look after her nana and then we revealed our intentions of moving back.

*This was a day we would always hold dear in our hearts. It was the beginning of another healing that we had convinced ourselves would never take place.*

CHAPTER 18:

# Things Happen Quickly

My mother was happy to learn we were there to stay, however, she was concerned we were staying with my brother. We told her we knew he was out of control with his drinking, but we could handle it until we found a place of our own. At the time, we had no idea as to the extent of the turmoil in their household. Over the next week or so, we would witness it for ourselves. We had started circulating résumés and looking for a place to live, but the shenanigans in the co-dependant household were getting the best of us. Their drunken marital spats were more like down-and-dirty, physical, drag-out brawls. Cops were called and things were thrown at each other. We couldn't take it anymore. My mother was aware of what was going on, so she offered us the second bedroom in her place until we found one of our own. It didn't go over well with the rest of the family because of what they knew of our past. How could they know things were different now? We held no resentment towards their attitude. We knew it wasn't going to be easy to shed any previously held feelings about us. Only time and perseverance would turn the tide.

My mother couldn't care less about what they thought. She saw the change in me, so we accepted her offer with the condition we would pay her rent while we were there. Within a few days, Kim and I both found employment. She found work in the bakery department of a long-standing grocery store. She was up at 4:00 a.m. every morning to drive the six miles down the hill to start at 4:30 a.m. She fit right in with the other "Bakery Chicks" as they called themselves. I found employment at a local mechanic shop, keeping care of the front-end and ordering parts when needed. Each night I would do all the cooking for the three of us, and the rest of the evening we would sit and chat. There was nothing earth shattering discussed; we were just getting to know each other again. It was the beginning of a healthy bond, unlike in the past. I never broached the subject of who my real father was or about the abuse as I felt it was a subject better left in the past. *If you leave old wounds to fester, they will only infect everything else in your life, including new beginnings.*

As for us finding a place, my brother's sideline job was being a caretaker of some local rentals and one was becoming available in three weeks. We drove past and saw it was located adjacent to the river. It reminded us of the place we had when we first got married. We could actually see it from this side of the river. We were told it had small living quarters, which was okay with us as just the view had us hooked. The rent was half of what we had previously paid before we moved back, so we told him we would take it sight unseen. We were looking forward to moving in three weeks and told my mother we would be out of her hair shortly. *But so much can happen in twenty-one days.*

Kim and I had a day off together, so we invited my mother to go shopping with us. As my mother was getting back in the car, she went limp and sat down holding her chest. We immediately took her to the clinic a block away. The nurse took one look and ushered her into the doctor's office. Paramedics were soon rushing inside and the next thing we knew, they were wheeling her out on a stretcher to bring her to the hospital. We were informed her heart was stopping from time to time, and she needed immediate care. We followed the ambulance up the hill and texted a few family members who started converging at the hospital to see her. In the meantime, we were already informed she was scheduled to have a pacemaker put in the next day. Her diagnosis was serious but stable.

There was a crowd outside, so we decided to leave in order to let everyone have a chance to visit with her, knowing they didn't want to be in the same room with us. As we were leaving, we were confronted by her brother. In an angry tone he said, "See what you've done. It's all your fault for moving back here." *Boy, that pissed me off. There was no way in hell I would ever again except blame I didn't own.* I turned and told him the doctor said if it wasn't for us getting her help immediately, she would be dead by now. Then I said. "You've always been here, so what's your fucking excuse for never visiting her?" Then we left. Was this the reason why we moved back home? Was it to be there in that moment so we could look after my mom as my daughter had asked? Nope. There was another.

The operation was a complete success. My mother had colour back in her cheeks and said she couldn't wait to get home so I could cook her another meal. I told her I would cook her anything she wanted upon her return. After recovering for a few days, she was released with more energy than ever and suggested she wanted to go huckleberry picking the next day. "Slow down, Ma. You just had a major operation." That night as she wished, I cooked up some lean chops in mushroom soup, topping if off with a perfectly cooked rice. "Best I ever tasted," she said. *Little did we know it would be the last time that I would ever cook for her.*

It was getting late and Kim needed to get to bed as 4:00 a.m. comes early. Mom told us she was just going to watch a little more TV and then turn in herself. It must have been about 1:00 a.m., when we were awoken by our door opening. The light from the hall shone on my mother's face, revealing she had blood on her chin. She asked us to call the ambulance. We bolted up with Kim following her into the bathroom. Mom crawled into the tub on her hands and knees with Kim following suit to hold onto her. She began violently throwing up blood. It was everywhere; both her and Kim were soaked by it. I was freaking out and pushing her alert button with one hand and phoning 911 with the other. *What the fuck was happening? She had felt so good a few hours earlier.* Kim was staying calm and comforting her as I began to move the furniture out of the way to get a stretcher around the corner. Knick-knacks were flying everywhere. Once the paramedics arrived, they relieved Kim. We stood outside the door holding each other, and my mother's blood was transferred from Kim's pajamas to mine.

We were both feeling helpless. Her vomiting subsided enough for her to be placed on the stretcher. We quickly put our shoes on and followed the ambulance down the hill. We went to the emergency reception to give them any relevant information. The nurse phoned my brother as he was listed as the only emergency contact. A little before he arrived, the emergency nurse came out to escort us in to see my mother. We both took one of her hands in ours and told her how scared she had made us, asking how she was feeling. She told us she was comfortable, and they were about to run some tests on her, but she was very tired. I informed her my brother would be there shortly, and we stayed with her until he arrived. Leaving her that morning we thought she was going to be okay.

We returned to her apartment where Kim changed into her uniform, and I drove her back down to work. I got a few hours' sleep before I went back down to pick her up to return to the hospital. Upon driving past the entrance, we noticed a large gathering of people standing around and talking. Kim recognized most of them as my mom's relatives and friends. I felt the blood drain from my face as I located a parking spot a distance away. I turned off the car, opened the door, and threw up. *I had seen a gathering like this once before outside hospital doors – the last time I saw my grandmother. I knew what it meant.* My brother saw us drive past and walked over to where we were parked. He informed us my mother was now in the family room. I guess after the pacemaker was put in, it forced an embolism to burst inside her abdomen, and she was bleeding internally. Nothing could be done but to say goodbye.

I didn't need to run away this time, not like I did when I was a child. Kim was right there to hold me and help me through whatever I had to face. Now we knew the answer as to why we had returned home. It was by greater design, just like everything else that guided us. It had to be. Why else did I reach out to her when I did? If we hadn't, she would never have known of our forgiveness. We also wouldn't be there at the end of her life to say goodbye, just as we were with Dad. *There was still one last thing I needed to do, which I believe now was the ultimate reason for us returning.*

Kim helped wipe my tears, and we made our way to her room. She was quite medicated but coherent. Kim approached first and leaned in to give her a kiss and I followed suit. We stood above her and let her speak first. She reached for Kim's hand, thanking her for being there for her that morning. Then she grabbed one of mine and placed it in Kim's, saying how proud she was that we stuck together all these years and she was sorry we didn't have more time together. *This was the moment.* I gently let go of Kim's hand and placed it on the back of mine on my mother's cheek. I leaned in to say something I thought I would never be able to tell her. It was something I had said so many times in my youth without knowing what it meant, but I did now. They were four words I waited to say all my life and feel the full effect. As I started to cry, I looked her straight in the eyes and said, "I love you, Mom."

I was truly saddened this would be the first and last time I could ever tell her. There were others waiting to say goodbye to her so we were prodded to hurry up. Kim and I gave her one last kiss and that was it. She passed away later that day. A cycle in my life had ended the best way it could. A mother and son were at peace with each other at long last.

I dreaded the conversation I knew was about to take place. Things had happened so quickly; the news of my mother's passing would be devastating for my daughter. She was so far away with no immediate family members to console her. I couldn't imagine how she was going to take it, but she was grateful we were there for her and also grateful Kim had stood by me all these years. It wasn't the best of circumstances, however, it quickened some sort of bond that was just getting started between the three of us. It was yet another blessing, and one for which we soon would be even more thankful.

## CHAPTER 19:
# The Better Only Gets Better With Love

Things for us started to develop in a seamless fashion. We were about to move into our new place, and I was able to secure a different job just across the street from where Kim worked. It was nothing spectacular – simply a sales position at a small dollar-store chain. It worked out that we could meet to have lunch together every day. Kim and I could never spend enough time together. As for our new residence, it was absolutely perfect. Yes, it was small in size, but we didn't need much space as we had very few belongings. We had just enough to be comfortable. We learned long ago that material things were of little importance, as long as we had a roof over our heads and daily meals. The most important thing was to have each other to love, and boy, did we ever love each other.

We made new friends through work, and they often asked us to attend various gatherings. However, we would rather sit at home outside, watching the river roll by, enjoying every minute we had together. I know it sounds mushy, but it was true. We were making up for lost time, so there wasn't enough time in a day to share now. Through everything we endured, we came out on the other side, where we were truly meant to be. We were two souls dancing in life, joined as one. We had our health and each other. What more could we possibly want? I wasn't standing still in anything anymore, including my employment, as I had secured a job at the local government liquor store. We were very proud of each other's work ethic. From the time when we first started working at that service station, not once did either of us miss a shift at any job we held. In fact, we hadn't even seen a physician in the last fourteen years. There was never any need as we never got sick enough to warrant seeing one. We were strong like bull. Anyways, things were great and all the perceptions my family members and people we used to know had dissipated. My brother and sister in-law were now back in our lives, and we began bonding with them.

Then one night, someone else came creeping into our lives. During the winter months we had a heater in an outside room where we shared laundry facilities. We never smoked in the house, so we used it as a smoking lounge. It didn't have heat or insulation, so we bundled up and had coffee with a little kick to it to keep us warm. At first, we thought a raccoon had entered in to join us. Whatever it was bolted in and jumped on Kim's lap. It was a furry little critter, and oh so friendly. It was a grey and black tabby, purring loudly as he nuzzled into Kim's lap, biting her fingers gently as she petted him. We knew he was there to get out from the cold and was probably hungry. Kim quickly handed him to me so she could go in the house and bring him out a dish of water. The only thing she could find for him to eat was a piece of cheddar cheese. He lapped up the water and devoured the cheese. Then he rubbed against Kim's legs and left out the door, leaving just as quickly as he came in. We figured he must belong to someone, but it was a nice interruption to the night. It made Kim question whether or not to get another kitty, however that wouldn't be left up to us. The mysterious tomcat would take full control of that decision. Night after night he would make an appearance. We had questioned the neighbours as to whom he belonged, but no one knew. Soon he became a permanent squatter. To commemorate the first night we met, we would crown him King Chedda. He was a cheesy little beggar. The bond between him and Kim was unbreakable. She spoiled him like crazy. *And just like everything else in our lives, we would realize it wasn't just by chance he had entered ours.*

Life was wonderful. Over the years I began to show my age. My hair, once brown, was now crowned with grey. Kim didn't seem to age at all. People couldn't believe she was past fifty. She never wavered in the routine I first witnessed so many years ago in that Calgary hotel room, taking care of herself no matter what. I wasn't out of vanity; it was just who she was. She believed God had given her one body, and it was her job to take care of it. It's what I alluded to earlier. *She walked with grace that emanated from within, spilling over into her physical beauty. Everyone could see it. Everyone could feel it.*

We couldn't have been more happy where we were in life, but life hadn't finished with its little blessings for us just yet. The town was all a buzz about a new store coming. A major dollar-store chain was going to open in our one and only shopping mall. They advertised employment opportunities for all positions – both clerks and management. Kim insisted I should apply for the manager position. I was apprehensive about it. I had come a long way, but I was still lacking confidence about my abilities. However, Kim wasn't. She saw more in me than I did myself. She always did. So I applied for her more than anything else. If I didn't get the position nothing else would change. I still had my other job, so no harm no foul. I was told each position offered would be decided during the set-up. Two weeks before opening, shelving needed to be put in place and the stock merchandized. It was a major operation to get the store ready, meaning fourteen-hour days to set it up. I figured that was that. I couldn't quit my other job on a chance I might be hired as the manager. Once I told Kim the process, she never wavered in her conviction that I would get the job. It was only because of her encouragement that I would take a leap of faith, but I was still worried I might let her down.

She told me if things didn't turn out the way we hoped, it wouldn't disappoint her. The only thing that would was if I remained standing still and didn't try at all. So I gave my resignation at the liquor store and waited for the call to begin the set-up of the new store. It came with a 7:00 a.m. start. Upon arriving, it was a little disheartening to see most of the town had turned out. Fifty-three of us had been called back for set-up, which meant I would have to beat out fifty-two for the position I wanted. Oh boy! I did have two advantages over everyone else though. First, I had previous experience in a dollar store; not of this magnitude but experience just the same. Second, I had something no one else could possibly have: the unshakeable confidence of Kim, which made me find the strength to get through the day. It was exhausting work, but I wouldn't quit. When everyone took their breaks, I continued working. Most nights, I went directly to bed as soon as I got home. Kim was so proud of how dedicated I was. She knew it was hard on me as I wasn't a spring chicken anymore. Every bone in my body ached, but just like Kim said, it would all be worth it. Three days before the grand opening, the head of the set-up crew offered me the job as store manager. The only thing I could think was that I didn't let Kim down.

After the first year, I wanted to do something for Kim. We had two vehicles at the time, but both were old and constantly needed fixing. I was happy driving mine, but I was concerned Kim's was unsafe. As I said before, materialistic things didn't mean much to us, but Kim's safety meant everything to me, so it was time to buy a brand-new car for her. This was something we had never owned in almost twenty-nine years of marriage. I convinced her there would be no harm for us to at least go and look at some. On the first lot we approached, Kim noticed one that caught her eye standing out from the rest. It wasn't about its design; it was all about the unique apple-green colour. She loved it. Go figure. By the time we returned from the test drive, she was in love with it. I think she would have loved any new car, but it was still the colour that gave it more cred. I was so happy to know she would be safe now. She was just happy about the colour.

But things didn't end there. Kim was now concerned for my safety and wanted me to get a new vehicle as well. I told her one new car was enough, but she wouldn't let it go, so I returned to the dealer to see what they had second-hand. It was ironic, but one had just been traded in, the same make and model as Kim's. It was one year older and without all the bells and whistles, but it still came with a five-year warranty. I snapped a few pics and sent them to Kim. Her response was, "Start the paperwork". So just as we shared everything else in our lives, now we would share matching cars: one that was suited Kim – beautiful and colourful – and one that suited me – basic and plain. That was my running joke anyways.

Surely nothing could get better in our lives, but we started a twice-a-year tradition. We would spend our holidays at a local hot springs and always rent the same self-contained condo facing the lake. Each and every time we treated it like a lover's getaway, which never went unnoticed by the staff at the springs. Now we were known as the "Honeymooners". We always had the best time of our lives whenever we went.

There was one sad event during that time that we had to face, however. It was another Lloss of a family member. My brother's liver decided it couldn't take any more, and he was admitted to the hospital with very little time left. It's strange how many types of grief there are. Of course we felt very saddened about his passing, but we also felt relieved his suffering had come to an end – not just through his illness, but what he had endured through his entire life. He was a very damaged man, who never received the help he desperately needed. *But for the grace of Kim and God, there go I.*

Besides dealing with his loss, everything else for Kim and I was as perfect as it could be. I was still amazed and grateful for the position I held. I never would have figured I could be leading a team responsible for over a million dollars in sales annually. I pinched myself on a daily basis. Adjacent to where I worked, was a twenty-four-thousand-square-foot grocery chain store. In the two years I worked at my job, I had never ran into the manager once. Then by chance one day, we were both outside having a smoke. After introducing ourselves, we would soon become fast friends. Unbeknownst to me, he had always watched me at work and was impressed by how I ran the store. He had been in the retail business for over thirty years, so the compliment meant a lot to me. He said that his chain was in negotiations to turn his store into a franchised one under the same umbrella, but more of a "No Frills" type of store. He would soon be the new owner. We sat and had coffee everyday, getting to know each other a little more. One day, he casually asked if I knew of anyone who could fill the position of bakery supervisor. Well, there was one person i could think of. I wanted to go outside and look at the heavens. Surely the stars were aligned once again. I knew this would be a step forward for Kim. It was now just a matter of me convincing her she was ready to take the leap.

Kim had reservations about the job, as she loved working with the gals. But just as she told me once, I reminded her there would be no harm in exploring the opportunity and weighing its pros and cons. Her wage would increase significantly. The 4:30 a.m. shifts would now move to 6:00 a.m. shifts. But the one factor finally making up her mind first and foremost was that she would be working right next door to me, meaning we could see each other during the day. She accepted the offer. From the time she started, we shared all of our breaks together. Any trepidation whether she could do the job soon disappeared. Her work ethic was an example and an inspiration to others. As time went on, the owner started broaching the subject of me jumping ship and working for him. Each time I would turn him down flat. I was excelling in my present job, receiving platinum business awards from the Better Business Bureau and monthly bonuses, so I was quite content where I was. As time passed, Kim tried to convince me to join her team. Then one day, the owner invited us to his place for some drinks. He offered me the manager's position. With it would come a complete benefit package, retirement plan, and a substantial salary increase. It was another step forward, and with Kim's full confidence behind me, I accepted. I then reminded

Kim I would become her boss now. Her response: "Only at work, my dear. Only at work."

I was like a fish out of water having to learn everything from top to bottom, but to the owner's credit, he never gave up on me. He was tough to work for, but outside of work, he was the most generous and loyal of friends. There would come a time in the future that I would forever be in his debt.

The one thing we appreciated most was the bonding between all of the major employees in the store. It was more of a family sort of atmosphere. The only downside was work always carried over to our home environment. We were always talking about it from the time we got up until we went to bed. It was getting in the way of any quality time together. It made us look forward to our honeymoon getaway at the hot springs even more. But once at home, we fell back into the work syndrome state. I was more secure in my job and the salary alone would be plenty to meet our daily needs. Besides Kim had worked so hard and endured so much over the years. It was time for me to carry the load now. I sat with her and told her what I had in mind, and she agreed that it would be the best thing for her to resign. I told her she could take it easy now and suggested she didn't even need to work any more. I still chuckle at her response to such a statement: "Silly boy."

Yes a silly boy I was. How could I ever think she didn't want to continue working? It was a rite of passage for both of us now: the new and improved us. She started preparing résumés with the local job centre and gave her two-week notice. There were those stars again. She answered a posting that was put up at an office-supply store. The manager talked to her and set up an interview two days before she would be unemployed. She was so excited when she returned from it. Not only did they sell office supplies, but a lot of art supplies as well. She said it was like she was in a candy shop. She truly wanted them to hire her and now all she could do was wait for a response. As we were shopping after her last shift had ended, she received a call. Kim never became unemployed. The job she wanted so badly was now hers. *It seemed like nothing could ever go wrong for us anymore.*

It wouldn't take long before the nightly stress we felt disappeared. Home was home, and work was work – never crossing over again. We had everything we could possibly desire: good friends, jobs we enjoyed, and our little place on the river. Plus now, my daughter was talking to us on a regular basis. She was even planning to visit us when she was coming up to see the other side of her family.

Whenever we sat outside watching the river roll by, it would give us pause to reflect on how far we had really come. There was nothing more enjoyable to us than that – except of course, the times we would spend at the hot springs, which was fast approaching. However, events leading up to it did present a small hiccup. The house we were living in had been sold, and we were given two months to vacate. We were sad we had to leave such peaceful surroundings, not to mention any suitable housing in town was far and few between, especially ones that would allow pets. Come hell or high water, Kim would never leave her beloved Chedda behind. He was an outside kitty, so where we were was perfect for him. I began searching through local rental web pages. We thought we might have to cancel our vacation, as we had only a month left before we had to move. *What in the hell were we worried about? Just as everything else, it was meant to be.*

A co-worker brought to my attention an ad that had just been posted. I knew it would be perfect and wasted no time inquiring about it. The landlord said he had an overwhelming amount of interest in us, and he would be in touch. We drove past the place several times which only made us want it more. Then we got the call for a date and time that we could have a showing, along with the rest of the applicants. The only kicker was our holiday was scheduled for the day before. If we left for it, we wouldn't make the showing. We told our perspective landlord of our plight, so he graciously offered us to show it to us before the rest of the applicants. Just that alone told Kim and I it was meant to be. We met the owner at the lower end of the property. There were a lot of steps going up, but that was appealing to us, as it offered plenty of privacy. He then told us they owned a local pet store in town and having Chedda was no problem at all. He showed us around, and it was absolutely perfect. It had a lot larger living quarters than we were used to and the yard was amazing. Not only was there a patio out the front door but also another behind the house and both were completely surrounded by trees. I knew what Kim was thinking: *A perfect jungle for our little lion king.* We told him we loved it, mentioning we had the deposit needed in hand. To our surprise, he said "Welcome home." We were over the moon. It was all we could talk about at the hot springs. We couldn't wait to move in. We were receiving blessing after blessing. It's truly amazing what happens when you have love in your life.

We all settled into the new digs immediately, with our Chedda never missing a beat. He quickly made the surrounding territory his own. All the other kitties in the neighbourhood would now bow to King Chedda. Kim was relieved he adapted as well as he did. Our first year there couldn't have been better. We even did something we had never done before. We hosted our own social gatherings. With our crew, it was more like drunk fests, but it was always a good time. No one died or got arrested, so what could be better? Kim and I never drank hard liquor – always just wine or beer. However, at each gathering, Kim started a new tradition and poured everyone a shot of her favourite liquor; something to warm up your innards. It was sweet and fiery just like her. Fireballs for everyone.

During our first winter, the snow covered the many steps leading up from the street, and I hated shovelling. Kim, however, enjoyed the exercise. She felt she needed it now, as she was not running around as much as she used to in her old job. She even mentioned she felt she was getting fat and was getting a little more of an extended tummy. I couldn't see It. Her frame was always beautiful in my eyes.

*You know how in life there are moments in time you would like to have back? Well for us, this was one of them – but neither of us could have known.*

# CHAPTER 20:

# A Moment In Time

Our days consisted of work we both enjoyed. Evenings were made up of a bottle of wine and elaborate meals I conjured up. We would end each night with our dance of love, and then every morning when we woke, we shared a more intimate type of dance. Now Kim had time to explore her creative side. She found a Nail Community Group on Facebook. Her art background was an added bonus. She loved every minute of it and it became a passion of sorts. Even her customers and coworkers were amazed she did her own nails. Seeing how happy it made her meant the world to me. We could live out the rest of our lives just as we were.

Winter came and went, and summer arrived in all its splendour. We spent it as we always did, sitting outside with a glass of wine or two until it got dark, then finishing the day off with a moonlit dance. We were so looking forward to our thirty-fourth anniversary coming up in the New Year. It was astonishing how time had passed so quickly. We endured so much over the years to be exactly where we dreamed we would be. It had been a long, hard journey, but we were finally home. We were in heaven on earth. We could see ourselves feeling the same way on our sixtieth anniversary and beyond.

*BUT LIFE CAN BE A FICKLE BITCH and maliciously tear apart everything you have built and all that you love. Everything we endured and overcame wouldn't measure close to what was about to happen. For the love of all that's righteous, please no!!!*

The end of August was upon us, and as so many times in the past, it was our cue to book our honeymoon for the third week in September. Kim had mentioned she felt a little sluggish and was having a bout of constipation. She ate more fibre to relieve it, but it still persisted. We agreed she should get it checked out. As I said, she had never sick a day in her life, so we didn't have a family doctor. Fortunately, we found one that was taking on new patients. An added bonus was that the doctor was female, which made Kim feel a little more at ease about seeing someone. She left her first appointment with the doctor with an order for blood tests and an X-ray, along with some laxatives. She insisted she felt well enough to wait to take the tests until after our vacation a few days later. The laxatives were starting to work, so she was convinced she was just bound up. She didn't want anything to stand in the way of our time at the hot springs.

The day we arrived, and we quickly changed into our swimsuits to enjoy the day at the pools. Not once did Kim mention she felt sick. That evening, I noticed she was looking very pale. She fluffed it off and said she was fine. The next morning, her appearance made it obvious **she wasn't fine.** I knew we had to leave. She was so upset that we had to cut our stay short, but she relented. I told her we could come up another time. I was only concerned about how she felt, so we made the journey back home. Back home, I told her to go and lay down, and I would bring everything in from the car. So with her beloved Chedda curled up beside her, that's what she did. I let her rest for a while and then inquired if she was hungry. She told me maybe she could have some soup, which I quickly prepared for her. She took a couple of spoonfuls of soup and then immediately ran to the bathroom to throw it up. We needed to go to emergency, and I wouldn't take no for an answer. We took along the requisitions the doctor had previously requested. The wait to get in was torturous. I had never seen Kim looking so ill. I was getting really scared!

Once inside, they took blood tests, wheeled her away for an X-ray, and then returned a short time later. I held her hand waiting for the emergency doctor to return with the results. As he entered the cubicle, he enclosed the curtain around us for privacy. He began relaying what the X-ray had shown. There were two things making him concerned. The first was a fluid build-up in her abdomen. The second was an anomaly lower down on her right side. What the hell did that mean? He could see the panic displayed on my face, so he offered some comfort by saying, "Don't worry... She's not going to die." However, the preliminary results showed something serious going on, and more tests were needed to get to the bottom of it. A CT scan and more blood work were ordered. We left the hospital and waited to get word about the scan. Kim was so exhausted that she fell asleep as soon as she lay down at home. I didn't sleep a wink. I brought a chair into the bedroom and watched her just to make sure she was going to be okay. The unknown was killing me inside.

When she woke up, she saw me staring at her. All of a sudden she bolted from the bed and ran to the bathroom and closed the door. I was worried she was getting sick again. Upon exiting, she looked at me, smiled, and said, "Woohoo. I'm not constipated anymore."

Not even realizing what I was saying, I responded, "What a relief that is."

She laughed and said, "Plop, plop, oh what a relief it is."

That was the Kimmie I know and will always love. Feeling better now, her only concern was getting back to work and of course starting a new set of nails. We had about a week to wait for the CT scan and she was determined to go on as usual. Of course, I knew she was worried, but she faced it like everything else she did in her life. We were doing all we could, and she wouldn't waste any time with unnecessary worry. After all, it might not be that serious. She was feeling better.

The day of the CT scan came and went. The following day, her GP called and asked us to come in the next day. This was it; we would find out what was going on. Her doctor went on to explain what they had found. The scan showed a few small growths on her ovary. There was no way to tell if they were benign or malignant or its progression without another blood test, but it was definitely cancerous. The doctor made a referral for Kim to see a gynecologist. She had blood drawn again and we went home. The reality of the situation didn't hit me until we sat outside with a tea. I think both of us were still in shock – myself more so than her. I broke down, got off my chair, and knelt down beside her in tears, telling her I didn't want her to die. She lifted my chin and responded, "I don't want to die either, babe, but it is what it is. There's nothing we can do but hope for the best."

I thought she was putting on a brave face for me, but it was how she really felt. There were no tears or self-pity. She continued exhibiting that grace she walked with throughout her entire life. One tends to think the worst in these situations, but her resolve made me shake those feelings off. Immediately I started finding out as much as I could about ovarian cancer, especially the survival rate. She wanted to think about it as little as possible, so she made me promise just to tell her the important things, good or bad. I spent hours that night googling everything I could. Her results said the growths were small, which was a good sign. I learned if caught in time, treatment would consist of a radical hysterectomy with chemotherapy. The prognosis was quite good. Okay, we could deal with that. I told her my findings and all she said was, "See, people can endure a lot worse. We're blessed if that's all I have to go through."

My findings did give us a little hope. It was a short-lived one, but it would carry us to her next appointment with the gynecologist. Her demeanour was just as gentle and caring as Kim's GP. She said she had the results of the bloodwork. Its purpose was to measure a certain marker that ovarian cancer had. Its clinical term was CA125. Basically it's a protein found on most ovarian cancer cells that are secreted into the blood cells. Depending on how high the count is, the more advanced the cancer is. Her count was borderline at best, so that was good news. At least on the surface it was, however, the doctor was still concerned about the fluid build-up in her abdomen and wanted to do several things. First was a complete gynecological exam, which was done during our appointment that day. In that regard, everything appeared normal.

The second was a pap smear and that revealed no anomalies either. The next was to forward her results to the local oncologist and set an appointment with him, and then he would decide whether to start chemo right away or not. At times, chemo is done before a radical hysterectomy to eradicate as much of the cancer as possible. Then bouts of chemo would follow after the surgery as well to remove any other cancer cells. To think this was our best-case scenario still underscored the seriousness of the situation. But as Kim said, many women had to endure such a procedure and came out cancer-free. We *could only pray she would be added to the list.*

The next thing the doctor wanted was a little more invasive. An appointment was set up for a biopsy of something called the omentum, which is sometimes known as the policeman of the abdomen. The doctor explained it was a large sheet of fat that stretches over the intestines, liver, and stomach like an elastic apron, and it's known to secrete hormones and toxins. It was the first time it was brought to our attention that the CT scan showed what was called a caking or thickening of it. This too can also be caused by ovarian cancer. A small non-invasive biopsy would give them a tissue sample to be put under a microscope, allowing them to gather more information about the cells contained within. While being under the CT scanner, the area would be frozen and then a long needle would be inserted to extract a sample. Maybe to them, it seemed a "little" invasive, but having a long needle thrust into your abdomen didn't sound very pleasant either. I felt so disheartened that Kim had to go through all of this shit.

She underwent test after test without any real answers yet. Kim was taking it in stride, but it was pissing me off.

*Just find out what the fuck it is and fix her.*

The biopsy was scheduled in seven days, and her appointment with the oncologist was in three. In the meantime, Her constipation was back. She was eating very little, but it didn't stop her from working. I think it was therapeutic, keeping her mind focused on other things. Everyone that needed to know about what we were going through did. My daughter felt so bad she was so far away and couldn't be here to support us, but we told her just having her reach out to us was a blessing.

Our appointment with the oncologist was upon us. We prepared ourselves for the possibility that Kim would start chemo in the near future, however with having only the CA125 counts to go by, he told us that it wasn't necessary. The count was low enough that any chemo before surgery wouldn't alter the outcome. It was a good thing. This way her immune system wouldn't have to take a hit from the chemo, allowing them to proceed with the operation quicker if need be. This knowledge allowed us to return home in better spirits. About an hour later, we received a Facebook message from my daughter, asking if we were home yet. She knew of the appointment, so we assumed she just wanted to be updated about the results. We responded we were at home and things went okay. We didn't receive a response right away, which didn't concern us, considering the time difference. But later that evening, she called. The first words she spoke were: "Dad, I need to make arrangements to return to Canada right away!"

Kim and I looked at each other with surprise, thinking the same thing. She didn't need to come to see us right now. We knew she couldn't afford it. Then... Boom! In a shaky tone, she told us her natural mother had just been admitted into Vancouver General Hospital with total renal failure. Her diagnosis was terminal kidney cancer, and she only had a short time left. Crap! I guess the years of living on the street and drug abuse had caught up with her. *When it rains, it fucking pours and pours.* We didn't know what to say. In that moment, our circumstances felt small in comparison, and we were so sad for both of them. All we could tell my daughter was we were here if she needed us night or day. But how could she afford the trip?

Remember how I mentioned my custody lawyer had done something remarkable way back when? Unbeknownst to anyone, it turns out he had applied for

Victims Financial Assistance over the abuse she received living at her Mom's. C was notified a month earlier that she would be receiving compensation. The cheque was enough to pay for the return flight. What would be the odds that after twenty-one years this would happen, exactly when it was needed the most? *It still boggles my mind.*

The very first thing Kim said afterwards was: "See hun... At least we still have hope." *Hope indeed, baby.*

Kim's biopsy day came and went. The procedure was quick and relatively painless. The sample had to be shipped to a special lab that specifically dealt with cancer cells and the results would take another seven to ten days. During this time, Kim began to feel sicker. She was unable to eat and also beginning to feel pain as her tummy started to grow more. We tried to convince ourselves it was just constipation, so we got the doctor to prescribe some painkillers and heavy-duty laxatives. We knew it was time for her to stop working. Her employer was fully on board, allowing her a leave of absence from work. There was no way I was going to leave her home alone, so I asked for one as well from my job. As I mentioned earlier, my boss was truly a loyal and generous man, so without hesitation he granted me one. Then he basically paid me out of his own pocket until things were squared away with Medical Employment Insurance, which gave us one less worry so I could direct my full attention to Kim."

Seven to ten days was like a lifetime to wait for the results. Kim's gynecologist sent a referral to the doctor in Vancouver, who would be overseeing her operation and of course I googled everything I could about her. Her credentials were impeccable. Just like us, she was waiting for the results of the biopsy. Kim was faring poorly and staying in bed most of the day. Her constipation made her feel uncomfortable, and more often than not, anything she ate would come right back up. I stocked the house with everything imaginable that she might able to eat: soups, protein drinks, crackers, anything I could think of. I felt so damn helpless. But despite how she felt, she would stand in front of the mirror, wash her face, brush her teeth, and apply her lotion everyday, just like everyday before. Knowing how terrible she was feeling, all I could do was stand there and help anyway I could.

*I can't lie. It got the best of me. Each time I knew she was sleeping, I bawled my eyes out. Why was this happening? She didn't deserve this. No one deserves this.*

I had to be even closer to her throughout the day. So with the help of my brother, we found a very large sectional couch to place in the living room. That way, she could sprawl out and watch a little TV, and I could be right there with her 24/7, keeping an eye on her. Chedda curled up and seldom left her side. Kim loved having both her boys constantly with her. One day, we had the TV tuned to an oldies music station. A song began to play that was familiar to me. It was one my Grandma used to sing and Kim had heard it before as well. We both started singing with its words making us choke up a little. After it was over, she turned to me and asked me to download it on my phone. She smiled and told me this would be our new song of love now. We couldn't dance to it... but we could sing it to each other. The song was "A Daisy a Day" sung by Jed Shrunk.[3]

Did she know somehow her condition was much more serious than we had thought? I can't say, but this song would be sung over and over again to each other from that day forward. Soon an entire community would be singing it. In the meantime, I was getting extremely anxious to know her results and a little pissed off, as it was taking so long. The day we did receive them only confused and worried me more. The biopsy showed a spindle lesion in her cells that was positive for high-grade metastatic carcinoma. What the fuck did that mean?

It meant the ovarian cysts were not the cause of Kim's illness, but only a symptom of an underlying factor. Basically, they still had no idea what was causing it; only that it was very serious and life threatening. They said they needed to eliminate as many possible factors before we went to Vancouver. One theory was that it could be caused by colon cancer. It made sense, considering Kim's constipation, so again, Kim had to endure yet another procedure – a colonoscopy. Now that we knew things were a lot more serious, Kim wanted to talk about the "what ifs" – something I had no desire to do. I couldn't think about ever losing her, but she knew it was a reality now, and she wanted me to be prepared just in case. *I wished she would stop being so concerned about me and be concerned for herself for just once. I wanted her to break down. I needed her to cry for herself, so I could cry with her.*

She had so much more strength than anyone could imagine. How could anyone be so strong? Deep down I knew where it came from – a place I so desperately needed to pray for now. Something that she never faltered in during the

---

3    Please give it a listen, as its importance to our story will be manifested in the events to come.

last thirty-three years was what carried her through all the tough times we had. The reason she walked through life with such grace was because she believed in God's grace. Pure and simple.

CHAPTER 21:

# Our Faith

Up to this point, I have shied away from sharing our religious beliefs and how we viewed life and death. However, it is extremely important for you to fully understand the underlying factor that carried us through from this point forward. Not to preach or convert, but just as I exposed everything else about our life, I would be remiss not to share this as well. It would become the only hope we had. I will keep it as brief as possible, so bear with me for a moment.

We believe when God created mankind, he intended for them to live forever on earth, without ever suffering sickness or death. However, Adam, the first man, disobeyed the Creator and lost the prospect of living forever. As descendants of Adam, we inherited death from him. It was through God's love of mankind that he offered his only begotten Son as a sacrifice to forgive us for our sins. This restored the hope to once again live on a paradise earth as God intended. We believe there will be a Judgement Day where God will destroy the wicked. Those faithful will make it through Armageddon. And as for those faithful who have already died... "The one who exercises faith in me, even though he dies, will come to life, and everyone who is living and exercises faith in me will never die at all." (John 11:25- 26) So no matter what the outcome of what we were facing, we believed that we would be reunited once again and live together forever on a paradise earth. Kim's faith had always been stronger than mine, but whether through selfish reasons or not, I found myself praying like never before to give me the strength to be there for my Kimmie and to have the peace of mind she was displaying.

By the time she was to have the colonoscopy, it was hard for her to even stand. But she was a trooper, and we made our way to the hospital for the procedure. It went quicker than we thought it would. The general surgeon told us everything looked normal. Really? Then where in the hell was this coming from? Unfortunately the doctors had no idea themselves. The only option we had left was to hurry up and wait for our appointment with the cancer specialist in Vancouver. We waited and waited with Kim only getting worse. She was losing weight everywhere except her tummy, which was now swelling out like a huge balloon, but not a single word of complaint came from her.

Then a moment would come that would burn a hole in my heart forever. I was in the kitchen, just a few feet away from her, and I heard her starting to cry. "Oh my God... Are you okay, honey?" Asking me to join her, she grabbed my hand and placed her wedding bands in it. "Promise me you will keep these safe. They're slipping off my finger, and I don't want to lose them." Oh, sweet Jesus, I lost it. I put my head on her chest and cried like a baby with her. It was the only time I had seen her really cry throughout everything. Not because of her physical pain or the prospect that she might be dying. She cried because a symbol of our love had slipped off her fingers. SHE NEVER TOOK THOSE RINGS OFF. *So what else world? Have you finished pummelling our hearts yet? I think not.*

Our trip to Vancouver relied on a few things. First and foremost, we were waiting for the call. Second, we would have little time to arrange a flight. And third, our finances were being drained, and the flight alone would cost close to $800. Fortunately a friend of ours mentioned a service called Hope Air. Go figure. Anyways it was a service that paid for flights for necessary medical appointments. The headquarters were located back East, which meant a three-hour time difference, but you could apply online which I did on early Friday morning. That afternoon we got word that our appointment in Vancouver was the following Monday. I explained to the receptionist we were waiting to hear back from Hope Air, but even if we had to pay for the flight ourselves, we would be there. She told us once we arrived, to go directly to the Emergency Department and check Kim in. Her doctor would be made aware of our arrival. Okay, that was a little progress. I immediately got off the phone and tried calling the 1-800 number of Hope Air again. It was past business hours, so I left a desperate sounding message. Within ten minutes, a volunteer called us back and told us we qualified for their assistance. They just needed to know our departure airport and time, and they would handle the rest. All we had to do now was get through the weekend.

I gathered up everything Kim wanted to take and then phoned a cancer house near the hospital, so I had a place to stay. We had no idea how long we would be there, but we were prepared for any eventuality. There was just one last thing Kim wanted to take care of before we left. A week earlier she had made me purchase do-it-yourself will kits. She said we only needed one, but I insisted she might outlive me, so I returned with two. *Just the reality of having to fill them out made me nauseous. I can't even imagine how it made Kim feel. I was so overwhelmingly sad that she even had to think about this.*

Where we live is surrounded by mountains, and the airport is very small. It hadn't snowed, so that was encouraging. There was a good chance the plane could land. Kim felt like crap, and was barely able to sit up. Just her getting to the airport would be uncomfortable for her, never mind the hour plane ride ahead of us. Once we got to our airport, she reclined on one of the benches and tried to make herself as comfortable as she could, but the waiting was torturous on her. Then an attendant approached us, saying the flight was cancelled due to fog and we would have to return the next day. *You've got to be kidding me? Oh my dear sweet Kimmie, but what could we do?* It was touch and go the next day, but the plane made it in. We were first to board with the aid of a flight attendant. Once we reached the platform to enter the plane, I realized it was a smaller jet and you couldn't even stand upright to be seated. Bending over was the worst possible position Kim could be in, never mind now having to shuffle along in that position to be seated. But as always, she managed without complaint. Once we were seated, the pilot came back and knelt down to talk to us, inquiring about our trip. We told him we didn't really know anything except about the ovarian cysts. He then told us his cancer story, saying he had stage four testicular cancer. His prognosis at the time hadn't been very good, but now he was cancer free. He encouraged us to never give up hope. Kim appreciated his encouragement and I pretended I did as well, but I just wanted him to get the plane in the air. So much time had been wasted already. Time was the only thing important to us now.

Once at the Vancouver airport, I called to say we had made it in, and then I hailed a taxi. Arriving at the Emergency Department gave us another nice wait, but at least we had made it. We were told a member of the doctor team would see her shortly. Well, that was encouraging. She had a team to help. A short time later, we were called in to an examining room. Waiting for us was an intern who asked the usual questions and went over what was about to happen the next morning. The surgeon would use laparoscopic surgery for a look and see, at which time they were going to remove the ovary in question and her appendix. "What the hell? Why the appendix?" We didn't ask, concluding they might as well take that out as well while they were already in there. She was about to be moved to her room on the cancer floor. It was getting late, and I had no clue where my accommodations were for the night, so Kim told me to go and find it. She reassured me she would be fine until I checked in. The cancer house was fairly close, approximately six city blocks down the same street. I checked in and made my way back. By this time, she also was settled into a private room. No matter how she presented herself, I knew she was nervous about the next day. I wasn't going to leave her that night to be alone in her own thoughts. She might not have shared them, but they must have been terrifying, so I curled up in a chair to be exactly where I should be.

Okay, it was the big day. The time had come for her surgery and to finally find out once and for all what was going on. I couldn't let go of her hand as they were preparing her. They told me I could follow her down to the surgery ward to wait with her until she went in. It was a whirlwind of nurses, anesthesiologists, and surgeons. We hardly had time to say two words to each other, but we managed just as she was being wheeled in. "I love you baby," and "I love you more." Then I saw her mouth the words, "I'll be okay, baby." I'm glad she didn't see my reaction. I cried throughout my elevator ride back up to the main floor and all the way down countless hallways until I reached the street. They gave no indication about how long it would take, so I googled my ass off once again. Without complications, it could take anywhere from an hour and half to two hours, so I set the timer on my phone. I couldn't stay still and began doing a loop of about ten city blocks. Each time, I returned to the hospital, making my way up to her room to see if she had returned. Every time, I was more anxious than the last. I held it together for a while, but as time ticked away, I was getting so worried. Now two hours had passed and still no word. I asked the floor nurse to check, but it was to no avail. She hadn't heard anything. I phoned back home in tears and talked to my boss, a friend, and finally my brother. They all assured me it would be okay, but now it had been over three hours. I was sure something had gone wrong. It was just taking way too long. I thought I had lost her.

I went back up to her room in a total panic, but just as I arrived, the other elevator opened. It was Kim, alert and smiling. She saw the tears in my eyes and reached out and said, "I'm okay, baby. I told her what I had thought. Chuckling, she responded, "You can't get rid of me that easily." That made the waterworks start again. As she was being brought back inside her room, I went to a bathroom nearby and threw up. I was so relieved. I closed my eyes and thanked God for bringing her back to me. I needed to hold her and let her know how worried I was. She said she was fine then lifted her hospital gown to show me her tummy and a few dressings covering where they went in. Her tummy was a lot smaller and not as bloated as it had been. *Okay, that was a good sign.* She said she hadn't felt this good for quite some time and in fact, she was even hungry.

We were so encouraged, thinking they must have taken her ovary out and whatever else they needed to do, but we wouldn't really know until her doctor paid us a visit the next morning on his rounds. But that was okay. She felt better and that's all that mattered. The only burning question left was what she wanted to eat when they allowed her. She was permitted fluids, so the first thing she wanted was a good cup of coffee. "Have no fear, your super barista is here." She savoured every sip. It had been so long since she could hold anything down. We were almost a little giddy, but we deserved it. The next step would be solid food. That night she insisted I spend my night in a real bed, saying I looked exhausted. I didn't care. I felt exhilarated knowing she was feeing better. I only agreed knowing she needed the rest a hell of a lot more than I did. So I stayed as late as possible and then left her to sleep.

She texted me to make sure I was in bed before she dozed off for the night. I took a selfie to prove it. She returned one adding a text that made me sob uncontrollably: "I love you so, so much. You are my alpha and omega. Thank you for loving me, my darling." Oh baby, you are so easy to love. Even though I was in a real bed, I still couldn't sleep. All I could do was worry about the meeting with her doctor in the morning and what she had to say. Was my Kimmie all fixed now? How much chemo would she have to endure? Was it ovarian cancer after all?" There were still so many unanswered questions.

Early the next morning, I heard a notification on my phone. I knew who that was. I opened it up and saw a selfie with a message saying, "Yum, yum." The picture was of a hospital food tray, for the most part being empty. Kim was eating again. I was so happy. She was even able to go to the bathroom. *Holy crap, literally!* I couldn't wait to get my ass up there and give her a kiss good morning. When I arrived, her spirits were better than I had seen in a long time. We sat and talked about getting ready to go back home. We just needed to wait for the specialist to see her and let us know what was next. I wish we could have held on to that moment in time when there was still hope and still in the eye of the hurricane already upon us. But it was out of our control. It was out of everyone's control, including one of the most renown cancer specialists sitting in the room with us now.

She eventually told us that Kim was in the last stage of her cancer. A lot she said was getting lost in technical explanations, but the bottom line was she believed the cancer began in her appendix and was very rare, affecting about one in a million. She told us the cancer lesions had covered everything inside her. *Does that give you a better insight in to how strong Kimmie had been to that point? But folks once again, you ain't seen nothing yet.*

We found out that Kim wasn't going to be cured. They couldn't fix her. She was going to die. My heart sank into my stomach. Kim didn't say a word, but we were both thinking the same thing. "How long then?" *Please tell us something could be done to prolong the final outcome.* I grabbed Kim's hand and asked, "So what's next?" The doctor told us she was going to set up intense chemotherapy treatments closer to home. This would give us a chance to slow down the cancer's progression. "So how much time, Doc?" Her answer was twelve to eighteen months. She then left the room to arrange Kim's release. I crawled up beside Kim and held her. "It's not fair, baby."

Without missing a beat, all she replied was, "It's all right honey. We'll get through this the best we can." She began singing our daisy song and I joined in with tears. We held each other ever so tightly. *It was the saddest moment of my life to that point, but there would come a time that would surpasses it.*

We sat and talked for a bit and agreed that at least we had a year, maybe more. There was nothing we could do except look forward to each day as a blessing. Besides, she was hungry again. I can't imagine how scared she must have been. I know I was terrified, but there was no time to think of that now. The only thing I could do was to be there for her, no matter what and face things with that same faith, strength, and grace she demonstrated all of her life. It wasn't a choice for her; it was just who she was. We knew the road ahead would be daunting as we were once witness to what chemotherapy does to the body. We were just hoping at least it would bring some days that we could enjoy together, without her feeling as sick as she'd been. We wanted some time to say all the things we held in our hearts and to enjoy one last summer and the simple pleasures of life we all take for granted. At least we had those to look forward to before we had to say our final goodbye.

Oh how I wanted to take her place. She deserved so much more. After everything she sacrificed for me, I would gladly offer my own life in exchange for hers. She knew I would, but she accepted what was and what was to be. She told me that it was a blessing that she would go first. She wouldn't have the strength to go on without me. But how could she ever believe that I could go on without her? She had always been my strength. Now I have to be hers.

We still had some time. Not as much as we would have liked, but some. Maybe we would have enough to celebrate our thirty-fourth wedding anniversary. That would mean so much to us. It was well within the parameter of her prognosis. So from that moment, she made me promise not to dwell on the bad things and to be thankful for each and every blessing ever bestowed upon us. We were souls that would always be as one. That is a blessing very few can ever achieve in this cruel world. But most of all she wanted me to have faith that God had witnessed our love and through his grace and forgiveness he would reunite us one day. We were meant to be together in this world and in the new one he has in store for mankind – a world where sickness and death will be no more and a world where we will never have to say goodbye ever again.

CHAPTER 22:

# What Courage Is Made Of

It was time to head home and wait for her chemotherapy treatments to be scheduled. In the meantime, we were told the fluid in her abdominal cavity would probably accumulate again. When it became uncomfortable for her, we could go to emergency and have it drained in order to relieve the pressure on her intestines and everything else inside her. Okay, that was a little good news. She would at least be able to eat somewhat and get around more until her treatments. The plane ride back was a lot more pleasant for her. I don't think I ever let go of one of her hands all the way back. She even joked with a little wink that we had a true excuse to go to the plane's lavatory together. Then she gave me a kiss and said she felt bad that we were unable to express our love physically in that way anymore. She knew it was of no importance to me, but for her to even think of such a thing spoke volumes of her unselfish nature.

However, there were a couple of little selfish pleasures she was looking forward to upon getting home. It had been ages since she felt well enough to do her nails and watch her *Coronation Street*. Besides cuddling her boy Chedda, those two small self-indulgences to keep her mind distracted would be the first thing on her agenda. She asked me to deal with letting everybody know what had transpired in Vancouver. She just didn't want to think about it. Lord, neither did I, but I knew it would take a burden off of her to not have to offer long explanations to those who loved her and re-live everything that transpired over and over. All in all, it was a small price for me to pay to let her have as much peace of mind as possible. She didn't want people feeling sorry for her even if it was out of true concern. She wanted to continue on as usual and not be a bother or bring anyone down.

I, on the other hand, wanted her to know how many people thought the world of her. If she didn't know how much she was loved, I sure did. It was time she did as well. Once word circulated, the outpouring of love and support truly humbled her. Everyone who knew her personally and all her Facebook friends rallied around to give words of love and encouragement with message after message. All reminded her that she was always there for them when they needed a kind word or a nudge to keep smiling. It touched her deeply to know how many people cared. She wanted to reciprocate the love and let everyone know that she'd be okay, so she decided to share her battle ahead. Not to receive pity but to show her appreciation for everyone who cared about her and inspire others to never give up.

However, we tried not to create any more heartache for my daughter, who was already facing her natural mother's cancer prognosis, as Kim's diagnosis wasn't as immediately dire as hers. She had made arrangements to travel back to Canada about a week after we found out about Kim, but we told her she shouldn't concern herself with making the trip to see us. The most important thing was to be there for her mom. When she did arrive in Vancouver, her mother was stable and being released to live out her remaining time at home. C spent as much time as she could with her before she had to return back to Australia. Kim and I couldn't imagine what my daughter was going through. We knew we were facing tough times as well, but her tribulations were two-fold. At least we had more time on our side – *or that's what we had been told.*

Kim was fine for a while, but her tummy was getting bigger again, making her feel uncomfortable and unable to hold any food down. It had been almost two weeks, and we still hadn't heard from the cancer clinic about starting treatment, but all we could do was wait. We needed to drain more of the fluid from her tummy, so up to Emergency we went. The wait was tortuous on Kim, with no place to lie down and countless trips to the bathroom to throw up. She was finally admitted, and they began prepping her belly. The nurse asked if I had a strong stomach and/or any history of passing out. *What the hell did that have to do with anything?* It turned out the procedure involved a very long and thick needle being inserted into Kim's stomach. Some previous onlookers couldn't handle the process and had fainted.

I told them there was no way I was going to leave Kim. Feeling a little uncomfortable was the least of my worries. I held Kim's hand as they froze her belly. A portable ultrasound was then guided over her stomach to find the best place to go in without damaging anything else. *Yep. There's that needle they were talking about.* I told Kim to look at me as they inserted it. She couldn't feel it going in. *Thank God.* After the puncture was done, they inserted a small tube attached to a retrieval bag. The nurse was holding the bag, but she had to leave. She asked if I would be okay holding the bag, so to speak. It didn't bother me. I just wanted that fluid out of her so she could feel better again. Out it came. The bag began to fill and fill. I couldn't believe how much she had been carrying inside her. Her stomach and intestines were being compressed by all the fluid around them. No wonder she felt so crappy. When it stopped draining, almost three litres filled the bag.

The next morning, you could tell she was feeling better. By this time, the doctor had prescribed pain meds. She took them only when necessary, knowing any medication could make her constipated; something to be avoided at all costs. She continued taking several laxatives a day, only eating soups and things with fibre, and drinking as many protein drinks as she could handle. We tried everything possible to keep her comfortable, including weed oil. That helped her sleep, but not much more than that. All we could do was carry on until we heard from the cancer clinic. I made numerous calls to see what was taking so long but to no avail. Then we received word from my daughter that her mother had just passed away. *Aw Jeez. What were the odds that both her and Kim had been diagnosed with incurable cancer at the same time?* We reflected on how things might have been different for C's mother if she had received the help she needed so many years ago. She always had a good heart, but the weight she carried was too much for her to carry alone. We hoped my daughter would find some peace that God knows all she had suffered.

C hoped that when she came up to make arrangements for her mother's funeral she could make her way to us. We wanted to help, but our finances were being drained as well, and it would cost close to one thousand dollars in travel and expenses each trip to the chemo clinic. Free healthcare was a Godsend, but all the other expenses were adding up. However, no amount of money would stop me from extending Kim's outcome for a single second, never mind the year we had been given. The hope of at least one more year was all we wanted now. That's what they said. They wouldn't be shitting us now, would they? Why would they give us false hope? But why hadn't we heard anything yet about her treatment? It made me think the cancer clinic knew more than what they were telling us. Maybe they didn't think we could handle the truth, and we would be devastated to know the true prognosis. Of course, we would have been, but at least we would have known so we could do and say the things we thought we had a year to do and not be blindsided about how little time we actually did have."

Kim began feeling better for a short time and was able to hold down some of the nutrients without feeling sick. Pure adrenaline kept me going. Sleep for me was an hour here and there, as I felt I should stay awake in case she needed me. I knew she would never wake me if I had fallen asleep, but nothing could burden me concerning her. However, I was also beginning to lose weight myself. Kim began to notice it as well. Her solution was to make me eat in front of her. Her concern for me was still foremost on her mind. She even tried to make me feel better about it by telling me I needed my strength to look after her. Sneaky girl. She knew that would do the trick.

Then she began to feel a lot more pain and had to take morphine tabs to relieve as much of it as possible. Her daily intake of laxatives would have unblocked an elephant. It was always a celebration when she was able to relieve even the slightest amount of gas build-up. Her other pills were for the constant heartburn she felt. It was hard for her to sit up and lying down only exasperated matters. It was killing me seeing her this way. Every time I thought I couldn't take it anymore and was about to break down, she would begin singing our song. For the love of God, she knew I needed to hear those words: "I'll love you until the rivers run still, and the four winds we know blow away." They gave me strength, as they did her, that no matter what, our love would never cease. It was her love that saved me, and now I couldn't save her with mine. But it was still everything we were, and it would carry us through what would come next.

# CHAPTER 23:

# The Season of Darkness and the Winter of Despair

In late November, Kim's pain was getting worse. It had only been ten days since she had been drained of fluid, but now it had returned quicker and more than ever. Her belly was so swollen, it looked like it was going to burst at any moment. She hadn't been able to eat in days, but that didn't stop the vomiting. We again went to the Emergency Department to have her drained. This time, however, the procedure didn't make her feel any better. She was still vomiting and in extreme discomfort. By the following day I knew I needed to get her back to the hospital.

I phoned her GP and explained what was happening. She told us to call an ambulance and she would inform the ER that she was on her way. I called 911 and waited for the ambulance to arrive. Kim was laying on her back, and for some reason, her boy Chedda was sprawled out on her tummy. He seldom bothered her that way, but Kim felt comforted by him being there. The paramedics arrived and wanted to put her on a stretcher, but Kim insisted she would walk down to the ambulance herself. It was strange, but her Chedda wasn't going to let her get up and started hissing at the paramedics, which was so out of character for him. I had to pull him off of her and enclose him in a separate bedroom. We never thought about it at the time, but her boy knew how serious things had become. He was just protecting her and didn't want to let her go .

Once Kim arrived at the hospital, she was admitted immediately. As she had been drained the night before, they needed to find the root cause of what was going on now. That meant more tests, including an ultrasound and a CT scan. These would take place into the early evening, and she would be admitted overnight. To relieve her nausea and prevent any more vomiting, she needed an NG tube put in place.[4] While she was undergoing this procedure, she wanted me to return home and get a few things. As I was about to return with her necessities, a notification on my phone alerted me. It was from Kim with a picture attached of her complete with the tube in her nose and the butterfly bandages holding it in place. She had a half smile on her face and was holding her hand up to say hi. The text read, "Feeling better now. Miss you, my Love."

4    A plastic tube put through the nose, down the throat, and into the stomach to suck out any stomach contents that were making her vomit.

Before I responded I sat on the couch and bawled my eyes out. I returned to the hospital as fast as I could. It was only a ten-minute drive, but my mind was already there. That's what I told the cop who stopped me for speeding, anyway. He graciously let me off with a warning. When I entered Kim's room she had a bottle of juice in front of her. She looked at me and smiled as she picked it up and said, "Watch this," pointing to the NG tube. As she drank from the bottle, the orange juice being consumed began to flow right back up through the tube and into a holding container. "Isn't that amazing?" she said with a laugh. *Little things like that made me be in awe of her attitude.* She told me the surgeon wouldn't have the results until the next morning. She couldn't eat anything solid, but she was able to drink anything she wanted without feeling sick. We just needed to let the nurse know when the NG container was full so it could be replaced. With everything that had transpired to this point, we had learned to appreciate any small blessings that were granted us. So that night we were thankful that she didn't feel uncomfortable anymore and could watch her *Coronation Street*. But more important to her was that she was able to respond by messaging her many friends and thank them for all the love received. It meant a lot to her just to do that.

There was one more thing she did that night; something that as I write about has me in tears. It was rare that Kim would make me promise anything, However, she knew what she was about to ask would take every fibre of strength I had and then some. She was preparing me for what we would learn about her condition in the morning. *I believe now that she already knew. She must have.* She told me that no matter how bad the news, she didn't want to see any tears from me. She wanted us to be strong together. We have been so blessed throughout the years to have each other, and we had to be grateful for that. She grabbed my hands tightly and continued, "I love you so much, baby. Everything will be all right." I couldn't let her down now. I didn't want to make her sad, no matter what, so I told her I would try my hardest.

Her response was, "I know you will, my prince. Now give me a kiss." Damn it. I started crying a little and told her she didn't say anything about not crying now. She wiped away my tears and told me she was confident one day we would be together again forever. Her total faith in that was everything that allowed me to continue on. That night was for holding each other close. I crawled onto her bed and never left her side until the morning light. I never prayed so much in my life. I begged for the same strength and faith she had, but most of all, offering my undying gratitude that a wretch like me was so blessed to have this angel in my life.

The next morning, I leaned over to kiss her good morning. She smiled and said, "Any coffee yet?" In that brief second, it was like the hospital room disappeared. It was just another day, like so many, starting off with a morning kiss and me turning on the coffee. I got up and went down to the lobby to the coffee shop. Waiting for the elevator, she texted me from her room. The doctor had arrived with the results, but she had asked him to return in a few minutes when I was there. We would face whatever it was together. When I was sitting and holding Kim's hand, the doctor relayed what the CT scan revealed. The cancer was now completely covering her small intestine, shutting it off from the rest of her colon. No operation or chemotherapy could help her now. It took everything I had not to break down. I squeezed Kim's hand and got up the courage to ask the question that I didn't want an answer to. "How long?" Very matter-of-factly, he said, "A few days to a week," then left the room. Immediately I looked to Kim and said, "That's bullshit. "Don't you dare believe that, honey." *Did he see her? Was he even in the same room with us? Couldn't he see how much life she still had in her eyes?*

I told Kim that I was calling her GP. I needed to hear it from her. Kim's demeanour never changed. Like I said, I think she already knew and all she said was, "Okay, babe." When her doctor came back to her room, she said the results we were given were unfortunately true, however, the surgeon may have spoken out of turn. He may have been under the impression that Kim wanted to spend her final days at home. If that were the case, indeed her days left would be significantly less. However, if she decided to stay in the hospital's care, mainly because of the NG pump, there was no way of knowing how much time she had. It all depended on her will to live and how long her heart could hold out. It could be weeks, maybe even a month. To go from days to a week, to weeks to a month, our decision was immediate. The finality of it all would be placed on the backburner for now. I knew Kim had the will to stay with me as long as she possibly could. She would never give up her strength. I had been witness to it for almost thirty-four years.

*Strength does not come from physical capacity. It comes from an indomitable will.*

—Mahatma Gandhi

Mahatma must have known her. As for her heart, it was without defect. The pure love held within it could nourish a thousand lifetimes. Don't get me wrong: I was fully aware there would be a day that her strength would become depleted and her heart would not be able to beat anymore. But it was not today. Not tomorrow. Only when it was truly time. Until then we would face each day as a gift.

# CHAPTER 24:

# Her Almighty Grace

The next day she was moved to palliative care. It was basically two hospital rooms joined together, one floor down. One section was for the patient, and the other was for family members. Dividing it was a short hallway with a bathroom in between. The family section was equipped with a long couch, fridge, microwave, coffee maker, and a TV. Her room was a standard hospital one. Both were familiar to us. It was the same room we visited the day we said our goodbyes to my mother and my brother. I hated that room then, but I would cherish it now. It would allow us to have more time and become our home. In a way, being there was a needed relief for Kim. I still can't get my head around everything she had to endure from the time she began to feel ill. It has been ninety-two days from just feeling constipated to where we were now. She had gone through all of the procedures, having constant degrees of pain, constipation, heartburn, vomiting, and sleep deprivation without giving up or uttering one word of complaint or self-pity. *Did I mention how strong she was?*

At least now with the NG pump she didn't feel nauseous anymore. As long as the pump was working, she would be able to be in any position she wanted. But there was something else that needed to be done, and the thought of it made me sick. As she was unable to eat solid foods, her stomach and intestines needed to be shut down so they wouldn't contract anymore. This would stop any hunger pangs. *Oh baby, I'm So Sorry.*

The first morning in our new room, they hooked up an intravenous to supply her with the needed nutrients to keep everything working and her pain medication. Thankfully, they could also administer some type of medication to take care of those hunger "pangs" as well. Now settled and feeling more comfortable, there were important things that needed to be done. First she wrote a list of everything she wanted me to retrieve from home. Second was to make sure her boy Chedda had fresh water and food. Last but not least, she was craving something bubbly. By this time our close family and friends knew what was happening, so before I left on my mission I texted a dear friend to come up and sit with her while I was gone as I wasn't about to leave her alone for one second. I retrieved everything she requested. The last on her list was the main one for me. She could drink anything she wanted, and fortunately, I ran a large grocery store with an assortment of beverages. By the time I got back to the hospital, I had to make three trips out to the car to carry all that I had selected: milk, chocolate milk, orange juice, grape juice, apple juice, root beer, ginger ale, peach juice, tomato juice, a can of her favourite coffee, and of course, something real bubbly – two types of de-alcoholized flavoured champagne.

Kim couldn't stop laughing, "Oh baby, is there anything left at the store?"

With a straight face I looked at her and replied, "If there's anything else you want I'll get that too." She laughed and told me to give her a kiss. It was so nice to hear that much laughter again. It was the first time I had heard it in a long time. That was the sense of relief I was talking about – just being able to laugh again. Her attention now turned to Chedda. She was worried he would get lonely. She asked if I thought it was too much for us to ask our friend to check up on him everyday. The friend in question was the only friend I would ask. She loved our CheddaBalls. I told her that she would probably be offended if we didn't ask. It was such a burden off of Kim. She loved her boy and thought she would ever see him again. Little did she know I wouldn't let that happen.

During the times she was asleep, so much went through my head. There was another coincidence that wasn't lost on me – one that I mentioned to you at the beginning of my story. The only woman figure in my childhood who had showed love had died of stomach cancer. Bloated belly, constipation, and no operation could help. Sound familiar? I had thoughts that something was linking the two together. What my grandma started, Kim was bringing full circle by teaching me what love was, fully and completely. I only just started loving my grandma, but it caused unbelievable sadness in my heart when I lost her. Now however, I had experienced everything love was in all of its splendour and glory. So how could I possibly be prepared for the sorrow and inconsolable sadness to come along with it? I guess Tennyson had it right: "I hold it true, whatever befall I feel it when I sorrow most. Tis better to have loved and lost, then never to have loved at all."

No truer words have ever been said, but they offered me little comfort now as we started the first full day in the death room. But there would be no time for sorrow – only time to continue to love and be loved. We would live each day as if it was the last, all the knowing it would be for one of us very soon. *Oh God, how I wished it was me instead.*

Besides being hooked up to the NG pump, Kim felt pretty good. Any nausea had disappeared and the pain was being managed. Twice daily she would need to have intravenous solutions to supply her with the needed nutrients. Some would also be absorbed into her system by the liquids she consumed. From the get go, we needed to record the amount of anything she drank. This way, the nurses could gauge what should be given to her intravenously. So I had a notebook dedicated to keeping track of even the slightest sip. Equally important was the upkeep of her NG pump. We would need to summon the nurse each time the container was getting full, because if it did, Kim would get violently sick and vomiting would be excruciating for her as a tube now ran down into her stomach. The pump and container was on the wall behind her, so it was my task to keep an eye on it.

She was able to respond to the numerous messages online that day, feeling it would be rude of her if she didn't. She wanted to make sure all the support for her was answered back. It meant a lot that she felt well enough to respond personally. While she was busy doing that, I was busy bringing her a selection of beverages. One minute she would crave something sweet, the next something hot. Whatever passed her lips was as if the world stopped for a brief second, so she could savour each taste, as if she were experiencing it for the very first time. It was one of the very few joys she still had left. And boy oh boy, she was experiencing a lot of joy. The NG container needed to be replaced on a continual basis. Each time after summoning the nurse, she would apologize for being such a bother. *Can you believe that?* Wow! There were times they couldn't come right away, and the container had become completely full. I could tell Kim was getting nauseated, so I would run to the hallway to hurry up the nurse. I was thrown into a panic each time.

I didn't want this happening anymore. Not if I could help it. Now each time they changed the container, I observed them intently, watching where they would take it and where they kept the empty ones. From that night on I would be her NG nurse, unhooking it when it got full and then replacing it. Once the nurses saw I was doing it correctly, they left me to it. She would never feel nauseated again. Not on my watch. Whenever she got tired and needed a nap, I would adjourn to the other room and watch a little TV.

Even though I hadn't slept much, daylight had come quickly. Kim wanted me to unhook the NG so she could use the washroom and continue with the same thing she had done every single morning throughout her entire life: standing in front of the mirror to wash her face, brush her teeth, and apply her lotion, never missing a beat, just like any other day. She would be damned if anything stood in the way of her routine. She always took care of herself. Why would she stop now? *Grace from within never does.*

> *Grace comes into the soul as the morning sun into the world, first a dawning then a light. And at last the sun is in her full and excellent brightness.*
> —Thomas Adams

After I helped her back to bed and re-attached the NG, we could hear a lot of commotion outside the room. I peeked out and saw it was the cafeteria crew delivering breakfast. It was nothing for us to be concerned about as they should pass right by as Kim couldn't eat solids. Nope. They came in with a tray anyway. I know it was their job, but it didn't sit well with me. I ushered the server into the adjoining room and curtly told her not to bring in any more food trays. She told me they had a standing order from the doctor to deliver it, which confused me. Why would her doctor do that? At the time it felt a little churlish to be parading food in front of someone who couldn't eat. I told her if they had to bring it, they should enter through the family room door, at least until I talked to her doctor about it.

Soon after, her doctor visited to check up on her. We went over how she was feeling and were told that her daily blood tests showed she was getting enough nutrients. That was good news. She also told us Kim was allowed to roam the hallways or even go outside. She would probably need the use of a wheelchair, but if she felt good enough, it was permitted. Just as I capped off her NG to go to the washroom, I could do the same when she felt like a little jaunt. The only restriction was the amount of time she could be unhooked. Depending on how long it took for the acids in her stomach to build up, she could have anywhere from twenty to forty minutes before she felt nauseous.

In what seemed like a very dark world at the time, the prospect of being able to go outside was a needed glimmer of light. "We know what's on the agenda today, don't we, honey?" Her doctor said she would be back the next morning to find out how our excursions went. As she was leaving, I followed her into the hallway as I didn't want Kim to hear what I was going to say about the damn food tray. I told her what had happened and questioned if she did indeed requisition it. She apologized that the server had used the door to Kim's room, however she verified that she had ordered it. She told me she was not only concerned for Kim but for me as well. She knew I would need to keep up my strength, so the food was for me covered under the hospital's umbrella.

So what I thought was churlish was anything but. It was a kind gesture from a very caring and compassionate doctor who was also trying to look after me as well. I think deep down I knew there had to be a reason for it. I just couldn't see it at the time. The last thing on my mind was my own well-being. It truly touched me it was on hers.

Upon returning to the room Kim asked, "What's up?" She knew the doctor and I had been discussing something. I told her what we talked about. At first she just laughed and said, "They want you to suffer too, do they?" That's my Kimmie. A good laugh heals a lot of hurts, and we could use as much of that as possible right now. She was touched her doctor was looking out for me. It would be the first time of many that she would make me promise to find a way to show our appreciation to everyone involved in her care. At the time, I was thinking it was their job to look after her, but I promised her just the same. If it meant that much to her, then I knew it had to mean a lot. One day I would be consumed by it. But for now, it was time to get Kim out for some some fresh air.

So with that, I scoured the hospital floor for an available wheelchair. Returning with one, I capped off her NG and helped her to put on her puffy red parka. "Your chariot awaits, my love." As I wheeled her outside the hospital doors, the winter weather couldn't have been more perfect. The air was crisp, and the skies were clear. Kim didn't want to pull up her hood, as she relished the cold on her face, but I made her anyway. I couldn't risk her getting sick. The only thing on my mind was the clock ticking away. I didn't want to push the boundaries of the first extended time she was without the NG, but she couldn't care a less.

She was aglow with the winter's day. I mentioned her cheeks were rosy, so she had to see. I wheeled her to our car in the parking lot so she could see herself in the side mirror. She covered each cheek with her hands before she looked. An unveiling of sorts, I guess. When she removed her hands, her smile was from ear to ear. Something so simple as rosy cheeks was medicine for the soul. She thought it was the perfect time to take a picture of her. Not for us, but to post it on her Facebook page and to let everyone know how much she appreciated their concern. So this is what she had me say along with the picture.

"Kimmie wanted to give everyone a big wave and is thinking of you all. You gave her the strength to make it out and about."

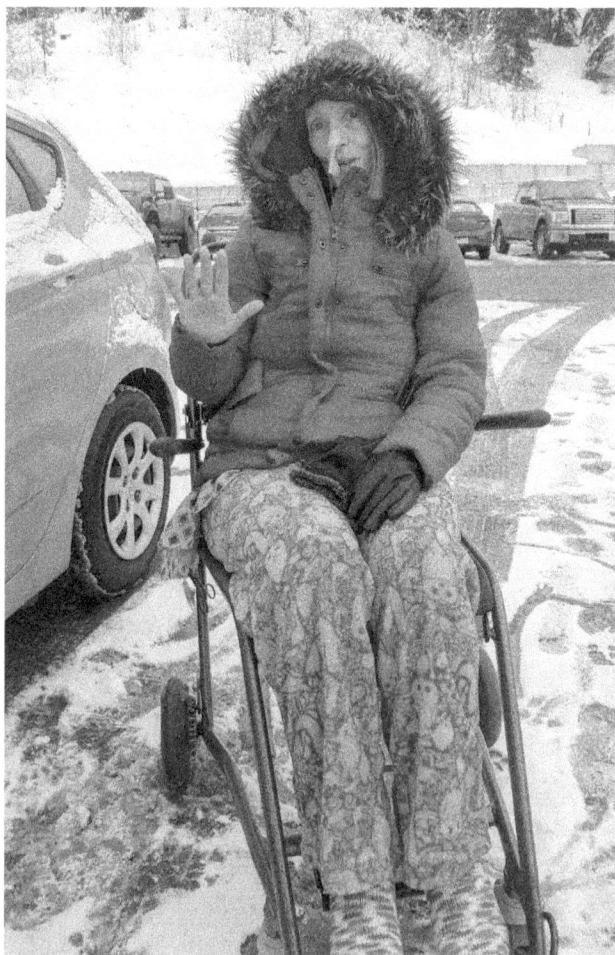

How could you not love this woman? How could I possibly live without her? I didn't want to think about that. She was so strong, and I couldn't imagine there would come a time when she wasn't. In a way, I still believed she could go on forever. Her strength made me a believer, and this belief would help carry me through each and every day. Shortly after posting it, she told me it was time to go back inside. That feeling in her stomach was beginning. If there was such a thing as championship wheelchair races, I would be crowned World Champion. We made it back to her room in no time flat. By the time I got her back on the bed and her NG attached, all we could hear was ping after ping on both our phones. I never had a Facebook account, but my phone was linked to hers. Everything she could read; I could read as well. She had no idea what an inspiration she was. The contents of the messages would surely let her know now. I read each on my phone as she was reading them on hers. For someone who said no tears, she was certainly holding back some of her own. She was touched beyond words and felt blessed. As for me, I was grateful that maybe now she understood what an amazing woman she was; not just to me, but also to everyone who knew her. I know I keep saying it, but when everything is said and done pertaining to life, isn't that the greatest gift for someone to know that they are loved? I will be forever in the debt of those who made sure she knew it. *It gave her an inner peace that her time in this world had meaning to so many others. There is no greater blessing than that.*

One of the private messages was from my daughter, asking if she could call us later. Kim responded in text: "Of course, you can call us anytime. Not like we had anything else planned. Lol." Then she looked at me and asked, "We weren't planning on going bar hopping tonight... were we? Me and my NG could drink anyone under the table now." Wow!

The rest of the day was filled with visitor after visitor: co-workers who were more like family, my brother and sister-in-law, my nephew, They just kept coming. Kim didn't mind. She was delighted they took time out from their busy lives to see her. As I stood back and watched each one spending time visiting, something became very apparent to me. As their visits ended, I saw a shift in each one of their demeanours. What started off as being solemn soon turned to joy and laughter. I'm sure their intentions in visiting Kim were to cheer her up. Don't get me wrong it did, however, it was Kim who turned the tables in that regard.

She would have none of the doom-and-gloom attitude. She made each visitor feel like it was just a visit between good friends and family. It was remarkable to watch.

As each visitor left, I walked them to the elevator. "Strong." "Amazing." "Beautiful." "Graceful." "Unbelievable." These were words I heard on a constant basis and attributes in her that I knew oh so well. It filled me with pride that others could see it. She had always been the light in the darkness. Each time I returned to the room, I told her that she was simply amazing and sealed it with a kiss. She always responded, "*We* are only amazing together, my prince." *Oh, so true.*

The expression "my prince" was new to me. The first time she spoke it was in conjunction with the news of her diagnosis in Vancouver. There were no secrets between us, so I had to ask. I needed to know why now I had become her prince. Her explanation was short and sweet: "Just like a fairy-tale, you've fulfilled all of my dreams in life." *Oh my love. Don't you know it was your magical lips who kissed this frog to turn him into a prince?*

As promised, my daughter called that evening. I put the phone on speaker so both Kim and I could hear. She said now she wished she had come up to see us when she was dealing with her mom. Kim reassured her not to feel guilty over it. At the time, there was no way of knowing it might be her only opportunity. Just the fact she was a part of our lives again meant more than she could possibly know. It was a blessing of which we never could have dreamt.

# CHAPTER 25:

# Crash Course in Nursing, Friends, and the Cheds

Kim had been kept busy all day with visitors and the occasional trips outside. It was time she got some rest. With that, Kim closed her eyes and fell asleep. I gave her a kiss and went to the other room and began watching a little TV. I must have been tired as well and drifted off. All of a sudden, I was awoken by the sound of Kim screaming my name in distress. I ran into her room and found the NG had stopped pumping. She looked at me and said, "I think I'm going to barf!" I quickly rang for the nurse, but by the time she arrived, I had already disconnected the NG and reconnected it, and it was pumping again. Within a minute or two, Kim felt better. The nurse informed us some air must have gotten trapped in the line. "Sometimes with these old pumps it happens."

Again...not on my fucking watch. Once was enough. I already felt devastated I had fallen asleep and hadn't picked up that the pump was silent. From that time on, I needed to be able to hear it and also see it. There was a fold-out chair in one of the common rooms. I wheeled it into hers and placed it right beside her bed with the head of it facing Kim and the wall behind her. I kicked myself for not thinking of it before, but from now on I would be where I was meant to be – always within arms reach of my Kim.

The rest of the day consisted of numerous little getaways from her room, wheeling her through the hospital's different floors, occasionally going outside, and of course visiting with family and friends. Some friends we could not have done without, beginning with Bella. If you were ever stranded on a deserted island and had the choice of having only one friend with you, it would definitely be her. Her exuberance and wit for life was infectious, and she was never partial in who she treated with kindness. She was a lot like Kim in that way. It could only be her with whom we entrusted the care of Kim's small creature. I had given Bella our house key in order to check up on Chedda whenever she could and make sure he was okay and had food in his dish and water in his wine glass. *Yes, wine glass.* Kim didn't like him having to bend over to get water. Also, its transparency allowed Kim to see if there were any kooties in it. Told you already, Chedda was her boy. Always the best for him.

So that night, Bella sent several messages with pictures attached. The first picture was of Chedda on her lap as they both settled in to watch a movie. Can you believe that? We only expected her to feed him, not have a movie date as well. Kim's heart melted. She missed her boy like crazy, but it gave her peace to know he had a surrogate mom who loved him just as much. The second picture however made me have an "uh-oh" moment. I thought for sure Kim would freak. Bella had of course brought movie time snacks for him. Instead of popcorn, he had his mitts in a bag of Temptations – a treat Kim refused to give him because she thought it would dampen his appetite for real food. However, now she was just happy to see him in good hands.

I knew seeing the pictures were bittersweet for Kim. She missed him so much, and I could see it in her eyes. Something had to be done about that. I would have a new mission for the following day. Maybe just maybe, I could convince her doctor to let Kim have a healthy injection of Chedda. After all, it was the family room, and he was family. I had to try anyway. The next morning after her doctor finished visiting, I once again followed her into the hallway. I told her how much it would mean to Kim if she could have a little visitor. She flipped back a page of Kim's chart, wrote something, then looked at me and said, "Done." She actually prescribed letting Chedda come up to see her. She stated it was highly unusual for a cat, but she saw no difference between that and a therapy dog. The nurses would be informed, but she asked to keep it on the down low. I couldn't wait to let Momma know. Returning to her room with a grin from ear to ear, I said, "Bet you can't guess what critter is coming to visit?" She thought for a minute, started smiling, and then said, "Really?" You know the look a child has when they are told they are getting a pet for the first time? Well, that same look was all over her face. She was giddy with delight. I told her we needed to be discreet, but her doctor had prescribed it. So again her response was to make me promise to find a way to show our appreciation to her. *I know, my love, we'll think of something.*

Another visitor coming that day who Kim was looking forward to was Kathleen , a young woman near and dear to Kim's heart. She was the girlfriend of an employee who Kim had worked with and was still working with me. Over a short period of time, they had become very close. Kim loved her take-no-prisoners attitude. Get on her bad side, and oh boy, watch out. However, if you were a friend, she would move mountains for you. She stood five foot nothing but her heart made her ten feet tall. She was working as a care aide at the time in various nursing homes, palliative care units, and at the hospital. Like Bella, she was just a beautiful person. Kim thought of her more like a daughter than a friend.

From the very first visit, she filled a lot of roles for Kimmie and myself. For me, it was the role of an outside care advisor. No matter how caring our nursing staff were, I could never be sure if there wasn't something more that they could be doing or that I could be doing. She knew most of the nurses personally, so she would speak privately to each one. I don't know what was said, but they became even more attentive to Kim's needs now. I could call her 24/7 to ask any questions I had regarding any procedures or if I just needed someone to talk too. As for Kim, Kathleen made her feel so loved every second she was there. She never needed a chair to sit and visit as that wasn't close enough for her. Because of her small stature, there was enough room on Kim's bed, so she would hop on up beside her and stretch out, always holding her close. It made Kim feel so loved to have her there. It also gave her a chance to forget about all the medical crap. It was just time to catch up on everything girlie: You know, gossip and the goings on of everyday life. Most times I would take my leave to go and have a puff and give them privacy to have a talk between BFF's.

So, we were seven days in, and for the most part, Kim still felt pretty good considering. I was making arrangements to get a cat carrier so Chedda could make a visit. Once so excited about it, Kim was now having a few reservations about how he would react. It might be too much for him. *Yes, she was more worried about her cat than any joy it would give her.* I assured her that he'd be okay, reminding her how adaptable the little bugger was. I told her if it was too much for him, I could just take him home again. That night, I asked Bella to come up and sit with Kim so I could make my way to the house to retrieve the boy. It went without a hitch. I passed the nursing station on Kim's floor with grins from the nurses. I entered through the family door and made sure it was tightly closed behind me. I could hear the excitement in Kim's voice. "Did you get him?" As soon as Chedda heard her voice, he began to answer her loudly, trying to push his way out of his concealment. I unzipped the entrance and he bolted out. He started off by exploring the new surroundings, then once settled, he jumped onto Kim's bed. "Oh, my Chedda." Kim began to well up with tears of joy as she had thought she would never see him again. He climbed on to her belly and stretched out with each paw extending around the sides of her. I had never heard him purr so loud. It was one of the most touching things I have ever seen in my life. Anyone who knew Kim, also knew everything about her boy and how much she loved him. She wanted to share her happiness of their reunion. With that, she asked me to take a picture to share online, adding this message: "Kimmie just wanted everyone to know she is comfortable and has the very best furry blanket she could possibly have. Chedda is making sure the nurses are taking good care of his Mommy."

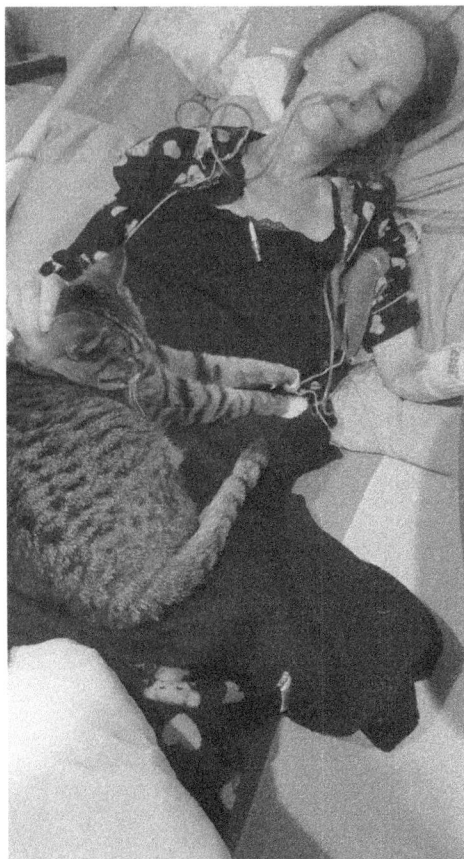

Chedda was there almost all night, but the hospital was awakening, and I needed to get him back home before anyone would be the wiser. The last thing I wanted to happen was anyone complaining. It meant so much to Kim to have him there as many times as we could, but that also would become bittersweet further down the line.

The next few days, we would have more pressing concerns. Kim's tummy was being expanded by the fluid build-up again, and we needed a long-term solution, involving having a permanent tap being placed into her stomach. *What's another hole now, I guess. At least she could be drained as need be.* So another holding container at the end of a tube was stuck in her. Every time I looked at her tummy, my heart would sink. Its mass was so much greater than anytime I had seen previously. I could only imagine how uncomfortable it must have made her. I could only imagine because I never heard her complain about it. I know I keep saying that, but it still amazes me.

CHAPTER 26:

# Blind to the Signs

It was getting harder for her to get up for our excursions to the bathroom. I would have to literally pull her off the bed so her feet could touch the floor, as she couldn't bend her upper torso. Our shuffle to the bathroom had become a little slower. Now she needed more help to sit down on the toilet and then stand. One of the nurses suggested it might be time to have a catheter. *Hell, double not!* As long as she could walk or even crawl, that wouldn't be an option. It was a piece of dignity she would hold onto for as long as possible. I knew she was getting a little weaker, but I would give her all the strength I had to keep her dignity in tact, even if it meant I had to carry her.

Have you ever heard the stories about how someone's adrenaline gave them super strength like lifting up a car when someone was pinned underneath it? Well, Kim was constantly pinned under the weight of her cancer. My adrenaline fuelled by love was carrying as much of that weight as possible. It was everything I was running on. I had very little sleep, but I was seldom tired. I seldom ate, but I was never hungry. Inspired by Kim's strength, those things were inconsequential to me. There were petty things in regards to what Kim was enduring. I needed to be as strong as she was – a truly formidable undertaking.

Daily visitors were always welcomed unless she felt tired. More and more, they would mention to me that Kim's face was looking a little more gaunt. "What are you talking about? She looks fine." They also mentioned I was looking worn out and thin myself. It was something lost on me how Kim and I looked. It had been a slow progression over months. We were with each other constantly, so it wasn't as apparent to us as it would be to someone who saw us occasionally. All I could ever see in her face was beauty and light. The weight she was losing didn't affect that. As for me, I did probably looked more worse for wear than she did. The state of my appearance would only come to have meaning to me when someone else noticed it. Not a visitor, but by Kim herself. She was about to put her foot down. *Uh oh.* "You know what would make me happy, my prince? I want you to go home, have a shower, and get rid of those awful jeans. I want to see you in a brand new pair."

Again her selflessness overwhelmed me. I arranged for someone to come and sit with her, quickly bought the first pair that would fit me, went home, showered, dressed, and returned to the hospital. I couldn't believe how happy she was just to see me in a new pair of pants. "Turn around and show me. Come closer." In arm's reach she extended her hand and pinched my ass. Then with a devilish grin said, "Now that's what I'm talking about." Can you believe this woman? How could I ever go on without her? But I still wouldn't allow myself to think about that. Someway a miracle would happen to keep her with me. But the real miracle was the promise of one more day, one more week, one more month. Where there is great love there are always miracles. It's just how they are perceived. You just have to open your eyes to see them. Kim taught me that everyday.

Maybe not a miracle, but a Godsend did come in the form of another friendship with a young man Kim and I cared for deeply. His name was Colton . Unpretentious and filled with kindness, he had another passion in life that filled his days – his love of playing guitar and singing. When visiting, he'd play her a song of her choosing. Each time, Kim would close her eyes to get lost in the music and be lifted to a different place and time. It was medicine for her spirit.

*Music is well said to be the speech of angels; in fact, nothing among the utterances allowed to man is felt to be so divine. It brings us near to the infinite.*

—Thomas Carlyle

It might seem like a small thing to most, but when you're counting each blessing as she did, being offered the love of a friend through music was nothing small. She felt blessed to know him. More importantly, she knew he would be there for me when she couldn't be. *If only she knew how true that would be, but we're not there yet. Just keep holding on a little bit longer, babe. Then a little bit longer after that.*

By the end of the second week, I had to face the reality that she was weakening. I was beginning to see physical signs of it: swelling in her legs, dry lips from dehydration, one or two bedsores, and the need for a higher dose of pain meds. The only thing not deteriorating was the light in her eyes and the beauty she still possessed. It was because of these I knew she wasn't done yet. I just needed to be more diligent in her care: making sure her legs were propped up or laid flat to promote circulation; always having ice cubes and a cold cloth to hydrate her lips, and making sure she assumed different positions to reduce bedsores.

As for the pain medication, it was half dozen of one, six of the other. It concerned me at times she was either getting too much or not enough. It would be a subject of a heart-to-heart discussion between the two of us. She didn't want to be medicated to the point of euphoria, clouding her reality and building up a resistance to it. So we agreed, we would monitor the dosage intake. She wanted only enough to mask the pain, but still have a clear head. She may not of had control of what was happening to her physically, but she still had full control over her mental capacity. The next day we relayed our wishes to her doctor. She wasn't surprised that we wanted to take more control over some things. She also knew I wouldn't let her suffer through one pang of pain, so the nurses would be informed to rely on our judgement about when her pain meds were needed

I knew some of the nurses didn't see some things the same way we did and were thinking it was selfish of us/me to prolong the inevitable. Walk a mile in our shoes and then tell me that. We were blessed with nurses always popping in just to say hi and asking if we needed anything. Many would say how they were inspired by our love for each other. It filled their hearts with joy to see such commitment. I guess they didn't think I was such a pest after all. A few of them even got together and awarded me with a name badge for going above and beyond in the care of a patient. Kim and I were touched by their kindness. So yet again, it was an opportunity for Kim to remind me we needed to find a way to pay it forward.

*Blessings are more cherished by those who bear the spirit of gratitude.*
—Edmond Mbiaka


She wanted me to keep my eyes open to those little miracles that still surrounded us and not be blinded by everything else going. Without her help, my tunnel vision blinded me to such things most of the time. I could never let myself slow down to see them. I was constantly moving, constantly thinking, trying to stay one step ahead of her needs. I could never do enough. Then there would be moments that would take my breath away. They would break my heart and fill it with such joy at the same time. Out of the blue, Kim asked me to bring her lotion. I thought she wanted to apply some to her hands and face, but as I handed it to her she patted the bed and instructed me to sit facing away from her. "Lift up your shirt, baby." She insisted on placing her hand on my back and began to rub some lotion in. Her weakened state didn't allow her to move her hand much, but she continued with all the strength she had. Tears rolled down my cheeks. I apologized for crying, saying I knew I promised her I wouldn't. She asked me to turn to her. Looking deep into my eyes, she said, "It's okay baby. I love you so, so much. Thank you for everything you've done for me."

My heart stopped. All I could do was to put my head on her lap and bawl my eyes out. She knew she was my everything and wanted to make sure I knew I was hers. It would be the first of many times that I would break down, but never in front of her again. I could feel my heart being ripped apart piece by piece. It was the first time I allowed myself to think about not having her here with me. I made a decision then to resolve that scenario. It was a secret and the only one I would never reveal to her. However, it would give me the peace of mind to do what I needed to do in the present and give Kim every bit of strength I had left. I wouldn't need it anymore after that. I wouldn't need anything."

Besides the little tell-tale signs I mentioned, things continued on the same for the most part. I thought it would be a good time to boost her spirits. Another visit from her boy was in order. However, this time it went differently. We had never seen him react the way he did. He didn't even want to leave his carrier, staying curled up in a ball and shivering at times. *Could he feel how sick his momma was now?* Seeing him distressed made Kim anxious, and she wanted me to take him back home right away. I could see the sadness in her eyes. She knew it would be the last time she would ever see her boy again. She put on a brave face, but I felt Kim's heart break and that was the last thing I ever wanted to happen. *I'm sorry, honey. So very sorry!* On the way back home to drop him off I scolded him, "Why couldn't you be like you were all the other times?" Can you imagine that? I felt so bad for bringing him this time and making Kim sad. Whether it was because of good intentions or not, it would weigh heavily on my heart.

When I was about to return to the hospital I received a text from Kim. Just two words: Strawberry Milkshake. It was her way of letting me know it was okay about Chedda. I stopped at the local fast-food chain to honour her request. Always thinking ahead, I knew it had to be made a certain way. So instead of the drive through I went inside to order. I told them I needed them to blend it thoroughly as I couldn't risk any chunks of strawberries to block her NG tube. I knew it was so much more than just her asking for a shake. It was her way to distract me from how badly I felt and keep my mind on those other little blessings I could still make happen for her.

That night, my phone rang when Kim was sleeping. I knew it was my daughter, but I couldn't understand what she was saying. The excitement in her voice combined with her accent made her words blend together. I had to ask her to slow down and repeat what she had just said. "Dad...Tell Mum to hold on, I'm on my way." She told me a friend had purchased a round-trip ticket so she could be here. She had contacted the airline, and she was to fly out the next day to Vancouver, and from there, she would take the twelve-hour Greyhound ride to us. Her arrival would still be days away, but she was coming. "Wow. Holy crap. Wow." I had no other words to express how much it meant to me, and it would mean the world to Kim. After everything she'd been through recently, she still wanted to be here for us. To think at one point in our lives we had given up any hope of reconnecting with her and now this. Yes, we had learned to cherish the many blessings already bestowed upon us, however this was so much more. It was a gift bestowed by God himself. I always had faith the Creator had a special place in his heart for Kim. This gift just acknowledged that her attributes hadn't gone unnoticed.

I couldn't wait to tell her. I grabbed her hand and said with a smile she must have some friends in high places because they granted a special wish and C was on her way. "No way."

"Yes, my love. She'll be here in the next few days."

She stumbled with her words. "But how? She can't afford it." I told her what had enabled her to get the tickets. She closed her eyes and put her finger up to relay to me that she needed a moment. I knew she was praying, giving thanks for His gift. A single tear ran down her left cheek. Many more ran down mine. Once she finished, she opened her eyes and said, "Come here you." She took some Kleenex and wiped her cheek and then mine. "Come closer." She placed each hand on either side of my face and brought me to her lips saying, "We are blessed, baby. You know that don't you?" I just nodded my head and started crying again. Once we gathered our emotions, I noticed something I hadn't seen in a while – a renewal of light in her eyes and a subtle glow of colour upon her face. The news gave her something to look forward to and rejuvenated her spirit. It couldn't have come at a better time.

The rest of the day, Kim seemed to have more energy. She wanted to do her nails again, a slow dance when moving from the bed to the chair, and there were more than a couple of trips outside. It was like the clock had turned back in time, adding more days to the count down. It was something I pleaded for in my prayers everyday. It was my turn to close my eyes and give thanks.

Her newfound energy was a boost to mine as well. Now whenever I entered her room I would do my silly dance and sing her our daisy song. I knew I could always make her smile with that silly shuffle, sometimes making her laugh out loud, which was my favourite symphony. The next day she wanted to prepare for C's visit and spruce herself up a little. She was unable to take a shower or a bath because of all the holes and tubes in her. She asked if I could find a way so she could at least wash her hair. The nurses and I collaborated to bring a salon to her. Two of our favourite nurses wheeled in a cart with a dry shampoo cap and various combs and brushes. While one was massaging her scalp, the other was helping Kim with her nails. It may as well of been an actual salon with all the gossip being tossed around. They made her feel like a princess.

On December 18, 2017, we had been here for fourteen days. Kim's vitals were still as strong as ever, and there was no sign of any of her organs shutting down. Once they started to go, others things would deteriorate rapidly, so as long as she could pee we were golden. That afternoon she was getting a new bed of sorts ordered by her doctor. It was a five-thousand-dollar air mattress that could be inflated or deflated with a push of a button. Its purpose was to relieve any undue pressure on her body, making her more comfortable and reducing the onset of bedsores.

Even though it appeared she had more strength mentally, her physical strength was lessening. It was harder for her to lift her arms for an extended period of time. Holding on to a cup with her beverage of choice was now becoming more difficult. No problem. I would just hold it for her whenever she needed a drink. She always used a straw as the NG tube covered a section of her mouth. I noticed when she put it past her lips she couldn't close her mouth enough to grasp it, causing the straw to move back and forth. All she needed was a straw that couldn't move, kind of like a sippy bottle. So I cut the length of one just enough to reach the bottom of the Dixie cup and had the flexible part extending from the top rim of it. Using surgical tape, I fastened it to the one edge and it worked like a charm. When Kim was resting, I assembled four or five at a time, so she could have a taped straw on each cup for every change of beverage. Kim thought I was nuts to use so many different ones but I didn't want any beverage contaminating the last. I wanted her to taste 100% of anything she craved.

# CHAPTER 27:

# So Little Time Together

The next morning, we anxiously waited to hear from my daughter when she landed in Vancouver. We were concerned because it was snowing like crazy, and we thought they might have to cancel the Greyhound Bus routes in our direction. C didn't have a choice about how long she was here for. Any time delayed by the snow would take away precious time she would have to visit with us. She had travelled a hell of a long way to get where she was and now we prayed she could make it the rest of the way. She arrived at the airport, and it was snowing there as well. By a strange coincidence, her brother was also in Vancouver, so C decided to travel by car to Kelowna with him and then bus it from there. She messaged us once she had arrived and told us the next bus wasn't scheduled until the following day. We could wait another day. That night, Kim and I passed the time as we always did with a little TV, a little messaging, and a tour of the hospital and its grounds. We usually saved our trips outside for when it was pitch black. She loved looking at the stars. I wish I knew what she was thinking when she gazed at them. All I knew was that one day soon she wouldn't be able to. She must have been thinking the same thing. I couldn't imagine how scared she was. How could I live without her for even one minute? I knew the decision I had made earlier was the right one now. But we still had some time, and our daughter was coming.

In the morning, we were excited about C's pending arrival. Again Kim wanted to spruce herself up a bit – just little things like brushing her hair, curling her eyelashes, and making sure she had a new set of pajamas on. Things that would have been so easy at one time, depleted most of her strength now, but she wanted to look her best for C. It was the same reason she wouldn't allow my daughter's kids to talk to her using the video app. She didn't want them to remember her this way, thinking it would scar them. Anyways, the snow just kept coming down. She was getting concerned for C's safety and wanted me to keep in contact with her as she travelled. I thought I would do better than that. I knew the first bus was already supposed to have arrived, so I went on the website to show her that it had made it safely, and I convinced her that the second one my daughter was on would as well.

*Oh crap!* When I checked I began to be more concerned than Kim was. I didn't let on but I learned the first bus had slid off the highway and flipped over on to its side. Fortunately there wasn't any report of injuries, but just the same, how could I tell her that? Then "ting"; a message popped up on my phone from C. She confirmed the news about the first bus but she was on her way. I was on pins and needles for the next few hours, secretly checking the website for any news. She was supposed to be here already. Then I received a message from her that the bus had been delayed, but she was here and ready to be picked up. I called my brother to meet her and bring her to the hospital.

Kim was overjoyed to see her. C wanted to make sure we knew she was there to help and not just to visit. She wanted to allow me to get some rest and at the same time do whatever Kim needed help with. So I went over all the necessary details with her. She was a second set of eyes, just in case I missed something. I still found it hard to sleep, but at least I knew someone was with her when I was in the other room trying to rest. It did take a little pressure off of me. I also knew this was all about Kim spending time with C. I think C needed that as much as my Kimmie did, so I left them alone as much as I could, even though it would take away some of the time from me. I knew it was the right thing to do.

When Kim was sleeping, it gave me and C some time together. On one occasion, it reminded me of how much I had hurt her. *Once one is damaged, they are always damaged to some degree. She may have been able to forgive, but she would never forget.* One night, when we were sitting together in the adjacent room, I started to break down and reached out to hold her hand. She held it for a while but told me it made her uncomfortable. I told her I understood and was sorry that things couldn't have been different between us. I wished I was the same person back then as I was now. I know she felt bad that it might have hurt my feelings, but it didn't. If there was anyone who could understand how she felt, it was me. There were no hard feelings on my part. *Her visit really had nothing to do with me anyway. It was all about Mum. That was the most important thing.*

The time she spent with her meant the world to Kimmie. It was a blessing not expected, but so much needed. It also gave me a little time to rebuild my strength for things to come. I would need every last ounce of it, plus as much adrenalin as I could muster to carry me through to the end. Beyond that, I had no worries.

It was December 23, and it was time for my daughter to leave. The mood was a sombre one for all of us, but I especially felt sad for Kim. I couldn't imagine how it felt to say the last goodbye to our daughter. It broke my heart that Kimmie had to go through this. I knew it was killing her inside. There was so much sadness in my heart, but I needed to keep as positive about things as Kim was. The last thing I wanted was for her to be sad about me being sad. Her plate was already overflowing.

Now it was just the two of us again. I focused on what needed to be done to make her more comfortable. When I helped Kim to the washroom or move to the wheelchair, it was becoming even more difficult for her to get out of bed. The medication administered to help the swelling in her legs and feet was becoming less effective and both were beginning to swell again. Their weight pushed into the air mattress, and she couldn't get traction to move them. I had to lift and swing them over the edge of the bed every time she got up. Also it was impossible for her to shimmy up the bed when she slipped down on it. The mattress wasn't working out, but I had to make sure that she felt the same way. "This mattress isn't very comfortable, is it?"

She looked at me and said, "No, not for days."

"Oh my God, honey. Why didn't you say something?" She said she didn't want to be a bother. It took so much work on the nurses' behalf to install it in the first place. What could I say? How could I be mad at her? I should have known she wouldn't complain. It was more my fault than it was hers. I should have been more intuitive about the little nuances she displayed. I made her promise to let me know if she ever felt uncomfortable again, no matter how much she thought it would bother anyone. She said, "Okay, honey," and then she pulled her NG tube covering her mouth to the side and told me she had a craving to taste my lips. *Already there, my love. Already there.* As always, she tried to slip me the tongue. My naughty girl.

Okay, time to get rid of that overpriced piece of shit. I phoned her doctor to ask to have it removed. She forwarded a requisition, and the duty nurse informing us it would be scheduled for the next day. They didn't have enough staff at the present time. *We'll just see about that.* By this time, I knew where and when all of our favourite nurses were working and what floor they were on. There were like roommates to us now. So the next time the duty nurse was in the room checking Kim's vitals, I excused myself and said I'd be right back. I proceeded to the other floors of the hospital, scouring the hallways in search of our favourite caregivers. When I found one, I told her the situation and that Kim had been uncomfortable for days. She gave me a hug and told me she would see what she could do. Within thirty minutes of my returning to our room, she entered with a brigade of fellow caregivers to help. She went over and gave Kim shit for not saying how uncomfortable she was. She told her she wasn't just any patient. She was the best patient a nurse could have, and an inspiration to everyone who was caring for her. *Yeah!! What she said!*

Now with the mattress gone, I took the opportunity to crawl up beside her. We held hands and gazed into each other's eyes. I wondered what she was thinking, but was afraid to ask. She broke the silence by telling me she wanted to smell the scent of a lemon again. It was one of her favourite aromas, and the smell had always been therapeutic to her. It was a request I filled with a quick call to my store by asking Colton to bring us as many as he could carry. From that day forward, they would become like smelling salts to her. Each time I would hold a half of a cut-up lemon to her nose, she would close her eyes and lose herself, remembering all the other times she smelled it: standing in our kitchen doing the dishes with lemon-scented soap, downstairs doing the laundry, and at dinner time when I prepared her salad. Something so small had so much meaning now. To this very day, my eyes well up whenever the scent crosses my path.

The removal of the mattress helped somewhat, making it a little easier to get her in and out of bed, but it didn't change the fact her legs and belly were still very heavy. Combined with her lessening strength, it was harder to support her own weight. The trips to the bathroom were becoming more difficult. I also had to keep her body lifted as she stood in front of the mirror to brush her teeth. *Yep. She was still brushing them.* When she was sleeping, I noticed her breathing was becoming more laboured; each inhale now taking longer to exhale. It didn't seem to happen when she was awake, so whenever I thought too much time had elapsed between, I would gently stroke her face to wake her up a little, just so she could catch her breath for a second.

Like running full force in to a brick wall, it began to hit me hard. It was the first time I'd thought that she was very close to running out of time. A request from her the next morning made me realize she knew it too. The one dignity she had left, would now be in question. She suggested it might be time for a catheter. Instead, I offered a compromise. Maybe the distance to the bathroom was getting too much, so how about if I brought the bathroom to her. Through my many strolls down the hospital halls, I noticed quite a few commodes and convinced her to give it a try for a day or two. Then if it were still too much for her, we would have the catheter put in.

There were other signs she was getting very tired of being tired. For the first time, she asked me to hold back some visitors except for the usual suspects. She didn't have the energy. It was as if once C had left, there wasn't anything to look forward to anymore. It took everything she had to get this far. She would never ever give up mentally, but so many things were happening to her physically now. The pain was increasing between the times the meds were administered by the nurses, so I phoned her doctor and asked for a morphine pump. This at least kept her pain on a level keel, but it also made her feel more comfortable to stay in bed. Even using commode became more difficult. It broke me in so many ways, but a requisition was ordered for the catheter. And if that weren't enough, her arms were skin and bone and the IV shunt fell out. Nurse after nurse tried to replace it without success. There had to be something we could do. *Oh God, please let there be a way to make it work.* My prayer was answered. One of Kim's nurses had already set things in motion by getting a hold of the doctor on duty, who ordered for a PICC Line.[5] So now she would have two catheters put in place that day. *Oh my sweet, baby, so much shit to go through. No wonder you were getting tired.*

---

5    A long, flexible tube threaded through a vein in her upper arm until it was in a larger vein in her chest.

CHAPTER 28:

# Things Deteriorate

They kicked me out of the room to give them more room to do the procedures, so I made my way out for a smoke, only to be stopped by one of our nurses. She asked if we could talk privately. *Oh boy, what now?* She it was beautiful to witness how much love Kim and I had for each other, and that I was strong in everything I did for her, and Kim was strong for me. She had never seen a couple so dedicated to each other. She said Kim had told her how proud she was of me. I stood there listening as my tears fell to the floor. *I knew all those things were true with every beat of my heart. It made me cry because no one could possibly know just how special our love was, how much Kim had done for me, and how much pain I put her through. So much time had been wasted because of my damaged soul, but she taught me how to love unconditionally through her love.*

Thanking the nurse for her comments, I knew this wasn't the only reason she wanted to talk to me. She asked me to have a seat. She sat beside me, then seemingly being at a lost for words, she reached into one of her pockets, removed a business card, and handed it to me. "You need to make arrangements for when Kim passes, " she said. On the card was the name and personal phone number of a funeral director. I told her I couldn't think about this right now. I would deal with it when the time comes. She grabbed my hand and told me that it couldn't wait. It wasn't about making funeral arrangements, but rather about what needed to be done to transfer her from the hospital to the funeral home once she passed and to give them the necessary information and permissions. She told me her body could remain in the hospital for days if it wasn't prearranged. Of course, I didn't want that. I thanked her for her candour and concern, reassuring her that I would do it. When I found a moment of spare strength, I knew I would have to make the call, but not yet.

I had been away from Kim too long. They must have finished with the PICC line and catheter by now. *Well, one out of two was done anyway.* Kim delayed the PICC line until I returned, wanting me to be there in case it didn't work. *Oh baby, I should've known. I shouldn't have let them kick me out of the room. It won't happen again, I promise.*

The nurse introduced herself, telling us she specialized in trauma and had worked in the ER for twenty years. Her qualifications made us both a little less nervous, especially when she told us she had never failed to find a vein to use. "This would be a piece of cake," she said with a wink. She explained each procedure, step by step, as she was doing it. Looking at the portable ultrasound monitor in real time, we watched the tube inserted into a small vein in her arm and then being threaded into a larger one inside her chest. She had to make several attempts to get it exactly where it had to be, but she did it. We were so very grateful and relieved. Yes, there was another reminder from Kim to repay kind with kind. This "kind" meant more to me than all the others. Kim would now be able to receive all of her solutions by intravenous again giving her a little more time. *Time. It was still the most important word in the human language to me.*

With so many tubes invading her body now, I was worried it might depress her, but I was wrong. She felt relieved about everything. She could still have her intravenous, and she didn't have to worry about when she needed to pee. She was at peace with the circumstances. The only thing concerning her was how it would affect her occasional wish to go outside. I told her I couldn't see a problem with that. The wheelchair chair had plenty of room to clip another bag to it. She didn't want to wait to find out, asking if we could try it. I felt so bad when I told her maybe we should wait for a bit. She had been without her intravenous for a substantial amount of time. I thought it was for the best to let her rebuild some more strength, at least for a few hours. She was a little disappointed, but she knew I was right. At least now she had something to look forward to again, which boosted her spirits. And so would something else – a visit from Kathleen. She needed a distraction while we waited to go outside and what better one than to catch up on all things girly, so I left them to it.

I went down to the car to inhale as many smokes as I could to calm my nerves. As I was pulling my lighter out from inside my pocket, a card fell to the floor. I knew what it was. I just stared at and took a few deep breaths to find that extra piece of strength. It was time to make the call. My hands were shaking, and I began hyperventilating. I couldn't settle down, but I tapped in the numbers to call. The funeral director answered, but I didn't know how to begin. He knew it was hard for me, so he helped by asking questions, which led me to explain why I was calling. He needed to know the spelling of her name, birthdate, and her doctor's name, but as I answered each one, it was bringing me to tears. I was talking about her not being here, and I couldn't take it anymore. I lost my strength to carry on the conversation. I interrupted him and told him I had to go, saying I would call him back. I sat there bawling my eyes out, hardly able to breathe. I opened the car door and began throwing up over and over again. *Oh God, why was this happening to her?*

The only thing that allowed me regain a little of my composure was the fact we weren't there yet. Kim was still in her room, and I had to get to her. I ran from the car and used the public bathroom downstairs to clean myself up. *Oh God, she's going to know I was crying because my eyes were so red and puffy.* I needed an excuse to tell her if she noticed. I couldn't tell her that I was making arrangements for after she was dead. It made me feel so dirty that I was even doing it. So before she even questioned me about my eyes, I told her I was crying because I was just so relieved and happy the PICC had worked. I think she believed me. She snapped me out of my sadness by reminding me it was almost time to go for a stroll, so I called in the nurse to disconnect her intravenous, something they wouldn't let me do on my own. I was, however, an old pro at everything else needed to get her ready. It took a little longer, but we were set to travel.

This time she had a specific place she wanted us to go – right to the edge of the hospital grounds. The property was elevated, and if you looked straight across, you were able to see our house. It took her a minute to locate It, but when she did, it brought a smile to her face. "We sure lucked out in finding the perfect place, didn't we?" she said.

"We sure did, honey." My heart was breaking for her. It gave me an overwhelming sorrow that she would never have the chance to ever set foot in it again. I know I couldn't either. Not for long, anyway. Then she asked if I would do something for her. "Of course, anything." She said she wanted me to stay there after she was gone. She said it would mean a lot to her knowing me and Chedda would be in the place we all loved so much. It would comfort her to know we would still be there. I couldn't tell her about the decision I had made earlier, so I promised her as long as I was alive, I would do everything in my power to stay there.

With that she wanted another kiss. It was delivered, sealed, and burnt into my memory. She started feeling queasy, so I brought her back up to the room and reconnected the NG. It was encouraging she felt well enough to sit in her chair for a bit while looking at her messages and responding to some, but the events of the day finally caught up to her. She was exhausted. As soon as I helped her to the bed, she drifted off, falling asleep for hours. I could tell at times her dreams were unsettling. So each time instead of waking her, I held a sliced lemon to her nose. It seemed to have the desired effect, calming down her erratic breathing a little. I just hoped it also interrupted any bad thoughts she was having. However, the next morning when she woke up, it became apparent her dreams weren't the only thing bothering her. She was experiencing a lot more pain. The doctor increased her dosage of morphine and shortened the time in between when it was released. I knew it would mean she'd be sleeping a lot more now. I also knew that I wouldn't be. I could sleep when I was dead

> *The mightiest power of death is not that it can make people die, but that it can make the people you left behind want to stop living.*
> —Fredrik Back

From here on in I find myself in search of the right words to express things that are indescribable, but I will try, so bear with me.

# CHAPTER 29:

# The Day I Died

The first day with her increased dosage didn't make her sleep much more, and she was still totally coherent when she was awake. I talked and talked to keep her mind occupied, but she didn't seem to have any fight left. Who could blame her? We were just passing time, until the time came when she passed. It destroys me to say it, but it would be selfish and unfair on my part to expect any more of her. While she was sleeping, I continued with the lemon, warm washcloths to soothe her face, and feet rubs. All the while, I sang to her: "I'll love you until the rivers run still, and four winds we know blow away." I knew she could hear me at times as her eyes wouldn't open, but I could hear her humming along. Those were the times I always kissed her. If she could hear me, maybe she could feel my lips as well. I just wanted her to know that even when she was sleeping, I was there to take care of her, just like she did me all my life.

Then on December 31, she became a little more awake at times and talking more. I had no idea what was happening. It was if she was getting a second wind, wanting to know it January the first yet? I told her not until tomorrow. She said, "Good, I didn't miss it." Was the new strength she was exhibiting about her wanting to make it to the New Year? I didn't know and I didn't care. Whatever the reason, I saw it as a blessing. That afternoon she made me promise to remind her when the New Year arrived. She had so much courage, so much strength, so much love in her heart. *How could this world do without her?*

HAPPY NEW YEAR!!! Yeah, happy fucking New Year. We'd been in the hospital for twenty-eight days, not that I was keeping count. I still didn't know why the marking of the New Year meant so much to her. When she woke up, I leaned in, gave her a kiss, and said, "Happy New Year, my love."

She smiled and said something that would confirm she knew how I was feeling about losing her. "I love you so much. I just wish we could go together." Was this her way of telling me she knew that I couldn't live without her. I was crying uncontrollably, trying to decide if I should tell her or not. Just as I was about to, she continued, "But we have to trust in God. He must have a plan that we don't know about yet." I wish I had the same faith she did, and I wasn't able to tell her I was struggling with mine. All I could say was that I wished for the same thing. She then told me maybe it was for the best. Someone had to look after our boy. She didn't know I had thought about that as well, having plans to give him the best home possible. Bella would make sure he was looked after.

It was quite an emotional morning, and I still didn't know why today was so important to her. I was afraid to ask. I didn't know if I could handle the answer. Throughout the day, she would tell me she was going to rest a little, wanting to build up her strength. *What the hell was she planning? What was so important to her?* All I could do was wait to find out. Whatever it was, she was bound and determined to make it happen. I sat beside her as she slept, thinking of our lives together. As the day turned into night, I sat staring out the window, watching the biggest snowflakes I had ever seen fall from the heavens. Then I felt Kim's hand moving in mine. I looked to her as she opened her eyes. She broke a little smile and mouthed the words, "I love you." Then she turned her head to look out the window. For what must have been ten minutes she didn't say a word, just watching each snowflake fall. Then she casually turned to me and said, "I'm ready."

I took a deep breath and asked, "Ready for what, honey?" She told me she wanted to go outside one last time and feel what 2018 felt like. *This was what meant so much to her.* Even though the logistics of it would be formidable, I had to make it happen. She hadn't been out of bed for days, and there was no way I could lift her from her bed to the wheelchair. It was then I remembered something the nurses had used with her a time or two when they changed her sheets – a rechargeable hoist with a hammock attached to lift her up. There was just a problem or two. They kept it in the basement of the hospital, and it was late with only two nurses covering the floor.

I was worried I couldn't make it happen for her, but I had to. It meant so much to her. She had prepared herself all day long for this. But if I was going to fulfill her wish, I would have to leave her alone for a bit, and that's the last thing I wanted to do. She assured me she would be fine as she was enjoying watching the snowflakes fall. Fortunately one of the nurses on duty was the same one who had the candid talk with me. I begged her to help.

There was no reason to beg. She would make it happen and called downstairs for them bring the hoist up. We slipped the hammock under Kim and attached it to the hook on the hoist. Then with a push of a button, we raised her off the bed and swung her over top of the wheelchair. Once seated, I ran down to the linen room and retrieved a few blankets. She wouldn't have been able to put her parka on, so I used the blankets to tuck her and keep her from getting cold. I disconnected the NG, and off we went. Once we reached the exit doors, all you could see was a blanket of snow. I thought she just wanted to be in the covered area as she watched the sky. Again I was wrong. She wanted to be right in the middle of the parking lot. It was a challenge getting there as the wheelchair wasn't equipped with snow tires, but I pushed it through. It was late, so we had the parking lot to ourselves to choose anywhere she wanted to be. She tilted back her head and closed her eyes. "Right here would be perfect sweetheart."

I didn't want to disturb her thoughts, so I just placed my hands on her shoulders and watched her catch snowflakes with her tongue. She untucked her arms from the blankets and placed her hands on top of mine, asking me to sing our daisy song. I'm sure she could feel my tears dropping from my cheeks. She kept her eyes closed and started humming along to help me get through it. It took every bit of strength I had not to break down before finishing it. She let the snowflakes fall on her for another minute or two, then with a gentle squeeze of her hand on mine, she smiled saying, "Thank You for being my World." I knelt on the snow-covered ground and placed my head on her lap and sobbed painfully. I could feel her hand stroking the top of my head and hear her saying over and over, "It's okay, baby. It's okay."

She said that it was time to head back in. I regained my composure and wheeled her back up to the room. She was totally exhausted, nodding off once or twice during the short distance back up. Getting her situated on the hoist to return her to the bed was a little more difficult, but we managed. I made sure she was settled again and then went and got a warm cloth to wipe the aftermath of the melted snow on her face. She could feel it on her skin, briefly opening her eyes and telling me she had always loved me, then drifting off again. *I wish I knew that was her final goodbye to me. I do now.*

That night her breathing became more laboured again. Anytime she did wake up over the next couple of days, she stared into space. She was aware of her surroundings, but wasn't able to say much. I think a lot of it had to do with the amount of pain medication needed now. It was hard for her to verbalize when she felt more pain, so I had to ask her by looking her straight in the eyes so she could concentrate on what I was asking. "Any pain?" It took all she had to answer me, gritting her teeth together and responding with either: "Yeeess, pain" or "Noooo pain." Each response hurt me to my core, knowing when she did wake, it was usually because of the pain.

I realized she was very close now, and her heart couldn't take much more. So I sat and watched her all night long and throughout the next day, applying warm washcloths, rubbing her feet, and sending text messages to answer some friends about her deteriorating condition. She didn't wake at all the next morning. I didn't know if she would ever again. But she had one more little surprise of strength to give, when Kathleen came up to visit. We hugged and talked quietly for a bit, then Kathleen moved to the side of the bed, and climbed on in to snuggle up to her. I went to other side and brushed her hair with my hand, letting her know Kathleen was here. Did I say a little surprise? Kim all of a sudden bolted up like lightning with a huge smile, looked straight at her, yelled out "WHOA!!!" and then fell back asleep.

We were both taken aback. She was still in there. Kathleen put her arms around her and held her close. I know I said I wouldn't leave her again, but I wanted Kathleen to have the opportunity to say goodbye privately. She had earned it for always being there for us. I know Kim would have wanted that. So I left them for a bit and then returned a while later. I hugged Kathleen goodbye and thanked her for everything. I continued watching each breath she would take. They were becoming so laboured. Hour after hour I watched, not realizing when the day turned to night. The hospital floor was as silent as it could be. I could only hearing Kim's breathing and the sound of the NG pump. I remember looking at the time. She made it to another day. It was January 4, 1:26 a.m.

The next thing I remember was being lightly shaken. It took me a minute to realize I must have nodded off. I was turned away from Kim, but my hand was still reaching back to her. I thought the nurse needed to get in to check her vitals, so I said, "I'm sorry, you have to get in here, don't you?" She grabbed my free hand and said, "I'm so sorry, Lee, but Kim has passed away. **PARDON ME...**

**WHAT**????" She had to repeat it before it sunk in. I turned to Kim and saw her laboured breaths were no more. The nurse was talking, but I had no idea what she was saying. I could only hear a continuous buzz in my ears. The nurse exited, leaving us alone. I sat on the chair holding her hand, continuing to watch her chest and mouth, just in case she started breathing again. *Why did I fall asleep? I should've been there when she took her last breath.* I looked at the time. 1:46 a.m. I had only fallen asleep for twenty fucking minutes.

Did she wait until I nodded off, so I wouldn't witness her dying. It would be just like her, wouldn't it? She didn't want my last memory of her to be that. Even when crossing over into death, she was thinking of me. In that moment, I remember feeling no emotion at all. I was dead and numb. I was outside my body and looked down at just the two of us alone in the room. Whether from shock or something else, I just calmly sat looking at her without a tear. I got up and folded the blankets on my chair, then sat back down again. I searched through my phone to group text everyone that she was gone. I phoned my brother to come and help me with all her belongings and messaged Bella to put our house key in her mailbox so I could get into our house. *There was still something I needed to retrieve there.* I walked down the hallway to the linen closet and retrieved a fresh washcloth and returned with it to our little bathroom. I ran hot water on it, squeezing it out over and over again, making sure it wouldn't be too hot for her. I sat beside her and oh so gently started rubbing it against her face. I would stop and give her a kiss, then another, just to make sure this was real and not a fairy tale where she could be awoken with just a kiss from her prince. *It wasn't working.*

I took the washcloth, put it on her night table, and got up to go to the other room to recover something I had hid in our gym bag. *It was a little secret I haven't told you about yet.* Before Kim had entered the hospital, she still had a supply of morphine tabs. We brought them with us when she was first brought in by the ambulance, just in case she needed them. I started taking a few every once in a while, whenever I felt emotionally drained, to get me through. But as time went on, I knew they would serve another purpose. I hadn't taken any for a couple of weeks, saving as many as I could just for a night like this. I brought them back and sat beside Kim, holding her hand and taking one at time until the container was empty. I don't recall how many I took, but I knew there was enough to ease myself into the next step I had planned. I got up and gave Kim one last kiss and told her. "Don't get too far ahead of me, my love. I'll be right behind you." Then some sort of intense feeling overtook me, and I needed to get the hell out of there as quick as I could. I couldn't stand seeing Kimmie's lifeless body anymore, so I waited in the adjoining room until my brother arrived. We packed everything up and brought it down to Kim's car. I went back one last time to see if we had missed anything. I don't know why, but I still couldn't look at her. All I knew was I needed to hurry up. Time was wasting. *I'd left her alone for too long already.*

I met my brother outside, and he insisted we go up and see my nephew who was working at a 24/7 coffee shop. I only agreed out of gratitude that he had come to help me. I told him I would meet him there after I went and got the house key from Bella's place. It was only a few blocks from the hospital, but even if it had been right next door, I still would have been lost. For the life of me, I couldn't find it. I'd been there numerous times, but nothing looked familiar. It could have been the morphine kicking in, but I lost track of why I was even driving. I don't even remember stopping when I did find it. The next thing I knew was parked beside my brother's car at the coffee shop and getting out to embrace my nephew. His mouth was moving, but I couldn't hear him over the continuous buzzing sound I heard the moment I realized my world was gone.

I was just focused on getting home as there was something I desperately needed to get and something I needed to do after retrieving them. On the way, I remember taking lip balm that she always had in her car's cubby-hole and pressing it hard against my lips. I was craving to taste where hers had been. I started feeling really relaxed as I parked her car in our garage. Sitting and trying to focus on the task at hand, I slapped my face to shake myself out of it. Then I slowly made my way up the stairs, sitting once in a while to give me more strength to make it the rest of the way up. I felt so weak.

I entered the house and went directly to where we fed Chedda and filled his bowl with food and then went to fill his glass with fresh water. By the time I returned, Chedda was already eating from his dish. I bent down and patted his head, telling him that Mommy loved him so much and not to worry, he'd have a good home to go to. Then I stood up and went to get what I had returned home for. I opened the jewellery box and gently pulled out her wedding bands and kissed each one. Then enclosing them inside my fist, I went and stood in front of our window that overlooked the downtown bridge with different colour lights illuminating its arches. It looked so beautiful. I stared for a moment and then looked up higher to get one last look at the hospital where I had left Kim. Then I said out loud, "It's a perfect night for a walk along the bridge."

I took a deep breath and made my way to the front door, still grasping her rings as tightly as I could. Just before I reached it, I heard a light knock and someone opening it to enter. It was Colton with tears streaming down his face. Immediately it triggered something in me. I cried out, "OH MY GOD, SHE'S GONE! OH MY GOD!" We embraced each other so hard, I found it hard to breathe, but I couldn't let go of him, crying like never before. I started feeling weak and I needed to sit down. If he wasn't holding me, I would have found myself on the floor curled up at his feet. We made our way to the room Kim and I always sat in. I took my usual seat, Colton took hers. We didn't say much as there was nothing that could be said. I knew he was at a lost for words as I was. There are no words.

He noticed I was holding something in my enclosed fist and asked me what it was. I raised it so he could see, revealing Kimmie's wedding bands. Without hesitation he unfastened the chain he wore that carried his St. Christopher's medal. He got up and approached me reaching down for the bands. He took them from me and threaded the chain through them. He went behind me to fasten the chain around my neck. *Now the symbols of our love were hanging down close to where my heart was.* I raised them to kiss each one. Underneath the tears that began to flow again, I got up to embrace him, telling him how much his kindness meant to me. The morphine along with my total exhaustion from the last four months hit me like a brick wall. Whether it was for ten minutes, or forever, all I wanted to do was sleep. I would have preferred the latter, but now, I was even too tired to move to do anything about it. I knew it wasn't a sign from Kimmie that Colton showed up when he did, but it did make me question if it was one from God on her behalf. I knew I couldn't think about anything right then. I didn't have the energy to, so I thanked Colton for everything and said I needed to lie down. We embraced once more and he left.

I stood in the living room feeling lost, seeing daylight creeping in through the window. The lights on the bridge were no longer visible. Not so beautiful anymore. I dropped to my knees beside the couch. Her pillow and blanket were still there from when we had used it as our bed. I pulled the blanket off and wrapped it around myself, wanting to feel where her body had been. I grabbed her pillow with both my hands and brought it to my face, squeezing it over and over, releasing her encapsulated scent held within the fabric. She became alive again in that moment. I could smell her there. I made sure not to touch it with anything else, or for too long, not wanting to soil it with my own aroma.

My chin fell to my chest, no longer able to carry the weight of my thoughts. My eyes were no longer able to hold back the dam of burning tears carving out their path down my cheeks and pooling into an ocean of despair. *I was nobody. All that I was is with her now.*

> *There is a sacredness in tears. They are not the mark of weakness, but of power. They speak more eloquently than ten thousand tongues. They are the messengers of overwhelming grief, of deep contrition, and of unspeakable love.*
>
> —Washington Irving

I don't remember falling asleep, but the next thing I knew I was awoken by my phone alarm, permanently set at 8:00 a.m. as a reminder when the coffee shop opened up in the hospital. I couldn't get off the floor to turn it off. Every bone in my body ached as I tried to move. It was hard to breathe. My chest felt like it was going to cave in and I was coughing uncontrollably. Thirty days in the hospital and I never had a sniffle. Now within a few hours, every cold, every flu I had fought off was exacting its revenge on me. I had never felt this sick in my life. I crawled up to the couch so I could have a soft place to die. I thought God had answered my prayers. He knew I couldn't live without her. *THANK YOU.* It was nothing in comparison to what she had suffered, but I wanted to hurt and feel the pain, wondering if I could be as strong she was. I wanted it to overtake me. I was at peace to leave this world. I begged God to let it happen."

CHAPTER 30:

# Not Done With Me Yet

Then a call I received a short time later, negated any wishes I might have had, making me realize I couldn't give in just yet. The funeral director had called to reassure me that Kimmie was no longer at the hospital. She was in his care now, and he wanted to set a time to discuss her "final arrangements". I needed to do this for her. She would expect me to. *Maybe that was the reason I didn't take that final walk. I wasn't finished looking after her yet. It's all I ever wanted to do my entire life was to take care of her, like she always had taken care of me.*

I made an appointment and curled back up on the couch with thoughts of what needed to be done the next day. I couldn't get the image of her being cremated out of my head. Ashes to ashes, dust to dust. *Oh Father, give me strength one last time.*

The rest of the day was somewhat of a blur. I remember numerous calls that I left unanswered. I didn't want to talk or respond to anybody. This was my sadness, my pain, and my grief. I was always selfish when it came to her, so why would this be any different? No one could possibly know how much we loved each other and the sacrifices she made for me. She was not just someone I loved, but the only one I had ever loved. She was the only one that had ever loved me. There was no choice about if I should go on or not. Emotionally I had already died with her. All I needed to do now was to have a little more patience for the rest of me to join her. *Perhaps after my morning appointment.*

That night I was about to feel another type of sick. The funeral home needed me to bring some necessary items. I took out her driver's license, SIN card, and birth certificate from her wallet. The picture on her license was staring up at me. I gently removed it from the clear plastic sheath, never taking my eyes off of her. I ran to the bathroom and knelt on the floor in front of the toilet to throw up. I remembered her doing the same thing over and over again. The bottle of cleaner she cleaned the bowl with was still beside it on the floor. I picked it up and hurled it against the wall above the bathtub. Its contents splattered everywhere. *WHY DID SHE HAVE TO GO THROUGH THIS???*

I wasn't hurting for myself but rather for everything she had to endure. I was having thoughts of missing my appointment at the funeral home so I could stop the pain now, but I knew the quicker I took care of the last thing I needed to do for her, the quicker I could take care of myself. I got up and washed my face to get ready to leave. I thought about changing my clothes, but I couldn't bring myself to get them out of our bedroom. There are so many memories of her inside those four walls. I remembered I had a clean pair of socks in the gym bag I brought back from the hospital. I was still wearing the hospital sock slippers that had been on my feet for the past thirty-one days. I sat down to remove them. Their fabric had implanted into the skin on the soles of my feet. It was a result of walking the miles and miles of hospital corridors. With one quick motion, I pulled them off and layers of skin were taken with them. It stripped away each day I had walked those tiles. The pain it caused was miniscule to what I was already feeling. There would be nothing that could strip that away. *Well, there was one thing, but first things first.*

I made my way downtown and parked outside of the funeral home. I prayed for the strength to go inside. I was already breaking down, knowing her body was on the premises, but I needed to follow through no matter how much it pained me. Her body was a vessel that held her soul and everything she was, but it was empty of those now. I knew that, but it didn't make it any easier.

The funeral director, Bill, treated me with the utmost compassion one could expect. Kim wanted a basic cremation without a service. She didn't want anyone to make a fuss over her. Exactly the same way she felt when she was alive. Bill filled out all the paperwork needed and applied for her Death Benefit on my behalf. Kim didn't have life insurance, feeling we would never need it. We always thought we would go together, or I would go first. I guess we thought wrong. I told him the last few months had been a hit on our savings. He told me there was no concern in paying him right away. I could wait until the death benefit arrived. Depending how much Kim had contributed to the Canadian Pension Plan, I could receive up to $2500. That's all good when said and done, however that would still mean I would owe $2400. Kim and I had always prided ourselves in not owing anything to anybody. Everything was delaying my decision to end my pain. I couldn't possibly leave behind any debt, especially where Kim was concerned. It would dishonour all that we'd accomplished. I could never let that happen. Oh shit. That meant I would have to wait to do her taxes as well. *I wasn't afraid of death anymore, but living was the ultimate suffering now.*

With everything taken care of at the funeral home for now, I went home to start my wait. That afternoon, Kim's doctor phoned to see how I was doing, knowing Kim's passing was devastating for me. As we talked, it became apparent to her that I was quite sick. She insisted that I go to my doctor and get checked out. I told her I didn't have one." She said she wasn't taking on any new patients but insisted on making an exception in my case. She had become very fond of Kim and I. She stood firm that I needed to come in and see her, saying there might be something else happening. *What else could it be?*

Now I was a little curious, so I reluctantly agreed to see her that afternoon. Once alone in her office I thanked her for everything she did for us. She took my hand, and said, "Throughout all my years in practice, I have never seen such devotion between a couple. I would often think of you at night when I was at home. It made me smile to witness such a love. You should be very proud of everything you did for her, and I'm so sorry it turned out this way." I listened with a stream of tears. I didn't know it at the time, but that was the reason she insisted I come in to see her. She wasn't concerned at all about my cold, it was my heart. When someone loves each other as much as we did, it can cause a very serious temporary condition – BHS or Broken Heart Syndrome.[6] *Okay, I could her concern now.*

It was the first time in my life I had wished for a positive diagnosis. There would be nothing more fitting for me to die of a broken heart. *Wouldn't that be the ultimate testament to our love?* It would also solve what was holding me back from doing myself in. My policy wouldn't cover suicide, but it did cover death by natural causes. I would leave enough money behind to cover both of our final expenses. It gave me hope that the universe was finally listening. She ordered a blood test and prescribed some antibiotics for my cold. She wouldn't have the results back for a day or two, but she said she would check up on me until then.

---

6    Broken heart syndrome is a real temporary heart condition often brought on by stressful situations such as the death of a loved one. The syndrome causes a disruption of your heart's normal pumping function in one area of it. If gone untreated, it can lead to serious damage and in some cases death.

It made me think briefly of how much she had always been there for my Kimmie. It wasn't lost on me how much both Kim and I appreciated her compassion. It reminded me of the promise I'd made to Kim to return kind with kind. At the time, I couldn't think of anything to do. My selfish grief wouldn't allow me. I was too lost in my own pain. But soon the first part of the question I had concerning why the universe was keeping me here would be answered. A thought in passing about a promise made would soon be the only thing I could think about. It would take a succession of events beginning with the reading of all the messages that had piled up on my phone over the last three days. "

## CHAPTER 31:

# Remembering the Promise

There were so many heartfelt condolences from everyone that knew her, all relaying how Kim had made them feel; how her sense of humour brightened their day; how strong she was; how beautiful she was inside and out. I read them over and over, each one making me cry, but no matter how heartfelt they were, they still left me feeling empty. Yes, she was all those things, but she was so much more. But they couldn't have known the depth of her grace. Only I knew what she sacrificed in life to stay true to herself and her unconditional love for me. I needed the world to know just how special she really was. I owed that to her. So instead of responding to individual messages, I began to write things and sharing them on her Facebook page. It was my way of talking to her and letting her know how much I loved her and in turn letting the world know.

**Trigger Warning**: What follows are things I posted, giving insight to the progression of my grieving process. It may hit a little to close to home for some. Each post is in chronological progression.

*Thirty-four years ago I met a girl. It would become the most important day of my life. The day I asked her to be my wife. Two complete strangers taking a chance on love. For those knowing my Kimmie, they understand why I was so captivated by her. Through her eyes and smile you could see her genuine heart filled with love for all who needed it. The battles in life would never dent her spirit, with the hardest battle just ending. Through it all, she was never concerned for herself but only others. To the nurses she would apologize she had to rely on them for her care. To me, that we didn't have more time together. Not once did she pity herself. In her strength she held on to give me time to let her go. I would've never of had enough time. I will never have enough tears to shed. I must keep her alive in the hearts of others as she is in mine. I will love no other until we meet again and renew ours. No matter where,*

*no matter when, I will find that vacant seat beside her once again, and we will sing*
*our song as we exchange our daisies. I love you. I love you more.*

The responses I received were emotionally overwhelming, It became cathartic for me that others could tell how much I loved her, while also giving hope that love like ours really existed in this world. I guess I will have more time to write to her. The results came back about my heart: Negative for any damage. *How could that be?* Kim was no longer here to talk to, and it was killing me. I know it doesn't make any sense, but just as we had shared everything with each other, I had to share my grief with her as well, so I just continued writing to her as if she could hear my words..

# REFLECTIONS IN THE DARK

My body has become an empty shell. Carrying only the weight that has been cast upon its shoulders. I can not sustain its density. My foundation is no longer made of stone. It has been hammered to dust. Where my feet once had a path to follow, they have now lost their direction, standings still in time. My eyes have been blinded from the scorching of a thousand suns, losing any vision to the light. The scars of darkness have fallen upon their lids. They are blistered by sorrow with rivers of pus continuously flowing down the crevices of my face. The atmosphere that surrounds me has become stagnant, leaving the taste of putridness in my mouth. It strangles the air I breathe. My chest heaves desperately trying to suck in any oxygen of hope. I am choking. My life's blood has become calcified. The heart that once pumped it through my veins has been brutalized, stabbed, and butchered beyond recognition. Its resuscitation has left it in the need of life support, only to be plugged into life's socket of despair. The white noise of its current humming in my ears is deafening! My human frame has lost its stature. It does not rise to normality. Its structure has been buckled by a ferocious hurricane. The calm before the storm has come and gone. All that held me together lays as waste upon the ground. Standing alone in its ruin. My mind held captive to ruminate the aftermath. "Oh, my Kimmie. You were the foundation of my life. Built of your unconditional love. I am so sorry I couldn't shelter you from the storm."
Then these...

# THE KISS

You do not scare me anymore. I have left my fears of you in the past. I will face you head on, eyes wide open so I can see the dark. I will not hide from you. Everyone hates you, but I will run to your arms. Lock your embrace around me as you did with her. I will not war with you as she did. Cloak your blanket around me to give me comfort. I will not cry that you have come. I cry now because you haven't. Invite me into your house as I'd rather not come uninvited. I am ready. You have prepared me well. My eyes have reflections of you in their stare already. My heart carries the weight of you in its chambers. You already took my soul and now hold it captive. Take the rest of what I have left. Take me. I am ready to walk with you and call you friend. Put your lips on mine as you did with her. Let it take my breath away. Let me share one last thing with her. **Let me feel the kiss.**

# THE BLINDS

In the morning...
The light searches through the blinds to find the beauty of your smile, the rays scour every darkened place not knowing all the while that no matter where it shines today, you are no where to be found, Except inside the prisms of my tears that lie upon the ground. As it stops its daily search and leaves the heavenly sky, it knows it will never shine as bright as the light between you and I.

In the night...
The darkness searches through the blinds to find the beauty of your form, searching through the silhouettes of things that once had been worn. It has no way of knowing you are nowhere to be found, except in the beating of my aching heart and the darkness of its sound.

In the window...
My eyes keep searching through the blinds to find you in some way, All I see are frequent passer-by's starting off their living day. And even though I can't find you, I hope in my escape, a glimpse of you may be hiding, inside a similar shape.

In the end...
For now, I must stop searching the images in the blinds. For all the things I crave to see, are only tricks of the heart and mind.

# THE SECOND CUP

The second cup on the counter is not as empty as it seems. I place it there each morning, with a little bit of cream. No need for sugar today, my love, is all that you would say. I have in you all the sweetness I need to make it through my day. The second cup on the counter is not as empty as it seems. It holds the words you would say to me, and all they have come to mean. A reminder of the little things that my heart will still allow are not so little anymore, not so little now. Every time you would call me back to steal a second kiss. This is for the first one, my dear, just in case it missed. And as I would turn to start my day heading towards the door, I offer the words, "I love you, hon." You reply, "I love you more." It's all the times I would tell a joke, as lame as lame could be. Your laughter would still fill the air, just because it came from me. It's all these things I remember now, and what they've come to mean, like the second cup on the counter, with a little bit of cream.

# SHADOW

I saw her shadow beside me dancing in the light, no cares of what's in front of her and not afraid of the cold dark night. She follows at my heels, with memories of days gone past, searching for that sunlight to make it forever last. And even as the clouds would come, weighing heavy with its rain, your shadow remains beside me to shelter me from this pain. And as the sun sets in the sky, and your shadow fades away, all I need to do is close my eyes to make your memory stay. And as the tears will forever flow, I feel your fingers as if to trace, every drop of sadness that has fallen from my face. So now I wait without you, with promises of things to be, a day that can't come soon enough when once again you'll be with me. So this I promise, my darling love, from the depths of my aching heart. I will hold on until the blessed day, when we'll never have to part. And even though you have left this world, your spirit still remains. It's in every ray of sunshine and every drop of rain. It's in all the friends you left behind, and the memories that they share. It's in every time silence is broken by the laughter in the air. It's in the shadow that follows me, as I dance across the floor. It's in the whisper of the words I pray to hear: "I love you more. I love you more."

Then a darker moment surfaced by a marking on a calendar. I had been without her for thirty days. It still felt like it was yesterday. The words I shared still hold true.

## WHERE I SEE GRIEF AT THE MOMENT

So today marks a month without her. 44,460 minutes and counting. People ask, "How you doing? A day at a time, eh?" When you grieve, it's not living day to day, but from moment to moment. The brain is truly miraculous. Everything you see, smell, hear, and taste over a lifetime is stored and then attaches an emotional response to each of those things. They are imprinted in our psyche and the way we see the world. When you grieve a loss, your mind becomes obsessed in searching every one of its senses. Everyday life becomes redundant, consumed by memories. Happy, sad, it doesn't matter. They are all a part of what you lost.

The last thirty-four years, Kim and I were inseparable. It didn't matter what the world laid at our doorstep, we overcame the bad times and rejoiced in the good. The one and only thing remaining constant was that we shared it together. Together doesn't exist anymore. So that's when the brain kicks in. It doesn't want to accept the truth. It starts living in the past, because the past is your reality. There is nothing else that you know. There is nothing else you want to know. Everything you lived and loved for has been taken away. They say there are four stages of grief: Denial, Anger, Depression, and Acceptance.

Let's see where I am at shall we?" Denial. I can't deny that I face life without her now. Anger. I'm angry it wasn't me instead. Bargaining. I have nothing left to bargain for. Acceptance. Nope, will never feel that one. Depression. That one I have. We all experience grief in our own way. There are no stages. It is something we offer up to give hope that things will get better with time, but time ceases, holding you captive. Now I have one constant left in my life. Time I can't share with Kim. Memories are all I have left. Why would I ever want to stop thinking of her? Even when sadness surrounded us, I pray to remember those moments as well. The moment when she insisted on rubbing lotion on my back when she barely had the strength to lift her arm. Or every time we kissed around the NG tube. It's all the times we would sing our song to say goodbye.

Are these happy or sad moments? A mixture of both? It's hard to distinguish happy and sad memories when it comes to grieving. Happy memories turn into sad ones because of what you had and lost. Sad memories, however, are greedy and don't turn into happy ones. But you can't have one without the other. Grief is all encompassing and unforgiving. Time will only magnify its existence. Once you realize that fact, you can take ownership of it. It will belong to you for the rest of your life. You don't get over grief. You become a victim to it. You become a Survivor. So don't ask me how I am doing. Ask me how I am surviving, and I will tell you the truth: Moment by moment. Second by second.

That's all I was doing – surviving from day to day. No matter what I did or wrote, it would never be enough to honour her memory or express the grief I was feeling.

Besides that, a reminder how cruel the world would come in the mail that day. Kim's death benefit had arrived: nine hundred, sixty-seven dollars, and twenty-nine cents.

It was a far cry from the twenty-five hundred that was suggested. She worked so hard everyday, and this was her reward. It was a fucking disgrace. It did however remind me of the debt I still owed. The funeral director had been so gracious in delaying any payment. I immediately went downtown and gave it all to the funeral home. Everything else about my financial situation remained the same. I knew I had to get back to work so I could pay off the remainder. I knew I wasn't ready to return, but now I had no choice. I needed to pay off the debt as soon as possible, and then I could finally have everlasting peace. So I had them put me back on the schedule for the following week. As I waited, I didn't do any more writing. Like I said, my letters and poems couldn't do her justice. The next couple of days I found myself just reflecting on all the messages and my writings and re-living our stay in the hospital day by day. It was as if I was looking for something. I felt it gnawing at the pit of my stomach, but I had no clue what it was. That is, until I heard a story being related on the news. It was about a home-less man who received a kind act from a stranger involving a substantial amount of money, but it didn't end there. Upon receiving it, he immediately went to a store to buy numerous blankets and pillows, but only one set was for him. He distributed the rest at the homeless shelter. When the reporter asked him why he spent all his money on others, his response was: "I'm repaying kind with kind." And there it was. I screamed out, "Oh, my God. How could I have forgotten?"

CHAPTER 32:

# All About the Daisies

The single wish Kim had me repeat over and over so I wouldn't forget was her desire for me to pay kind with kind. It awakened a new sense of purpose in me to do one last thing for her; the one she wanted more than anything and to show how grateful we were. From that moment on, I was consumed in making it happen. But there were just so many to repay on an individual basis. *Think, Lee. Think.* I went over every person who showed us kindness, and besides those close to us, for the most part they all had a common thread. They were all her caregivers and the hospital that allowed us to have more time together. There had to be a way to pay them back all at once. I racked my brain for anything I could do, but I couldn't think of a single thing that would express the magnitude of our appreciation. As if it was meant to be, I started singing our daisy song, just as I do each and everyday. Then it hit me. I had a perfect way to give tribute to Kim and in turn do something significant for her caregivers and the hospital.

*It was all about the daises. A symbol of our love.*

In no time I had formulated an idea. I wrote down every detail of my plan, never really being sure if it could be carried out. Ironically it relied on the kindness of others. It could be shut down before it even got started, so I needed a trusted second opinion, and there was no one better to ask than our Bella. After all, I would need her help as well to carry it out. She thought it was an amazing idea. The only obstacle now was convincing my boss. A phone call from him revealed he'd already been talking to Bella. She had mentioned what I wanted to do, and before I got a chance to go into any further detail, he reminded me he was much more than a businessman. He was our big-hearted friend. He told me I had no reason to explain it further and any resources he had were mine. Anything I needed to do, he would be behind me 100%. Remember when I told you there would come a time I would be forever in his debt. Well this was it. It was the first time I felt I had a way I could honour Kim properly, and he was allowing me to do it. This would be a kind hard to repay.

I instantly had more energy, with so much to do in so little time. I guess you're wondering what it was all about. Because of our song's promise to give her a daisy a day, I thought how special it would be if an entire community could give her one as well. This was the core of the campaign I was about to execute. By the kindness of my boss, I would have the platform to make it happen. Our store would hold a charity event for the local hospital. It would be a "GIVE YOU A DAISY MEMORIAL CAMPAIGN". All proceeds would be donated to the Oncology Department on Kim's behalf to provide the monetary support they needed in dealing with cancer patients. Maybe they could even purchase a new NG pump or two, depending on how much we raised.

There were so many factors that were needed to make it a success. As I said, I had very little time as I wanted it to correspond with the week of our thirty-fourth wedding anniversary. First I reached out to Kim's co-workers to design and print paper daisies. Then I had to get the word out as soon as possible, only having a little over two weeks. I began posting about the campaign everywhere, explaining what it was all about. Then something truly amazing happened. What started as a snowball effect, turned into an avalanche of kindness. Once word had gotten out, I had an influx of personal messages all wanting to support the cause in any way they could.

Owners of local businesses offered goods and services for our prize draw. We had to stop updating our website because we couldn't keep up with them all – everything from half-day guided fishing trips to gift certificates for services. Kim would have been so humbled her story struck a chord with so many, but it was just the beginning. Within a week, our prize list grew to more than forty-two things being donated. *If that doesn't give you faith in humanity, I don't know what will.* Something has to be said about living in a small community. One business even donated a twenty-foot-long banner designed by Bella's daughter to hang at the front of the store. *It was the same print shop that made our "I Love You" banner thirty-four years earlier.* It was special because it had my favourite picture of Kim embossed in one corner of it. The paper daisies were designed and ready to go with a border print containing a beautiful single daisy inside of it. The colour of the border was one that represented Kim's type of cancer. It was finished off with a script saying, "Thank you from Kim." It was absolutely perfect.

Everything was falling into place. Colton even offered to play some songs outside the store in the mall at the end of the campaign. And get this, as his gift to Kim, he learned our daisy song. I didn't think I could be there when he played it, but I'd try. There was just one more thing I had to do. The local paper wanted to do a story about us to let everyone know about the campaign. I sent a synopsis to the reporter of what led to its creation. I explained all about the promise I made to the love of my life and the final wish she had asked me to fulfill for her. The reporter wanted to include some sort of a picture with it. I told her about the banner that was already hanging in the store and maybe that would be fitting. She came up to the store to snap a picture, wanting me underneath it, looking up at Kimmie.

You already know how I feel about my picture being taken, but this was one time I would make an exception. This was for Kim. I would do anything for her. Everything was set. The campaign would run from Sunday the fourth to Saturday the tenth. It would end one day after what would have been our thirty-fourth wedding anniversary. I was so nervous. I had no idea what to expect or how many daisies we would need. I just hoped we could sell the 500 the girls had already made. They told me they were on stand by if we needed to print more, and all I needed to do was call down, and they could have them ready for me in a couple of hours. *Wouldn't it be so wonderful if we needed more? Oh God, please let this be a success. I was just hoping I wouldn't embarrass Kim's memory.*

The Friday before the campaign I was making sure everything was in place at the store. I received a message from my nephew asking if I had seen the newspaper yet. When I told him I hadn't, he replied, "You better go and get one. Dude, your story is the only thing on the front page." *No way, really?* I hung up and ran down to the bookstore in the mall to buy one. Okay, all they had. I couldn't believe it. The picture the reporter had taken covered the width of the top of the page. To see Kimmie's picture made me cry instantly and the story the reporter wrote was heart wrenching, but so beautiful.

This was the article.

"Used with permission of Black Press"

### "Daisies Help Man to Grant Wife's Last Wish"

Proceeds from the daisy fundraiser will go to KBRH Oncology unit, as a thank you from Kimberly. Honouring a last wish of his wife, Kim, is the one thing that has kept Lee going since February. Kim asked her husband of thirty-four years to find a way to let the doctors and nurses at KBRH know just how grateful she was for their compassionate care in the last days of her life. So for one week, beginning Sunday, March 4, Lee is holding Kim's "Give You a Daisy" Memorial Campaign at No Frills located in the Plaza. All proceeds from purchasing a $5 paper daisy will be donated to the Oncology Department in the Trail Hospital for new equipment or any other need of the unit's choosing.

"For thirty days I was at the hospital 24/7. I never left her," Lee began. "Even though we knew the outcome would be dire, we couldn't have made it through as well as we did without the doctors' and nurses' true care for our well being."

Kim was always healthy; she only began feeling unwell in September. Within months, she was hospital-bound by a rare cancer called Pseudomyxoma Peritonea, or cancer of the appendix. After a whirlwind of medical treatment and a trip to Vancouver, the couple had to face the truth. Kim wouldn't have one year of life as originally hoped; an operation would be futile and aggressive chemotherapy would now not take place.

By December, Kim and Lee were told she would never go home from the hospital again. "It was that quick; the cancer that vicious. My wife needed constant attention, and they always went above board," Lee shared. "She was truly grateful for their compassion. She wanted me to think of a way to return the kindness after she passed, so this is her wish."

For weeks, Lee has kept himself occupied in body and spirit by collecting prize donations as part of Kim's memorial fundraiser. He's also planned live entertainment by local talent during its last two days. "This campaign is in memory of a woman who truly always thought of others before herself," Lee said. "I have no words to express how grateful I am in the outpouring of community spirit and to all those who have donated fabulous prizes."

The purchase of a $5 paper daisy from March 4 to March 10 will give one entry into a draw and the chance to win a growing list of prizes, all generously donated by forty-two-plus local businesses.

"We have all been affected by cancer, in one way or another," Lee said. "Let's remember their battles with a daisy. With this small gesture we can honour all those who are still fighting or have lost the battle to this ugly disease," he added. "In turn, we can help give the hospital the tools necessary to look after the ones we love, and together we can raise awareness to fight this horrible disease."

By the time she was diagnosed, Kim's cancer had advanced to Stage IV. That means the cancer had spread from where it started in the appendix to elsewhere in the body. This is also called secondary or metastatic cancer. "It's one of the rarest cancers; only 600 to 1,000 people are diagnosed with this annually," Lee explained. "There are no symptoms until it's too late, so her wish is by telling her story, that it may save a life. Please do not wait to see a doctor. A simple bout of constipation was the only sign we had."

Sunday marks two months to the day Kim passed. March 9 would have been the Pages' thirty-fourth wedding anniversary. The "Give You a Daisy" moniker comes from a popular 1973 ballad that was special to the devoted couple. "Each day we would sing that song over and over to each other; it was our way of saying goodbye," Lee shared. "This story is a sad one and devastating for me. However, through telling it, my hope is that a may save a life." Story by: Sheri Regnier.

I had to leave the building after I read it. I walked through our store to go out our back entrance where my car was parked. I sat there reading the article over and over, crying each time as I did. Then a co-worker came out and tapped on my window with a big smile and said, "You need to get back inside right away. There's a line-up of people wanting to buy daisies." The campaign hadn't even started yet. I didn't even have the daisies at the tills. I ran back inside to where the cashiers were located and was swarmed by customers all wanting to shake my hand or give me a hug. Most remembered Kim from when she worked with me and others were her customers from the office supply place. Then there were complete strangers who were touched by the article. People were crying and at times I almost broke down and joined them myself, but I didn't. I had a promise to keep. I looked behind the crowd and brought my eyes upward to the banner. Kimmie was looking down at us all, overseeing everything. I could swear the smile in her picture just got a little bigger. I remember thinking, *This is all for you baby.*

By this time, our Front-End Supervisor had already brought the daisies out to each of the six tills. The cashiers were fully on board with customers buying three and four at a time. They just kept coming. I knew most of my day was going to be at the front of the store, so I brought out a chair and placed it directly below Kimmie's picture and personally thanked each customer as they folded their daisies and dropped them inside the container. Before long, one of the cashiers blurted out she needed more daisies. *Oh crap!* We still had quite a few, but the way things were going, we wouldn't for long. I phoned the girls and let them know the campaign had started already, and we would need more daisies for the week. I think they were just as shocked as I was, but they would have some ready in a few hours. Kim would have been so proud of her girls. I know I was and so very grateful.

I began realizing something as I sat at the table that day. There were so many other people also hurting. Whether they had a friend or loved one battling cancer or had lost someone to it, they were opening up about their pain. Not directed just to me, but to each other. I had never seen so many people hugging and sharing tears. This campaign was so much bigger than just Kim and I. It was bringing people together and giving them permission to talk about their own experiences. Some had buried their hurt deep inside for years. If Kim only knew what she had started with her unselfish wish. The entire town was now paying kind with kind to each other. It was something to behold.

There was so much generosity and compassion from everyone. Customers would be dropping twenties and fifties in the draw box, and we now needed someone sitting at the table all the time. Volunteers from the hospital foundation were already scheduled to take turns daily, but that wasn't supposed to start until Sunday. But as I said, kind for kind was everywhere that day. A couple of my employees came up on their day off to sit there, when I needed a break. I was overwhelmed. I actually felt a moment of joy for the first time since Kim had passed by seeing her wish come true, but I was devastated to have to fulfill it in the first place. One thing gave me a little solace now: I knew I wasn't alone. Grief and sadness is universal, linking us all as humans. However, we are taught to suppress the feelings. It's a stigma that needs to stop. I know it certainly did that day. Thank you Kimmie, for teaching us all.

> *Life is short and we have never too much time for gladdening the hearts of those who are travelling the dark journey with us. Oh, be swift to love, make haste to be kind.*
>
> —Henri Frederic Amiel

I went home that night, needing to write to Kimmie again. I missed her more than ever and March 9 was fast approaching. That was the most important day of the year to us and always celebrated with a shared joy and love. Now it would be filled with sadness over the joy and love that we couldn't share. *It was breaking my heart.*

I wrote her this...

> Hi My Love. I'm taking time out now to write your anniversary letter. As you know, I will be extremely busy the day of. You wouldn't believe how many people brought you a daisy today,

and we're just getting started. But don't worry, I'll make sure I keep a few for myself, so I can deliver them to you personally. Usually by now we are getting ready for our getaway to the hot springs, but with your prior engagement, it just wasn't in the cards.

We did try to make up for it a few months back, but unfortunately our trip had to be cut short. I know you still feel bad about it, babe, but it wasn't your fault you fell ill. We should have cancelled the trip in the first place, but you had to be hard-headed and put on a brave face about how sick you really felt. But that's okay. I can't be angry. when I know you kept quiet out of love for me. I love going there as much as you do, but it doesn't matter where we are, as long as we're together. That's how we live everyday of our lives. We truly are Blessed, babe, having shared so much love for each other.

It's amazing that just when I think I couldn't love you anymore, then I do. All I have to do is think of you, and it becomes so easy for me. After all these years, I still don't know what you see in me, but you always say the same to me concerning yourself. We have gone through a lot over the years, and the one thing always constant was our undying passion for each other. Yes, of course that kind of passion, lol, but more so the passion of just being with each other as much as possible. Like we say when people asked why we didn't have kids, never revealing the real reason. "Total selfishness," we would say. We don't want to share each other with anyone else. Raised a few eyebrows, eh? But at least we were honest.

That's why I am finding it so hard to be away from you now and can't wait to join you as quickly as possible. I've put in numerous requests through prayer but haven't heard anything back yet. I can just hear you now: "Patience, my dear. Patience. I know I know, but sometimes patience sucks balls.

But I digress; let me continue with the real purpose of this letter. As always I write because my heart cannot contain the love I have for you. It pumps blood through my veins providing me with the oxygen needed to breathe. It is and always will be my life source. The simple elegance in which you walk only reflects the surface of your grace within. You are the epitome of what our Father in the heavens intended when he created woman. The fragrance of your beauty permeates all who behold it and yet you walk in humbleness. I am witness to your compassion. I will testify to its perfect nature.

By God's grace you fell to my feet, not too revere me, but to hold fast to my foundation. To strengthen me. To drape my nakedness. It is in you that time has no beginning or end. Each second ticking aloud with the beat of my heart. Your gentleness whispers upon my skin. And when I was a barren desert, you planted your seeds deep inside of me, watering my soul so I may bloom each day in the garden of life. You are my protector. Hardened steel bends to your strength. You will allow no foe to permeate our union. To death do us part and then forever after.

Happy Anniversary, my Sleeping Beauty. I love you more. Talk to you real soon. Forever Yours.

*It was a blessing the campaign got off to an early start. Besides our wedding anniversary corresponding with it, so did another date. Sunday would mark two months to the day she had been gone. Two anniversaries. One symbolizing our beginning, the other marking its end.*

Almost immediately after I wrote the letter, I soon spiralled into a very dark place thinking about it. Organizing the campaign had become a distraction, allowing me not to think about myself and how distraught I was, but in reality, nothing had changed. More than ever, I just wanted to die. After the campaign what was there? There was nothing left for me to continue on. There couldn't possibly be. I was close to paying off Kim's funeral expense and I thought of a way to cover mine as well. I would leave both our cars to my brother so he could sell them to cover the costs. But in the meantime, I still had a promise to keep that I would run into head on and deal with the crash later. So without any sleep, I returned to the store early, wanting to be there when we opened our doors.

I was sitting at the table and watching customers going through the tills, hoping they were holding a daisy in hand to bring to Kim. A customer I had always taken the time out to talk with was making her way through. She was in her eighties and quite frail. Often I would help her to her car with her groceries. Standing up to see if she needed any assistance, she waved me back and said she would come over and talk to me. She was carrying a big black bag in one hand, her groceries in the other. She put both on the floor near where I was sitting.

Before I could say anything she grabbed my hand and placed a hundred dollar bill in it. "I can't take that." I knew she was on a limited pension, so I handed it back to her. She asked if I could spare a moment to sit and chat. She grabbed my hand again and held it in hers and began to tell me her story.

"You know I was married once. We had forty-five years together. He passed away from cancer twenty years ago. Not a day goes by that I don't think of him. We were a lot like you and your wife, but I just needed to let you know something. Time doesn't make you miss them any less. I feel as sad today as I did when I lost him. We never had any children so I'm all alone. When I read about you and your wife in the paper, it made me cry for you. I know what your life is going to be like now. Just like me you are going to feel so alone. But you know something? Every time I come into the store, you always talked to me. You don't know how much that means, and that's why I need to give you and your wife the money. My husband would have wanted me to in order to say thank you from both of us in making a little old lady feel a little less lonely."

It wasn't even 9:00 a.m. and I was breaking down already. I had no idea how just talking to somebody can make a difference in their lives. *Maybe that's a lesson for us all. Bless her heart.* We got up and hugged before I escorted her back inside. Then seeing the black bag she had brought made her say, "Oh, I almost forgot. This is for you." She reached in and pulled out a sealed metal container. She told me she knew I was probably to busy to cook, so she had made me a roast beef dinner to take home. Now it was 9:30 a.m. and here I go again. I'd only been there an hour and a half and already needed a break to compose myself.

This is going to be a very long day. There were so many other touching moments, but I made it through. I wasn't looking forward to the night ahead. The eve of a darkness. I was so tired, but I wouldn't allow myself any sleep, not like I did two months earlier. I should have been awake for it. *Why wouldn't she let me share it with her? I'll never know the reason now, but it still weighed heavily on my heart.* So I promised myself that on the fourth of every month I needed to stay awake between the specific time of 1:25 and 2:00 a.m. to imagine I was awake to witness her last breath. This time I began writing, needing to express how that day affected me. "I was lost and never coming back."

# TAKEN

You took my joy with you. It leaves this barren space. No longer does it fill my day, as each time I saw your face. My heart is completely broken. There is nothing left. but pain. Every living moment without you fills it with disdain. You took my light with you. The darkness has set in deep. The only time I see any light now, is in the dreams of you when I sleep. The music has stopped playing. The conductor has retired her baton. The orchestra pit now empty, leaving only memories of her song. I replay its sad melody to capture its refrain. No matter how I try to change the words, the chorus remains the same. You took my world with you. It spins for me no more. How could it revolve without its axis, generated by its core? The spectrum of a perfect rainbow is no longer in my sight. Its colours against the stormy sky have turned to black and white. You took the sun with you. It does not rise nor does it set. It hangs without any meaning and shows me no regret. When I look to the heavens in search of the stars on high, the North Star is always missing. You took it in your eyes. It leaves me without direction. I remain lost without a way. Time is always standing still, as the night turns into day. These things you took with you. There are only two you left behind. One is slowly becoming lost, but it's only in my mind. The other is inconsequential now, no matter to me at all. My death is all I wish and pray and beg its final call. Oh, my love, I know it wasn't you; it was never in your control. I was left with all the treasures a man could want. You filled me with your soul. I promise I'll bring it back to you, when my time on earth is done. Then we will meet under the moon and stars and bask beneath the sun. I just pray to the Almighty above and all the mercy he can bestow. He'll understand the reasons why I have to leave his show.

Of course I thought about how Kimmie would view my decision. I know she would expect me to try and go on as long as I could. But when do you stop trying? How much pain is enough? If you are 100% sure you will never find any joy in life ever again, then what's the point? She wouldn't want me to be sad forever. That's the last thing she would wish on me or on anybody. There was no doubt in my mind now. Finish the campaign and wait on a few more weekly checks to pay the funeral home, and that would be it. For the first time since I lost her, I felt an overwhelming sense of peace run through me. I was no longer feeling the burden of life on my shoulders. I had no use for it now.

The campaign remained as strong as ever. So much so, we needed to replace our draw container with a thirty-gallon Rubbermaid Tote. My days were spent thanking everyone and lending an ear when they wanted to relay their own stories. I wasn't as anxious about things anymore. I remained in the calm before the really calm. I knew I wouldn't be suffering much longer. I did feel proud that Kim not only got her wish, but now her legacy would live on without me. I'll say it again: "She deserved that and so much more."

The weekend came and offered a celebration of sorts. Colton lifted everyone's spirits by providing live entertainment with everyone singing along. I know Kim didn't want a service, but she got one anyway. It was a celebration of life in her honour and the whole damn town came out and sang our song. *How about that, babe?*

On 9:00 p.m. Sunday, the campaign came to an end. I waited at home for the call from my front-end closer to tell me what the end results were and how many people brought Kim a daisy. Remember at the beginning of the campaign I was hoping we could reach 500? Well, we surpassed that by a few. Allow me to let you read the results from the follow-up story in the newspaper a few days later.

*THE TIMES*
*"Used with permission of Black Press."*

> The Give You a Daisy Memorial Campaign, in memory of Kim Page, raised $13,105 for the KBRH Oncology Department by selling 2,621 paper daisies. Lee, Kim's husband, (right) presented the proceeds to Lisa, Director of Development Trail Health Foundation. We would like to thank everyone who

donated in Kim's memory during this week-long campaign and also supported Lee in his quest to pay tribute to Kim.
- Story by Sheri Regnier.

2,621 daisies. The population of the town was only 7000.

"Pretty amazing, eh?" I should have been overjoyed. Don't get me wrong, I knew it was special with the results more than I could have imagined, and I know Kimmie would have been humbled by it all and proud at the same time: Not about what her wish had accomplished, but how her core belief in the goodness of humankind had been proven. She lived her whole life as an example in that belief. So yes, the campaign allowed me to express our gratefulness to others, but the real reason behind it for me was a selfish one. It was all about how grateful I was to her.

*The highest tribute to the dead is not grief but gratitude.*

—Wilder

# CHAPTER 33:
# I Think I'm Done Now

I knew there could never be enough ways to express my gratitude for all she had done for me and truly honour all the qualities that made her who she was. I was hoping the campaign would do that in someway, but how could it? It was never really about her, but what others did for her. I know her last wish showed a small part of her unselfishness, but the world still had no idea what it had lost. What could I do to show them?

*I hope she knew I tried. Maybe I'll ask her if God forgives me for what I was planning and reunites us one day. Perhaps I'll know very soon. I was certainly dealing with the crash now and had no intention of surviving it.* Now my main focus was paying off our last bills and deciding which was the best method to end my life. There were so many factors to consider. Even though ironic, it was the most important decision of my life at that moment, and I didn't want to fuck it up. During the day I worked, and at night I would google different methods to help me make up my mind. It would be hard to get the pills I would needed. I didn't want to leave a mess by slitting my wrists. Carbon monoxide didn't have the highest success rates. So I guess the first idea would be the best fit. The only downside I could see was that it would take so many resources to recover my body – boats and maybe a helicopter.

I'd have to leave a note and apologize for being such a bother. Now that the logistics of my decision were final, I could do what I had always done. Spend all my time thinking of only Kimmie and filling myself with her before I left. It wasn't hard. Everything in the house filled me to the brim. Her clothes I had found so painful to look at, now I held each piece. I needed to touch everything of hers. I began sleeping on her side of the bed. I searched to find any memory of her that I could, even those from the hospital. Her pajamas, toothbrush, anything and everything. But out of all her possessions, there was one I spent most of my time with that meant more to me than anything. Her thoughts on any given day in the past were all contained in her cell phone.

She left a lot of herself in her messages and posts, and I needed to read every one of them. Each one had just as much significance to me, but in different ways, all bringing me back in time to when I was happy and had joy in my life. Each picture brought me back to the moment when they were taken; each comment to when they were said. But it was the ones I didn't know about that interested me the most, like personal text message between friends. Most were mundane everyday things. Some were of a supportive nature to whomever was in need. But there were more than a few that talked about us that I didn't know about. One in particular would be the beginning of something else for me. The universe would speak to me once again, delaying any plans I had concerning the immediate future.

Kim had lost contact with an old childhood friend. It wasn't until about ten years ago they reconnected through Facebook. They began texting each other to catch up on life and sharing their stories of what had happened over the years. Her friend was dealing with some hardships that I will not mention, but I will share Kimmie's response.

**Written by her Own Hand** from 2008

> My philosophy on life, is our philosophy on life. If you have that one person that surprises you every day, whether it's menial or not, it still rocks your world. Twenty-four years of everything the world could throw at us, I realized I have Teflon undies. If you have one person in your life, whether brother, sister, friend, or significant other that you would do anything for, you have been blessed. We could write a book about the hardships we endured, but in the end it will turn out to be a love story like no other.

> Love conquers and heals all wounds. I believe we are all a part of a larger family and there are so many things we learn from each other. It is not about what we have, but what we give. I can't remember who said it, but they are words I try to live by.

"Don't judge each day by the harvest you reap, but by the seeds you plant."

So girl, no matter what you're going through, remember these two things: There is always someone worse off, and with a little help from others, we can get reach the destination of where we want to be. We just have to let the love in and return it in kind. I am always here for you when you need a little love or just an ear. I promise things are not as bad as they seem. Let your love shine, girlie.

Love and kisses,
Kimmie

There was just something about this message that penetrated deep inside me and ignited a flame. Her words had an elegance to them that were spoken from the core of her soul. Every word told of who she really was and who I knew her to be. I couldn't stop reading it over and over. *Why does this mean so much to me?* I spent days pondering over it. It was always there in the back of my mind, burning like a small ember. It wasn't until I was going through all the comments from the poems and letters I had posted about her that the ember would turn into an Inferno.)

(Responses)
"So beautiful. Love wins!"

"Lee, thank you for posting everything you write - it is an honour and a privilege to witness the beauty of your love with Kim!"

"Humble, raw, and real. It doesn't get any better than that! Thank you."

"Lee, your words are a raw depiction of a true love. Imagine if everyone was so lucky to have that... what a wonderful world it would be."

"Your tributes are so painfully beautiful. They are an inspiration to all who read them. I hope you find peace in your heart one day, Kim would want nothing less for you. Take care."

"You have been gifted, Lee, to be able to describe what some of us feel because we love as truly, deeply, madly, fully and forever as you do Kim! May I say that if you had not had the most magnificent love of all time – you would never grieve like you do! It is even more special how you share it with others. Your words give love meaning. So from me I want to thank you for sharing. Your love has touched many more than you could possibly know. Keep sharing."

*This is why I'm still here.* There were so many comments like these, but my grief blinded me when I first read them. The words I shared were out of selfishness, with the only purpose being to express how much pain I was in and for everyone to know it. As I read the comments back now, I began to see how our story affected others. The ember Kim had ignited with her words made me realize how I could show my gratitude for everything she did for me and for all the kindness she had in her heart. *I MUST RETURN IT TO THE WORLD.* Just as Kim had said, "We can all learn from each other. It's not about what we have, but what we give." There would be nothing more fitting than to honour those words and to give the world our story and to plant a seed of hope for others that true love does conquer all. Our lives are a testament to it. I was about to do the most unselfish thing I had ever done in my life: TO SHARE MY KIMMIE WITH THE WORLD.

I began formulating things in my head, knowing I couldn't leave anything out and needed to be true to every little detail, no matter the pain it would ignite. I would share the darkness I endured for so many years and what and who brought me from the depths of it. I knew it would be one of the hardest things I would ever experience besides losing Kim. But love was never said to be easy. As Kim so elegantly said to her friend, "We could write a book about the hardships we endured, but in the end, it would turn out to be a love story like no other."

I was writing as if my life depended upon it, and in a way it was true. If the universe hadn't spoken to me when it did, I would have carried through with my life-ending decision. All the other things that had delayed me from carrying it out were allowing me time to discover the real reason I had to go on. It was to share with the world a love story like no other and give others hope. There is nothing greater we could mark our existence in this world with than that. So besides work, all my time would be spent writing.

I wrote every word on my cell phone, so I could write at anytime, no matter where I was. I had no idea how long it would take for me to finish it. How much time does it take to describe fifty-seven years of one's life, especially when there was so much to share? All I knew was that it had to be completed before January 4, 2019 – the one-year marker of Kim's death. If I didn't have it done by then, I would stop writing, knowing beyond that, I wouldn't have the strength to continue. My process would tax my emotional well-being to the limit. I had already relived the sexual abuse and the aftermath it caused once before through therapy. That part of my past had already been dealt with emotionally, so the words came easily.

It wasn't until I started writing about Kimmie that I would break down on a daily basis. All the things we had experienced earlier on were as real to me now as when they first happened: our first meeting; the first time we made love; when she lost the baby; and all the pain I caused her by my actions concerning my daughter. Depending on what I was writing about, I could be bawling my eyes out up to ten times a day, which emotionally exhausted me, but I had to continued on. Just like the campaign, **our story is much bigger than just about us.**

I knew soon I would be at a place in our story that would have less tears shed. I was almost ready to talk about the "Best Of Times". That's where I would have some time to catch my breath. Those years were filled with nothing but happiness and joy. I wasn't looking forward to writing about what came after that. But just like her campaign, I had to give it everything I had, running into it head on and dealing with the crash later. It had taken me nine months to get to that point, but I was there. I had spent approximately sixty-four hours a week writing, which translated into 2,496 hours combined or 103 twenty-four-hour days.

That left me with 28 days before January 4. I had twenty-eight days to re-live: "The season of our darkness, the winter of our despair, the epoch of incredulity, and the worst of times" all at once. I began feeling sick to my stomach every time I sat down to write. My process was no longer working. I cried thinking about what I was going to say and cried even more writing about it. I began having vivid nightmares of our stay in the hospital, waking up drenched in sweat every morning. My thoughts were becoming uncontrollable. Once consumed with my daily writing, I was now trying to avoid it at all costs. It felt like I was losing my mind. All those hours I spent were now in real jeopardy of not having their conclusion. *WHAT THE FUCK WAS WRONG WITH ME?*

I didn't know what to do. I thought the universe might be telling me it was time for me to go. Maybe what I was trying to do wasn't that important after all.

But I just couldn't believe that. I knew in my heart how important it was. As Kim said, "We just have to let it in and return it in kind."

I had to find out what was happening to me as quickly as possible, so I made an appointment with the doctor. She didn't need any tests to diagnose me and was surprised it took me this long to come in and see her. She began by asking me how I occupied my time since Kim had passed. She knew all about the Memorial Campaign, but she wanted to know what I had been doing since then. I told her besides work, I spent all my other time writing an autobiography about Kimmie and I.

"And how's that going?" she asked. I told her it was physically and emotionally exhausting, and I was so close to finishing it. But now, the things I was experiencing were stopping me. She asked if I had written about our stay in the hospital yet. "That's a coincidence. That is exactly where I am now."

She said that's what she thought and then gave me her diagnosis: "Lee, you are suffering from PTSD." She went on to explain what I was trying to recount was at the root of all my symptoms. In simple terms, my mind was trying to make sense of the traumatic experience I witnessed. I had watched someone I loved more than life itself die, and there was nothing I could do about it. Just like when some soldiers come home from war, their brain stores all the horrific things they might have witnessed or done. It's not until something sparks the memory that it comes back to them in vivid detail. She ended her explanation by saying, "Writing the end of your story is the **Trigger.**"

Of course it was. Now it all made sense to me, knowing all about triggers and what they could lead to. Kim and I had been in the worst battle of our lives with neither us given the time to really process everything that was happening. Four short months were all we had from start to end. When we knew there was no hope for her, my undivided attention was consumed by making her as comfortable as possible and fulfilling her smallest of wishes. I wanted to make her feel every bit of love that was overflowing from my heart every second of the day. I was blinded to everything else and all the other things that would have overwhelmed me if I had thought about them at the time.

But I was subconsciously witnessing every little detail. The medical procedures, the weight loss, her pain, and most of all, that I was losing her. I was recording all these things and so much more to play back at a later date. I was the instigator of my own trigger by pushing the play button over and over again by writing about it. All I could see were things that devastated me, but now I knew what the trigger was. Just as Kim and I had to deal with my other triggers in the past, it gave me the confidence I could deal with this one as well. It was more important to me than anything now. I needed to overlook the grief I was feeling and compartmentalize it. I was just looking at it in the wrong way. This was still about her being alive. It wasn't about her losing the battle, but rather about how she fought it tooth and nail. That's how I had to describe it. I need to show how she was a hero in life and an inspiration in death. She had to be remembered that way.

I went home and took the picture of her in the living room to my writing room and placed it directly on the windowsill in front of me so all I had to do was look up to see her. The words began to flow from the depths of me, passing my tears and on to my phone. I wrote until it was time to go to work in the morning, continuing when I got home. In my mind I was at the hospital again. Just as I was caring for her then, I was taking great care in what I was writing about her now. Soon I would have every one of her personal belongings from the hospital in the room with me. I would place each one on my lap as I wrote about them – her bottle of lotion, her nail file, the half-finished bottle of bubbly that she craved so much that I still had in the fridge.

At times, I even brought Chedda into the room when I was writing about him. I didn't want to miss a thing, needing to spark even the smallest memory I had. I started fasting and only eating enough to keep me going, just as I had in the hospital. When it snowed, I would go outside and let a flake fall upon my tongue as she had. What once made me afraid and broken-hearted to write about was now giving me a sense of overwhelming pride. I was so very proud of how Kim never wavered in her grace and her unimaginable strength, but most of all, I was reminded of how grateful I was to have had someone as special as her.

It would give me the adrenaline to finish the last thing I needed to write about: **A grief like no other.** I was embracing it this time, knowing that I grieve so much because I loved so much. It would be one of the hardest things I had ever done, but I am finished now. December 23, 2019 at 7:02 p.m. The same day last year my daughter had to leave to return to Australia. The same day Kim began losing any of the strength she had left to continue her journey in this life. She had been getting ready to go home, having no choice but to leave ours. She had given it everything she had to stay with me as long as she could, but she was becoming too tired, just as I find myself now. **So very, very tired.**

I started out in this world damaged and alone, searching for the love that would redeem my soul and restore my innocence. By the long suffering and grace of one woman, I would finally be exactly where I was meant to be. The love she clothed me with has given me the greatest joy and the greatest pain at the same time. I experienced everything it had to offer and then some. It was everything that made life worth living, but now, everything that makes me not want to live. However, if given the choice to not experience the pain of my past and not meet Kim, there would be no choice. If it meant I had to suffer through one thousand times the damage to finally end up with her, I would endure it with a smile and without complaint. Just as she did.

*Thank you, my love, for being my alpha and omega.*

**Be ever so grateful for what you have, because one day, you might not have it anymore.**

# Epilogue

So what lies ahead of me now is questionable. After Kimmie's story gets out to the world, I think the universe will be done talking to me and giving me any more time, but I've been wrong before. I'll need just a little more patience to find out and just long enough to honour Kim's first wish a second time. What had given me the inspiration to start writing our story in the first place is about to be held again: the second **"Give You A Daisy Memorial Campaign"**. It may take the rest of everything I have left to continue on any further. Whether or not I'll survive the crash this time, I'm pretty sure of the answer. When the campaign comes to an end, there will be no writing of a book to keep me going until the next one. Everything is said and done. Our book of life together in this world has already written its final chapter. The only thing left is for me is to finish the epilogue in my own book of life and tidy up all the loose ends, bringing it to its conclusion.

I'll know when it's time. There will be no second thought. I will start a new journey. It is one that will bring me to be exactly where I was always destined to be: To be together forever with my Kimmie. **Such a beautiful thing.**

**IT IS A FAR, FAR BETTER REST I GO TO THAN I HAVE EVER KNOWN.**

*As this book was being prepared for publication, another paragraph or two has to be added before print.*

Two years to the day from when we learned of Kimmie's true diagnosis, I learned of mine. I will share one last thing with her. Our cancers are different in nature, but in the end, they will have the same outcome. I will do my best to have the same strength and grace she displayed. I'm not afraid of the dark anymore. God works in mysterious ways. Thank you Father.

If our story has touched or helped you in some way, please return kind with kind. Reach out to someone with a kind word or genuine smile. Hold your loved ones a little tighter. Don't be hasty to judge, but most of all as Kim said, "Let the love in, so you can return it in kind."

Thank you all for sharing our lives. I can only pray something can be learned from our journey.

*See you on other side.*

# The Broken Can Become Unbroken. Reach Out.

Crisis Services Canada: 1-833-456-4566
Child Abuse Hotline: 1-800-422-4453
National Suicide Hotline: 1-800-273-8255
Canadian Cancer Society: 1-866-786-3934
Hope Air: 1-416-222-6335

CPSIA information can be obtained
at www.ICGtesting.com
Printed in the USA
LVHW091922240320
651075LV00001B/1/J

9 781525 570322